Freedom Within the Margins

The Politics of Exclusion

Editors

Caterina Pizanias

James S. Frideres

Detselig Enterprises Ltd.

Calgary, Alberta

Canadian Cataloguing in Publication Data

Main entry under title:

Freedom within the margins
Includes bibliographical references.
ISBN 1-55059-127-4

1. Multiculturalism – Canada. 2. Canada – Ethnic relations.
I. Pizanias, Caterina, 1946-   II. Frideres, James S., 1943-
FC104.F73   1995   305.8'00971   C95-910585-9
F1035.A1F73 1995

Detselig Enterprises Ltd.
1220 Kensington Rd. NW, Unit 210
Calgary, Alberta T2N 3P5

Detselig Enterprises Ltd. appreciates the financial assistance
from the Department of Canadian Heritage and The Alberta
Foundation for the Arts, a beneficiary of the Lottery Fund of the
Government of Alberta, for its 1995 publishing program.

Printed in Canada   SAN 115-0324   ISBN 1-55059-127-4

Table of Contents

Foreword

As the margin or outside enters an institution or teaching machine,
what kind of teaching it enters will determine its contours.
--Gayatri Chakravorty Spivak *Outside in the Teaching Machine*

During the nineties, the concepts of interdisciplinarity, multiculturalism, borders, boundaries, and difference began crowding
the syllabi of course outlines and the programs of conferences and
symposia across Canada. To be inter-, cross-, or multidisciplinary
in one's work is almost expected in some academic circles,
particularly the area of multiculturalism. Overcoming
disciplinary ethnocentrism is expected, but how one accomplishes
that has yet to be settled, especially since the number of vested
interest groups that have become major players in developing our
institutional and political arrangements has increased over the
past two decades[1].

Both multiculturalism and interdisciplinarity as theory and
practice are in transition, much like the fabric of Canadian society
and the Canadian academy. Although notions of
interdisciplinarity have come from abroad, aspects of
multiculturalism have had their roots in Alberta and The
University of Calgary. Because of the transitional character of the
times as well as multi-culturalism's roots in the Prairies, two years
ago we saw an opportunity to attempt an unusual intervention, a
fishing expedition of sorts, to see how "multiculturalism" was
understood and made use of in the Prairies. Our "experiment"
came nearly twenty-five years after multiculturalism was
institutionalized with the 1969 publication of the first issue of the
Canadian Ethnic Studies journal by the University of Calgary's
Research Centre for Canadian Ethnic Studies. Dr. Alexander
Malycky, the editor of its inaugural issue, wrote that the main
objective of the new journal was to "stimulate, promote, coordinate,
and conduct research on all facets of Canadian ethnic groups, and,
in doing so, to contribute to the development of the multicultural
nature of the Canadian identity."[2]

As for the "multicultural" nature of Canada, it also received a
helping hand from Prairie intellectuals of Ukrainian and Jewish
descent who, under the political leadership of Senator Paul Yusyk of
Alberta, spearheaded opposition to the federal government's
redefinition of Canada as a bilingual and bicultural country.

During the late sixties and early seventies the notion of multiculturalism under the metaphoric banner of the "mosaic" increasingly captured the political *and* academic imagination of Canadians.

The 1963 Royal Commission on Bilingualism and Biculturalism initiated efforts from the top down to come to terms with this new "multicultural nature of Canadian identity." Successive government policies inspired projects like the Research Centre for Canadian Ethnic Studies. Later, new associations were established, such as the interdisciplinary Ethnic Studies Association in Toronto in 1977 (with the late Howard Palmer, History Department, University of Calgary, as one of its staunchest supporters), the Centre Internationale de Recherche sur le Bilingualisme (1967), the Institut Quebécois de Recherche sur la Culture (1979), and the Laurier Institute (1983). Other countries have since followed our lead with the creation of such institutes as the Centre for Research on Ethnic Relations (U.K.), the Center for Migration Studies (U.S.A.), the Center for Research in International Migrations and Ethnicity (Sweden), and the Institute for Migrations and Nationalities (Croatia). The creation of twenty-six ethnic chairs throughout Canada (currently eighteen exist) and the continuing funding of ethnic research by Heritage Canada further support our commitment to multiculturalism. Today we also find that all major publishers in North America have sections or divisions that deal with multi-culturalism.

Multiculturalism is supposed to have been realized within the bilingual/bicultural framework; interdisciplinarity is supposed to have been achieved also, except it has been practised from the theoretical and methodological vantage points of many disciplines, with some supporting data and/or references from one or two neighbouring disciplines.[3] Increasingly many have come to realize that any serious attempt to examine multiculturalism and/or interdisciplinarity must start by looking at both practices as being socially produced and reproduced--who/what is included/excluded and at what price? We need to make clear the connections between theories, policies, and the empirical worlds from which they emanate and in which they purport to have purchase.

As social groups undergo different experiences, they begin to develop symbolic orders that shape their perspectives; in addition, each group attempts to frame issues that will direct resources towards itself. Within Canadian society there is an implicit moral contract between Charter and non-Charter groups. There is a mostly unspoken belief that not all groups are equal, and newly emerging groups must conform to the more established entities. In being "multicultural," one is expected to take for granted the asymmetries of power between the European founding groups and those of aboriginal or non-European origin; any differences are obscured by the colourful images of the expressive multicultural mosaic of heritage events. In similar manner, asymmetries of theoretical and methodological disciplinary practices have to date been submerged in the lively rhetoric of interdisciplinarity, an interdisciplinarity that ignores the empirical world: theories, methodologies, and rewards are based on a mono-disciplinarity and are territorially controlled by the number of practitioners and funding sources. The fundamental questions of what and how one is to translate, transport, or eliminate practices, rewards, and power from one ethnic group or discipline to another have not even been dealt with, in either multiculturalism or interdisciplinarity: we continue to practice variations of disciplinary ethnocentrism in our multicultural discourses.

For our intervention, we took advantage of the Association for Canadian Studies Regional Development Programme when we organized our "eccentric" experiment, a two-day conference entitled "Freedom within the Margins: The Poetics of Multiculturalism in the Prairies," held at the University of Calgary in May 1992. The conference was organized to bring together different, usually disconnected groups of people all of whom nonetheless shared an interest in representations and aspects or analyses of "multiculturalism."

Instead of running away from the specific, concrete and particular, we invoked a transformative praxis that was political-- the academy and community at large would get equal billing; partial--we concentrated on the Prairies; and crisis-centred--we simultaneously positioned ourselves within and alongside the mainstream academic practices, following the lead of Trinh T. Minh-Ha, who has so aptly said, "To cut across boundaries and border lines is to live aloud the malaise of categories and labels; it is to resist simplistic attempts at classifying, to resist the comfort of belonging to a classification, and of *producing* classifiable works."[4]

Our use of the word "poetics" was inspired by its Greek root of *poesis,* which means both making and imagining; our understanding of "margin" is not the usual one of dependence on a centre of any kind, but a fragment on which resistances might emerge. Therefore, our politics were not exclusionary: we wanted to hear once again from the "experts," but also we wanted to hear from the "subjects" of their expertise. We wanted to create opportunities for engaging in multidisciplinary discussions, exchanging skills, and sharing insights. By ignoring the walls between the academy and the community, by trespassing on disciplinary borders for a short period of time, we wanted to create a space where the empowering poetics of the margins could begin to take root. In the end, our fears were unfounded: our experiment was a success.

Over forty papers were presented, along with workshops, panels, performances, and lectures by academics and community activists on aspects of multiculturalism and ethnicity, on participatory knowledge, art, homophobia, and xenophobia. The areas examined were those of "ethnic" experiences in everyday life and literature, indigenous issues, francophone communities outside Quebec, feminist research, women's spir-ituality, community health, and educational systems.[5] Contributors were solicited from a wide range of sites, disciplines, and perspectives, from within and outside the university community; the selection process reflected our belief that historically grounded and socially salient interdisciplinarity must involve basic categorical representations from many different vantage points. The enthusiastic response of the conference participants encouraged us to put together this volume; we present it to you as a document of the trajectory of different social and disciplinary practices and as a seed for the future.

With this project, we challenged ourselves as much as we are challenging others. Rather than taking interdisciplinarity in an essentialist, static manner from which "multiculturalism" could be spoken about and fixed, we want to show interdisciplinarity as a social construction and one in which we have decided to participate with minimal intervention. This new knowledge should--at best-- be polyphonic, thought through and negotiated in genuinely new ways, ways that will involve intertextuality not only at the level of naming, but rather as an integral part, a coming together with incommensurable practices.

This volume is located in a specific historical context--the Prairies in the 1990s and a specific philosophical context--the belief that a polyphonic discourse can be found within disciplinary margins. It is an account of developments/issues related to multiculturalism and can be heard as a report from a variety of positions within and outside the academy. It is an attempt at re-working, shifting, or ignoring the frameworks that structure our notions of identity.

We have arranged this volume of essays in loose groupings with minimal editorial intervention in order to show the irreducible diversity of current practices, and in recognition of the difficulty of producing a generalized interdisciplinary text without suppressing alternative voices and practices. To understand, let alone assimilate, the practices of other disciplines one must abandon the sort of judgements that we might apply in our own discipline--in our case, sociology. We believe that new insights can be gained from such eccentric collections of disciplinary hybridity, "rhizomal" texts as Gilles Deleuze might call them, because what "is at stake, therefore, in this inter-creation, is the very notion of *specialization* and of *expertise*, of *discipline* and *professionalism*."

All the authors, performers, and artists in this volume respond to and work within specific contexts as participants in the social relations and practices of power in different disciplines/locations within the university and community. Our organizational and editorial interests lie in providing exploratory readings on how these disciplinary works rebound against each other, and in so doing generate implications for the practice of an active interdisciplinarity: How can we overcome disciplinary boundaries without coming to terms with incommensurable practices? How can we build coalitions within and outside the university so as to include as many voices as possible, shedding light on "multiculturalism" from different vantage points? How should we include experiences and analyses that are rarely voiced in the academy, yet not exploit the "marginal" experiences simply as exemplary data to disciplinary theories? How can we produce a discourse open to the play of contending tendencies and possibilities? The essays in this volume, while focusing on one or another aspect of multiculturalism in the Prairies, all share a consciousness of the interrelatedness of the multiple aspects of identity, whether personal, collective, or disciplinary.

As editors, we offer this volume as a fulcrum to use in looking for possible entries, embraces, or problematics for a new interdisciplinary relationship(s). If each of us begins to compare what we do in our disciplines with what others are doing in theirs, we will begin to see how we need to change in order to collectively and collaboratively develop new knowledge-construction methods without appropriating, co-opting or eliminating practices, references, and meanings of other disciplines. With this volume we raise some questions, although we have not attempted to answer them--there is so much more work to be done. But as Stanley Arroyowitz has recently commented "the energy is going to remain at the margins for a long time."[6]

Both the conference and this book would not have been possible without generous grants from the Association for Canadian Studies, the Alberta Multiculturalism Commission, the University of

Calgary Special Projects Fund, the Calgary Foundation, the United Way of Calgary and Area, the Calgary Immigrant Women's Association, the Calgary Multi-cultural Centre, the Calgary Aboriginal Awareness Society, and the University of Calgary Sociology Department. We appreciate their support--it enabled 150 participants to engage in lively debates arising from the varied and interesting sessions. We wish also to thank the other members of the conference organizing committee: Terry Armstrong, Joanna Buhr, Olivia Busby, Cecille DePass, Elsy Gagné, Caterina Greco-Mangone, Robert Laboucane, and Lisa Lucuik.

Caterina Pizanias
(Simon Fraser University)
J.S. Frideres
(The University of Calgary)

FOOTNOTES

1   See Alan Cairns, *Charter versus Federalism: The Dilemmas of Constitutional Reform.* (Montreal: McGill-Queen's University Press, 1992) and J.W. Berry and J.A. Laponce, (eds.), *Ethnicity and Culture in Canada: The Research Landscape* (Toronto: University of Toronto Press, 1994).

2   Alexander Malycky, "Introduction," *Bulletin of the Research Centre for Canadian Ethnic Studies*, 1 (1969): 2.

3   See Gilles Paquet, "Political Philosophy of Multiculturalism," in Berry and Laponce, *Ethnicity and Culture in Canada,* 60-80, and Jill Vickers, "Where Is the Discipline in Interdisciplinarity?" in *Papers on Interdisciplinarity* (Montreal: Association for Canadian Studies, 1992).

4   Trinh T. Minh-Ha, *When the Moon Waxes Red: Representation, Gender and Cultural Politics* (New York: Routledge, 1991), 107, 108, emphasis in original.

5   Ibid., 108.

6   Stanley Aroyowitz, *Dead Artists, Live Theories and Other Cultural Problems* (New York: Routledge, 1994), ix, emphasis in original.

PART I

JUXTAPOSITIONS

Morny Joy
Department of Religious Studies
The University of Calgary

1

Multiculturalism and Margins of Intolerance

Multiculturalism, a contemporary applied version of pluralism, could be considered as a modern variant of the old problem of *the one and the many* - a conundrum that has challenged Western philosophy since the time of the Pre-Socratic philosophers.[1] Difference, alterity, or otherness - all terms employed to refer to the strange or alien - have not fared well in the history of Western civilization (according to the official version). This is because, until very recently, it has predominantly exalted the values of white, educated, upper-class males.

Minorities within its domain (such as women, the old, the impoverished, slaves) suffered, though perhaps not in the same way as those deemed utterly foreign (including indigenous peoples) or enemies. Exclusion, intolerance, indifference have been the tools of the privileged majority. If these forms of control failed, then persecution or warfare were employed. Over time, the goal was that of domination and/or incorporation. Perhaps this movement is best represented by the philosophy of Hegel, where difference or distinction was acknowledged as the second movement of his dialectic, only then to be reabsorbed in the dynamic, unifying process of *Geist* or world-spirit.[2] This oppositional formula probably reached its extreme expression in the early philosophy of Jean-Paul Sartre, who declared "Hell is the others" and any encounter with another was viewed as a struggle for supremacy.[3]

Today, such automatic presumptions of superiority are being questioned. The unique or special status that has been accorded the Eurocentric and Christian perspective (particularly in the countries of the new world) is being undermined by the access to education and relative prosperity of those who would formerly have been disregarded or disdained. But it is not as if a new multidimensional model is ready at hand, eager to assume the mantle of tolerance and progress, where all are now deemed equal.

Life is far more complicated than that. Perhaps just as
postmodernism puts into question all former philosophic certainties
and truth-claims, so does multiculturalism dispute the notion of a
single superior social form. But neither postmodernism nor
multiculturalism provides a solution, and perhaps, it needs to be
admitted, there is not a *single* one. The question of determining
acceptable criteria of evaluation then becomes urgent if this
pluralism of perspectives is not to degenerate into mere anarchy.

How is it possible to provide standards that allow for the
polyphonic voices of a multicultural world without falling victim to
old antagonisms or simply repeating them in new guises. For it
seems that as long as oppositional modes of thinking predominate
in the West, little can change in the radical way that is required for
our present needs.

One area where this difficulty can be illustrated graphically is
religion, where the question of pluralism, in the form of
interreligious dialogue, has been a major preoccupation for the last
fifteen years. In a survey of religious pluralism published in the
Encyclopedia of Religion, John Hick provides a telling, if
unintentional, summation of the problem.[4] He describes both
exclusivism ("my way is the only way") and inclusivism ("my way
can incorporate yours") with some clarity. He then discusses the
apparent diversity of contemporary religion, which any simple
observation of the phenomenon can demonstrate, and then finally
states that the issue has not been effectively treated according to
philosophical requirements. But this is perhaps more a measure of
the inadequacy of Hick's own brand of Western analytic
philosophy, which is permeated by the subject/object dichotomy that
is characteristic of dualistic thought. Hick, as a tolerant liberal
Christian, wants to allow a form of pluralism that acknowledges
that all religions are various apprehensions of one ultimate
Reality.[5] This concession to pluralism, however, is at odds with the
theoretical parameters of his thinking which cannot entertain
sameness and difference at one and the same time. Thus Hick can
only conclude that perhaps it is on a practical rather than a
theoretical level that the question of pluralism can be resolved, and
that the search for a satisfactory philosophical definition can be left
aside for the time being. But this seems an abandonment of
philosophy as an effective manner of reflection, as well as a refusal
to examine new developments in philosophy that could supply a
more appropriate account of the situation. In this regard, it would
appear that is not just in the sphere of religion, but also in the area of
multiculturalism, that this theoretical deficiency has become

apparent, if its adherents persist in employing traditional philosophical formulas.

Before turning to the emergence of alternate philosophical view points from those that have predominated in the past, one other facet of multiculturalism needs to be addressed. This is the fact that multiculturalism itself is not a monolithic entity, as the name and usage in official pronouncements would seem to imply. There are many cultures. Each culture not only makes its own claim regarding its religious and social heritage but also has its own formulations of otherness and exclusion. To give but one example, women both from Western and non-Western immigrant communities are questioning not just the inferiority conferred on them by a colonizing nation or by the patriarchal system of countries where they have immigrated, but also their inferior status within their own communities. This issue of sexual stratification is but one area of social and cultural consciousness. Other variables, such as race, religion, class, age (or generation gap) all indicate that multiculturalism is a not blanket term that refers to a uniform challenge to Western hierarchy and uniformity. (Even this latter postulate has became suspect, for Western civilization itself, on closer inspection, cannot be regarded as a uniform cultural entity, but rather as a multifaced construct). Both the structures of sameness and difference, then, are in a constant state of evolution so that if there is to be an acceptable philosophical rendition of proceedings, it obviously needs to take these fluctuating circumstances into account.

One likely philosophical prospect for accommodating such a constantly shifting scenario is that of postmodernism. Particularly in its form of deconstruction, as articulated by Jacques Derrida, it defers to difference (in the guise of the neologism "différance"[6]) as that which indicates the inability of any conceptual construct to contain the infinite dimensions of reality. It focuses on the multiplicity, the irreducibility of that which philosophy has believed it has defined and controlled according to reliable standards. But in undermining these values, deconstruction can be viewed more as a caution against monopolistic tendencies and as a disruptive strategy, rather than as an exercise in accountability. As such, deconstruction does not support the articulation of a creative and/or comprehensive position. Yet such articulations are necessary - even if they are qualified as provisional insights rather than absolute definitions - if there is to be constructive debate in public forums on the issue of multiculturalism. Thus, if deconstruction cannot be of assistance in such a project, where can one turn for help?

Another recent proposal that has generated much interest is that of *narrative* as a form of personal and collective representation. The narrative mode allows for a plurality of perspectives, while not endorsing any one as the only or most viable version. This appeal to narrative, however, must not be dismissed as a simplistic retreat to self-indulgence, nor as a repudiation of the need for evaluation, so that the result is an "anything goes" or relativistic type of philosophy. To counteract such a trend, in the past few years, a number of philosophers have been exploring the territory of narration and its philosophical potential. One of the most prominent of these is the French philosopher, Paul Ricoeur, who undertook a vast study in his trilogy *Time and Narrative*.[7] In this work, Ricoeur elaborates how narrative modes can sustain, if not resolve, the seemingly irreconcilable depictions of time that can be observed between the object, chronological record (as in archives, calendars, monuments, clocks) and subjective and autobiographical reflections. In Volume I of this three-volume work, Ricoeur also observed the need for narrative (as history) in contributing to a form of self-understanding that acknowledges a debt to the past. He related this specifically to a growing awareness that, for many people today, finding a sense of identity often involves a reclamation of lost heritages, whether personal or collective, that have not been allowed their impact on the stage of history.

> We tell stories because in the last analysis human lives need and merit being narrated. This remark takes on its full force when we refer to the necessity to save the history of the defeated and the lost. The whole history of suffering cries out for vindication and calls for narrative.[8]

But Ricoeur was not satisfied with the rudimentary notion of identity that he proposed in this work. It is in a more recent work, *Oneself as Another*[9] that Ricoeur develops a more nuanced understanding of identity that he terms the "narrative self." For Ricoeur, this idea of self is both a mediation and a form of response to contemporary debates on the notion of identity. The postmodern challenge, in the context of identity, has rendered obsolete the former ideals of the self as a timeless essence or as an inherent psychological potential. Very few people, however, are comfortable with the postmodern alternative, which declares that there is no self at all - just a continuous flux of experience determined by forces over which there is no control. To resolve this impasse, Ricoeur proposes the model of a "narrative self." Here the construction of identity is regarded as an on-going project, where the task is to integrate, on a continual basis, the many themes (or plots) that comprise our lives. Thus, at one particular instance, a person may place emphasis on a certain aspect of his/her existence to the exclusion of others, but this could be regarded as a temporary focus on one plot among the many whose cumulative effects designate the unique combination of an individual's life. Ricoeur's description of a *narrative self* does not favour the belief that there is a unitary or specific identity that must be sought, but acknowledges instead the diversity and change that is basic to human experience.[10]

Ricoeur does not elaborate on this model in other than a subjective mode, but I believe that his appreciation of the coexistence of *the one and the many* as part of a constantly interweaving process has a distinct contribution to make to present discussions regarding multiculturalism. For just as narrative identity can preserve, on the personal level, disparate aspects of an individual's life without imposing a definite standard, so can it also encompass, on a cultural level, the multiple voices that contribute to a variegated society. Cultural identity, then need no longer be conceived according to a single and desired form, which all should strive to imitate, but can be regarded as a matrix of multiple elements that continually interact in ever new and unpredictable combinations. Cultural diversity mirrors personal versatility and it is the narrative mode that can accommodate its seemingly incompatible components in an existentially grounded philosophical format. This format circumvents the old philosophical dualism and its allegiance to the law of contradiction. From this perspective, philosophy, as it relates to the existential or lived world, needs to be appreciated as a means of focusing and reflectioning on the inherent ambiguity of life itself, instead of as a protective retreat to abstract formulas. But the Western philosophical heritage, particularly as employed in English-speaking countries, has a great difficulty in reconciling this conception of philosophy with rules of argument and logic. It regards ambiguity or paradox as messy and beyond the confines of *true* philosophy. Yet, it would seem it is necessary to move beyond such narrow definitions and sterile requirements, if philosophy is to help people of all denominations and all walks of life achieve a measure of understanding, both of themselves and of those with whom they daily come in contact.

And it is in this connection that I believe the work of Paul Ricoeur has been exemplary. For though his work in its initial phase was rooted in existentialism and phenomenology,[11] he soon became aware that mere description was an insufficient basis for philosophy. Language is not a transparent reflection of reality, anymore than the facts of a person's life are automatically indicative of his or her character. We do not always say what we mean, nor do we always mean what we say (or do, for that matter). There is self-deception as well as self-interest involved. This observation led Ricoeur to view all philosophy as a form of interpretation, although many who believe that knowledge is always the result of objective, empirical research have difficulty in conceding this point. To support his awareness that knowledge always involves a dimension of interpretation (however subtle and unconscious) Ricoeur turned to a form philosophy termed "hermeneutics."[12] Traditionally, "hermeneutics" was a technical term used to describe the interpretation or exegesis of texts, but in the last forty years the word has come to have a much wider application. Hermeneutics, as the act of interpretation, can refer to any aspect of understanding - be it that of a text of oneself, or of the world. In this vast domain of ways of understanding, the narrative mode figures prominently as one of the principal ways people have of depicting in a meaningful way the various moments, or succession of events that have occurred to them, i.e., a means of making sense of their lives. This may not always be logical, or sophisticated, in its presentation, but it will reverberate with a person's particular experiences. Yet Ricoeur will always insist that such instances, however unique or personally significant they may seem, are always a matter for interpretation. By this, Ricoeur wants to infer that none of us lives in a vacuum - that most of our expressions are determined by our past experience -both by the influence others have had on us and by the specific cultural ambience in which we have been raised. No one has escaped this often elusive indoctrination which is the basis of every act of interpretation.

While Ricoeur's hermeneutics has obvious relevance for any discussion of narrative, there are two further elements that I believe are of special significance for multiculturalism. The first of these is evident in Ricoeur's earliest explanation of texts. Here Ricoeur understands the relationship involved in interpreting a text as comparable to that between oneself and an alien object - the text functions as an other. Ricoeur endorses a disposition of openness to this other entity that has the potential for change, even to transform one's present outlook on the world. This is because any text (be it historical, philosophical or whatever) in and to itself can comprise a world-view that is totally different from the one people accept as a given or normal. Ricoeur believes that in approaching a text, a reader should be sufficiently receptive to its suggestions so that, as a result of the encounter, this reader could conceive of the possibility of alternate points of view, or different ways of acting.

But some qualifications are needed. Not all texts portray desirable realities - and discernment is required. Ricoeur introduced the term "a hermeneutics of suspicion" to describe the wary attitude one needs to adopt, particularly with regard to texts that are authoritarian or biased in an ideological fashion.[13] Rather than emphasizing this suspicious approach, however, Ricoeur is far more concerned with counteracting the rigidity and closed mindedness of many readers for whom anything that indicates change of even the slightest variety is immediately dismissed or classified as inferior or unacceptable.

As a way of mitigating such protective or hostile barriers, Ricoeur promotes a form of self-awareness which admits the fact that a particular background (be it cultural social, sexual, racial, religious, etc.) usually inculcates its members with selective attitudes. Each person no doubt incorporates a myriad of such influences, and Ricoeur suggests that it is each person's responsibility to become conscious of the pressures exerted by one's background and environment which may predispose, if not predetermine, one's attitude. The challenge of such self-knowledge has been incorporated by Ricoeur into the task of hermeneutics, so that ultimately it becomes not just an act of interpretation of a text, but a form of self-interpretation.[14]

This move towards critical self-reflection is the second element that can make a contribution to multiculturalism. It marked a change in Ricoeur's own appreciation of hermeneutics as an approach that pertains not only to objects such as texts, but also to persons.[15] And it is this complex application to the personal and subjective dimension on the part of Ricoeur that I feel could inform in a profoundly critical and meaningful way, those stereotypical and predictable responses from both sides that have typified the present multicultural debate. For there are not many participants engaged in this process who are willing to introduce the possibility that one could be ultimately enriched by respecting the position of another - to the point of admitting that an encounter with difference could be enlightening and life-enhancing. Participants are often more concerned with staking claims or guarding territory already controlled than hearing what the other has to say. This indicates that undertaking any such procedure of openness is not going to be easy. But Ricoeur would insist that, if there are to be any further developments in mutual comprehension, this delicate and demanding exercise in hermeneutics is necessary.

Ricoeur's principal recommendation is thus the need to alter our accustomed habits of thinking and acting. This is a type of hermeneutics that is not satisfied simply with an intellectualized theory of difference which remains removed from the intricacies of life itself. It is not enough to express verbally the benefits of tolerance. To some extent, this has been the basic fault of liberal pluralism - where life continues as normal with no real change in behaviour, though all sorts of pronouncements occur. Such conduct does not engage in a direct manner with the challenge that the utterly different offers. In contrast, Ricoeur's work respects the tenuous links that are always being negotiated between two people engaged in honest dialogue. It respects the fact that such encounters are not always successful - there are misunderstandings as well as lack of resolve - but the effort fosters further explorations in hope and trust of that dangerous territory that constitutes human relationships. It is never an easy thing to let oneself be vulnerable to another. It is an exacting task, requiring patience, risk-taking and often frustrations, but it is also a rewarding one, where heightened awareness both of oneself and of the other can compensate for the anxieties and discomfort involved. Perhaps it is the only way to confound the grievances that have been harboured too long, and honestly confront the other.

But it is the benefit of increased knowledge of self that also needs to be stressed. As a consequence, if not a corollary of an open-ended orientation towards the other, enhanced self-awareness should be emphasized, particularly in relation to the demands of genuine effort at multiculturalism. Within a hermeneutic framework, Ricoeur describes this revised notion of the subject that results as one that no longer imposes its own agenda on proceedings. Thus, the subject/object dichotomy of the Cartesian act of knowledge is surpassed, as is any notion of triumphalistic progress of type envisaged by Hegel. Instead, the type of subject or self that is constructed is less autonomous and more attuned to the vicissitudes of existence. Ricoeur describes this chastened version of the self as a non-egoistic, non-narcissistic and non-imperialistic mode of subjectivity.[16] (And it is this receptive demeanour, present from his earliest excursions in hermeneutics, that Ricoeur has only lately come to discern is more appropriately designated by narrative formulations.)

Ricoeur's more recent work compares this qualified and fluid form of self (as is depicted in narrative) with cultural identity. As such, there is an obvious parallel between persons who become more accepting of otherness in its many guises and cultures that become more tolerant of expressions at variance with their own. In Ricoeur's program, a necessary ingredient to assist the tolerance necessary for cultural diversity is a revised understanding of the term "ideology." Ricoeur understands that most cultures operate with a positive sense of ideology, though at times this can degenerate into unwarrented intrusion and regulation.

> The function of an ideology is to repeat and confirm a society's identity with what I would call founding symbols. An ideology's function is to identify a society and to preserve that society.[17]

Ricoeur allows that every ideology, however, has the potential to develop in a perverse manner.

> An ideology is pathological when it is twisted, held captive and monopolized by dominating groups in a society. And so an ideology that began as a preserving and justifying functions becomes a means of conservation.[18]

The question, of course, is how a culture can preserve its original impetus, while accommodating others, and not become defensively protectionist. Ricoeur is conscious of the fact that when a society changes too quickly there will be resistance. But how can moderation be achieved in a society between a form of tolerance that does not condone everything, and a short-sighted counter-action. For Ricoeur, a society should become cognizant of its own prejudices and weakness in the same way that a person becomes aware of his or her predispositions.

> I would say that every tolerant society must know its pressure points of intolerance because, after all, there is no-one who just tolerates everything. To be tolerant is to know where you are intolerant.[19]

Such a finely attuned knowledge would seem absolutely indispensable if cultural reciprocity is ever to be achieved. But this task would seem to be rendered all the more difficult when it is part of protracted on-going negotiations. This is because different cultural communities have varying thresholds of patience along the tolerance/intolerance continuum.

> In the end, we are all living in societies that are seeking their true pressure-points of intolerance. That is a very difficult *family* debate because we do not all locate these pressure-points at the same place.[20]

This acute observation would seem extremely pertinent to all those engaged in multicultural communication. There is a need for careful discernment not only of one's own weaknesses but also of those with whom a measure of accord is sought. In this regard, Michel Foucault's detailed studies of the machinations of power may be helpful.[21] Foucault has brought to our attention the fact that power need not operate only from superior positions. Power insinuates its way into all forms of social formations so that no class or race has a monopoly on its effects. Even within those communities and cultures deemed to be minorities or on the margins of a dominant structures, there are relations of power that operate in insidious ways. Thus, though a group could consider itself in an inferior position with regard to a more powerful organization, it exerts power on its own members to conform to certain standards. Power is pervasive throughout all levels of societies and their network of infrastructures. This double-sided nature of power, which puts each individual in an ambiguous position as to its operations of both acting out and being acted upon, also must be acknowledged. For all too often other cultures become the scapegoat for the perverse machinations of power by manipulators within a dominant culture who monopolize resources. At the same time, there are those on margins who sometimes blame the dominant culture for all the problems that occur within their own ranks, though often these are caused by similar abuses of power within their own communities.

Multiculturalism, when viewed from these various perspectives, constitutes a minefield not only for the establishment of relations of mutual regard and support, but also for adequate and appropriate philosophical expression. From a personal standpoint, the interweaving of the margins of tolerance and intolerance need to be scrupulously deciphered, otherwise backlashes can easily occur. But what is more important, on a social and cultural level, is that the diffuse, if not ambiguous, infiltrations of power be traced (wherever possible) to their sources. This knowledge could help prevent catastrophes of misunderstanding and alienation. It would also serve to indicate the various movements of criss-crossing, the bilateral shifts of power and the countervailing trends that permeate any multicultural enterprise. Narrative and hermeneutics can provide a measure of philosophical awareness that helps to illustrate the pluriform nature of multiculturalism, but neither form presumes to capture all the nuances present. Multiculturalism, in the end, is a vibrant challenge to the accustomed orthodoxies of Western thought and attitudes. It is a needed corrective that counteracts   self-satisfaction   or   cultural   stagnation.

Multiculturalism is not a dangerous or destabilizing development, it is rather a barometer of the prevailing conditions of the most affluent countries in the Western world. It is an indication of their readiness to foster change rather than remain obstinately inflexible - which they do to their own peril. Multiculturalism is a precursor of things to come - as such it must continue to test the margins of intolerance and the limits of philosophical speculation if this new order of things is to emerge without destructive conflict.

FOOTNOTES

1   For a good survey of the Pre-Socratic philosophers and their varying opinions on *the one and the many* see John Mansley Robinson, *An Introduction to Early Greek Philosophy*,Boston: Houghton Mifflin Co., 1968. See especially Heraclitus, p. 97; Parmenides, p. 107ff; and Zeno, p. 127ff.

2   G.W.F. Hegel spelt his version of dialectic, presided over by *Geist* in *Phenomenology of Spirit*, trans. and annotated by A.V. Miller, Oxford: Oxford University Press, 1977.

3   Jean-Paul Sartre, "Hell is Other People," *The Philosophy of Jean-Paul Sartre*, Ed. and introduced by Robert Denoon Cumming, New York: Vintage,1965, pp. 185-187. See also, "The Encounter with the Other," Ibid., pp. 188-208.

4   John Hick, "Religious Pluralism," *The Encyclopedia of Religion,* Editor-in-Chief Mircea Eliade, New York: Macmillan, 1987, Vol. 12, pp. 331-333.

5   John Hick, *God Has Many Names*, Philadelphia: Westminister, 1982.

6   Jacques Derrida, "Différance," *Margins of Philosophy*, trans. A. Bass, Chicago: University of Chicago Press, 1982, pp. 1-27.

7   Paul Ricoeur, *Time and Narrative*, Vols. I-III, trans. K. McLaughlin and D. Pellauer, Chicago: University of Chicago Press, 1983-1988.

8   Paul Ricoeur, *Time and Narrative*, Vol. I, p. 75.

9   Paul Ricoeur, *Oneself as Another*, trans. K. Blamey, Chicago: University of Chicago Press, 1992.

10   Paul Ricoeur, "Life: A Story in Search of a Narrator," in *Facts and Values: Philosophical Perspectives from West and non-West Perspectives,* ed. M.C. Doeser and J.N. Kray, Dordrecht, The Netherlands: Martinus Nijhoff, 1986, pp. 121-132.

11   A good introduction to the type of philosophy called "phenomenology" is *An Invitation to Phenomenology: Studies in the Philosophy of Experience*, ed. J.M. Edie, Chicago: Quadrangle Books, 1965.

12   Paul Ricoeur, "The Task of Hermeneutics," in *Paul Ricoeur, Hermeneutics and the Human Sciences*, ed. and trans. by John B. Thompson, Cambridge: Cambridge University Press, pp. 43-62.

13 For a description of the "hermeneutics of suspicion" see, Paul Ricoeur, *Freud and Philosophy: An Essay on Interpretation*, New Haven: Yale University Press, 1970, pp. 24-27.

14 Paul Ricoeur, "The Hermeneutical Function of Distanciation," *Paul Ricoeur: Hermeneutics and the Human Sciences*, pp. 142-44.

15 Paul Ricoeur, "The Model of the Text: Human Action Considered as a Text," *Paul Ricoeur: Hermeneutics and the Human Sciences*, pp. 197-221.

16 Paul Ricoeur, "Philosophical Hermeneutics and Theological Hermeneutics," *Studies in Religion/Sciences Religieuses*, 5/1 (1975-6), p. 8.

17 "History as Narrative and Practice," Peter Kemp talks to Paul Ricoeur, *Philosophy Today*, 19/3-4 (1985), p. 8.

18 Ibid., p. 8.

19 Ibid., p. 9.

20 Ibid., p. 9.

21 Michel Foucault, Part III: Practice: Knowledge and Power, in *Language, Counter-Memory, Practice,* ed. and intro. by D.F. Bouchard, Ithaca: Cornell University Press, 1977, pp. 199-233.

Branwen Stonecipher
Clergy, Covenant of the Goddess
Kate Slater
Pagan / Occult / Witchcraft Special Interest Group of
American Mensa

If You're White You Can't Be Pagan

The 1958 edition of the Oxford International Dictionary provides this definition for the word "Witch":

> "A female magician or sorceress; in later use, especially a women supposed to have dealings with the devil or evil spirits and to be able by their cooperation to perform supernatural acts."

Perhaps we could define "Witch" as a follower of a European aboriginal nature religion. The dictionary's gratuitous reference to the devil or evil spirits is offensive in the extreme, considering that there is no devil in the pantheon of European Witchcraft.

The most common public image of the Witch in the North American patriarchy is the green or grey-skinned, warty, misshapen, snaggle-toothed, smirking hag of *The Wizard of Oz*. We see her image emblazoned on shopfronts every autumn, along with the usual assortment of bats, black cats, haunted castles, and monsters.

Recently, an Alberta weekly attempted to find some Witches willing to pose for it, to illustrate an article on Canadian Witches. When none could be found, the magazine used a painting, *The Witches' Sabbath*, by Francisco, circa 1790, of witches offering babies to a goat-like creature. Goya is said not to have believed in the existence of Witchcraft, and he, in creating a series of hideous pictures for the Osuna Palace, used what he thought of as the mythology of the Inquisition as an expression of the evil that lurks in the hearts of every human being.

The tabloid press prefer to portray Witches as ugly old hags who consort with demons, sacrifice small animals, and kidnap children for unspeakable ends. At the opposite pole of stereotyping, quite a few of us will remember the 1960s television show "Bewitched" in which the Witch was portrayed as an everyday housewife whose magical powers kept her house sparkling clean and her bumbling husband out of trouble. The real Witch is none of these things.

Out of 242 Witches known to us in western Canada, the vast majority are married, lower-middle-class parents, struggling to raise children while holding down a full-time job. The ones that we have been privileged to meet don't have obvious facial deformities nor are they given to abnormal outbursts of cackling or of boiling frogs in a pot. They would be reliable babysitters, but could not clean your house by twitching their noses, even collectively. Most of these 242 Witches have college educations. Ninety-two per cent are employed, in sixty-three different occupations, but only nine persons have the occupations popularly expected of Witches: herbalist, fortune teller, or full-time priestess or priest.

The good news is, Witches do seem to manage to make themselves useful to the society in which they live. The bad news is that they may live in fear of persecution. The European Witch-hunts ended three hundred years ago, but the fear remains very real and very realistic. Consider the following three case histories, all of which took place within Alberta and within the last five years.

CASE HISTORY NO. 1

A tornado strikes a city, destroying houses and causing immense property damage, numerous injuries, and several deaths. One of the areas devastated by the storm is a mobile home park. A few days after the tornado, a resident of that park is severely beaten while resisting attack by an angry mob. She ends up in hospital, and her trailer is burned by the mob. The victim of the beating is a shopkeeper who sells, among other things, books on occult subjects. She is unable to identify her assailants, and no charges are laid.

The mob's justification for the destruction and the beating? Her attackers considered her to be a Witch who caused the tornado by magical means. As "proof" of their charges, they note that her trailer was left essentially untouched by the tornado. The outcome: The woman, who considers herself a radical feminist rather than a Witch, leaves town the following week and sets up another shop in eastern Canada, where she expects her neighbours to be not quite so violent.

CASE HISTORY NO. 2

A group of Witches, all women, decide to incorporate as a church so that they can raise funds towards a temple for the Goddess. They duly sign the articles of incorporation with their names and addresses and send them in to the government for registration. After some preliminary quibbling, the government accepts their application.

A couple of months later, incidents of vandalism occur at the rented hall that they use for their rituals. At first these are minor: For example, red pain is splashed on the building's steps. Then the incidents begin to escalate. The building's are glued while people are inside. Fires are lit on the steps of the building. Crude leaflets saying "Burn Witch Burn" are scattered about the grounds of the building and stuffed in the letterboxes of some of the original signatories of the church's articles of incorporation.

At this point the police are contacted. Since the leaflets have clearly expressed threats of injury, the police stake out the building. During the following week's ritual, the police notice two people hiding in the bushes near the building, search them, and find that they have glue and paint in their possession. A check of the apprehended people's identities reveals that they are education workers at a neighbouring church that had recently held a crusade against Satanic influences in Canadian society. The pastors of the church, when told of the apprehension of their employees, express dismay but note that they cannot be held responsible for the privately held beliefs of their employees.

The outcome: The people are released, without charges being laid, after being given a very stern warning by the police officers who promise to "throw the book at them" the next time they catch them near the building.

CASE HISTORY NO. 3

A television station decides to present a special news story about Pagan celebrations of Hallowe'en. After some searching, they manage to find a willing Witch, who consents to an interview on condition that the television station not film her face. Up to a point, this works out okay. Unfortunately, a couple of profile shots of the Witch, together with her distinctive accent, are sufficient for her co-workers to identify her. Three days later, her boss's manager, who is a lay reader at a local church, organizes a prayer meeting in the Witch's place of employment, which culminates in an attempt at a lunch-hour exorcism within the Witch's office as she is eating lunch at her desk.   The prayer group brings a bell, Bible, and candles into the room and makes quite a racket while dripping wax on the carpets and furniture. Nothing much seems to happen and the manager eventually retreats in embarrassment. Both the Witch and her co-workers are predictably unimpressed by the failure of the exorcism.

Three months after the television broadcast, the Witch finds herself out of work after her boss's favourable appraisal of her job performance is revised downwards by the company's manager. Coincidentally, the firing occurs three weeks after the Witch succeeds in discovering a new oil pool for her employers. She later finds out that the company had been recruiting her replacement since early November.   The outcome: The Witch's lawyer negotiates a settlement from the company. Her former co-workers support her in setting up a small business, and she learns to stay off of the television news.

WITCHES IN THE REAL WORLD

Most western Canadian witches have learned to be very cautious about revealing their religious preferences to their neighbours or their employers. Some younger Witches, who aren't particularly afraid of starvation are sufficiently enthusiastic about their faith to wear costume jewellery in the shape of a pentacle (a five-pointed star within a circle) in much the same way that some Jews wear the Star of David and some Christians wear symbols of the cross, a dove, or a stylized fish. Thus far we seem to have been spared the spectacle, increasingly common or the United States, of the black-robed Witch showing up at civic meetings and screeching at politicians whenever they seem to be getting out of line.

The Artists, musicians, and bus drivers may do perfectly well as public Witches, since their religious beliefs are not commonly held by their customers to have any bearing on their capabilities. Consider, however, the likely outcome of public exposure for the college professor seeking tenure, the medical student seeking a residency, or the geologist trying to survive in an oil company.

The problem that some of these people face is that the market for their job skills is sufficiently tight that the slightest nonconformity may spell the difference between a job offer and a form letter. Given the information that a prospective employee is a Pagan of any sort, the employer is likely to conclude that the candidate is either thoroughly evil or thoroughly dizzy.

This particular difficulty does not affect only Witches: our newspapers tell us enough stories of people from ethnic minorities who are denied fair access to employment and housing.

Canadian human rights legislation prohibits discrimination on the basis of religious belief. The courts, nevertheless, have been inconsistent in their recognition of European aboriginal religions such as Witchcraft, while at the same time steadily extending protection to North American aboriginal religions. It is as if the courts are telling us, "If you're white, you can't be Pagan." Why must this be the case? It could be a matter of simple religious prejudice. Canadian law is derived from English common law, which draws heavily upon the Bible and its basic precepts of human conduct. Most of the behavioural prescriptions of the Bible are derived in turn from common sense and civility, but a few of the biblical rules display a certain lack of tolerance for non-believers:

Thou shalt not suffer a Witch to live (Ex.d. 22:18). There shall not be found among you *any one* that maketh his son or daughter to pass through the fire, *or* that useth divination, *or* an observer of times, or an enchanter, or a witch. (Deut. 18. 1.) Given that our most vocal politicians and much of the western Canadian press are regularly heard to proclaim that Canada is a God-fearing, Christian land, and given that the most rapidly growing federal political party in this country seems to wish Canada were populated exclusively by whites, there are two conclusions that the average Canadian might draw on the subject of Paganism in general and Witchcraft in particular.

1.   Any sensible God-fearing Canadian would never dream of being a Pagan.
2.   All Pagans are Indians, or black, or whatever else the mind can conjure up.

Perhaps a better explanation of the indifference of our courts to Witches and Neo-Pagans in general is that it is administratively convenient to ignore new religious groups. It is quite probable that every crackpot and would-be New Age guru in Canada has considered the benefits of incorporating a church. A charitable registration number is indispensable to anyone trying to pry money out of tight-fisted donors. To be recognized as a church by Revenue Canada, a religious society must fulfill two criteria: provision of public religious education and performance of charitable acts. Merely gathering together to worship the deity or deities of your choice is not sufficient basis for a tax number. Most Witches have no objection to the performance of charitable acts, but the provision of public religious education is a bit more difficult. Given that Witches (and most other Neo-Pagans) don't enjoy a high level of legal protection, public services are vulnerable to the sort of disruption that we described earlier. Revenue Canada also applies a rule of thumb that calls for a would-be established church to have been in existence for one hundred years and have one hundred members. The first criterion isn't too difficult for any aboriginal religion to satisfy. The second, once again, is a problem because many Witches are understandably loathe to reveal the nature of their religious belief to a government agency.

Given all of these obstacles to official recognition, it is little wonder that many white Canadians have turned to Native American aboriginal religions for spiritual solutions. Having been raised to explore issues in a rational fashion, middle-class whites often find themselves torn between their yearning for comfortable roots in a nature-based spirituality and their insistent denial that their own ancestors in Europe could ever have been so irrational as to have had their own aboriginal cultures. The solution to this middle-class dilemma is to transfer yearnings onto Native American cultures, which are perceived as being attractively primitive and therefore lacking in any need to maintain rationality. A censorship process is clearly operating here: white middle-class aspirations to "get in touch with the earth" have no room for the notion of European tribal religions. This whole process is in essence a form of spiritual racism. Nevertheless, real Witches don't want to be Indians any more than real Indians want to be Witches.

While, middle-class Canadians are starting to catch on to the fact that they do have their own authentic aboriginal roots. Being born and raised in Europe, I can assure you that there are such things as white aborigines, and we are collectively conscious of the fact that we are visitors to North America. An increasing number of scholarly books are being written on Witchcraft by Witches. These books certainly are an improvement on the lurid Witchcrap" that's been flooding bookstores and libraries for the past twenty-five years. Given twenty-five more years of solid scholarship, it may finally become acceptable, although perhaps never fashionable, to be white and Pagan in Alberta.

WHAT IS PAGANISM?

My favourite definition of Paganism is "personal religion." All of us have highly individual concepts and faith; we seek what resonates for us, on a deep level. During the past nine years, I have participated in four sociological or anthropological studies of Pagans and ignored two other questionnaires. A tongue-in-cheek summary of what was asked would be: "How did you become weird and what is your net annual income?" Always afterward I have thought bemusedly, "Those weren't the question I'd have asked," and not the things I would have considered worth saying about my religious beliefs. I proposed to speak for types of Paganism in which men are a vital part–probably one in four Pagans is male. For one, the sexes are even; we are all marginalized here.

I am a priestess of the Old Religion, whatever that means. Like my peers, I am still learning, trying to understand what it means to be a "priestess"–this word of archaic power. I study partly for myself and partly as a junior member of our clergy; I am one of the people available to consecrate hand-fastings and funerals for Pagan friends or perform other functions of clergy. Within my faith this is not exceptional; since we believe that divinity exists within us all, we are each able to act as our own priestess or priest. My faith is both old and in a continuous process of invention. Many people, of different kinds and in different countries, are working on this process, with the main developmental period starting about twenty-five years ago. We borrow from many sources: Cabbala and chakra systems, meditation techniques and old melodies that have been used as Christian hymns. Yet the Pagan cores are quite unique and distinct from any of these, and are being built from our individual and collective insights and by the deliberate experiencing of mystery, ritual, and magic as well as from analyses by scholars in the fields of anthropology, psychology, theology, and the sciences.

What, then, is Paganism, especially those neo-pagan branches relating to old or modern Witchcraft and Druidism? In this section, share some of the images, myths, hopes, and theology that form a living stream from which differing persons and groups draw symbols and concepts and to which they constantly add their own contributions.

For ease of reading, I will often say "we" or make apparently general statements; it would be more appropriate to keep repeating "Some of us think this some of the time." Pagans link at a grass-roots level; we have few, if any, spiritual leaders; and our individual understandings evolve and change with time. Therefore, I want to let individual Pagans tell you for themselves what they believe, to give you a sense of why they choose what, today, is a difficult path. I will do this by presenting some of their music, chosen for its focus on Pagan religious and attitudinal content.

North American Pagans are distinctive in the amount of singing they do, in religious services, and socially. Most of our songs are short, heavily harmonized, and carefully worded chants or they are long ballads. From the longer songs only excerpts appear, in order to include a wider range of ideas in this paper. Singers are mostly Pagans or friends of Pagans–Witches, Druids, people following paths based on Native American spiritual beliefs, and people who would simply describe themselves as Pagans or practitioners of earth spirituality. A few describe themselves as synthesists, or will include Christian or Jewish faiths within their broader polytheism. Modern Pagans are creating a large body of music and ritual and visual art. A small part of this is commercially available, most is privately circulated. Recordings vary in quality: a few were produced in studios by professional musicians, most were made by Pagans writing for themselves and for each other, sharing their work with cassette recorders in their homes.

RELIGIOUS CONTENT WITHIN SON LYRICS

Lyrics by fifteen different authors follow, with brief commentaries on the themes to look for in each.

Witches, Druids, and other Pagans face with rueful humour and frequent frustration the task of explaining ourselves to incredulous or suspicious families and communities. We know that it would be simpler to simply call ourselves by labels that aren't loaded with problematic connotations. Among ourselves we argue whether it makes sense to stubbornly try to reclaim words that have been so defamed as "Witch". Branwen will say, "It's what I am; I will say, "But nothing else fits so well." Bonnie Lockhart speaks to our feelings in this excerpt from her ballad, "Who are the Witches?"

... Some people thought that the Witches were bad,
Some people were scared of the power they had–
The power to help and to heal and to care:
It's nothing to fear, it's a pleasure to share.

Who are the Witches, where do they come from?
Maybe your great, great grandmother was one!
Witches are wise, wise women, they say–
There's a little Witch in every woman today.

Pagan concepts of deity feature immanence and sometimes also transcendence. We generally polytheistic and to varying extents animist; we tend to believe that all things—people, spirit, land and its life forms, and the sacred—are interconnected and are one. One concept holds that deities are aspects of central realities—all gods one God, all goddesses one Goddess—and there is one Initiator or source or centre where everything joins. In another description, everything is part of a good and beautiful pattern like that of the star-filled sky, and as in Zen philosophy, matters that affect one part of the pattern or web affect all its parts.

This idea is beautifully expressed in the song "One," by Seattle singer-songwriter Co'Lo'neh. Her spirituality is now primarily influenced by Native American practice.

> One God, many ways,
> One Goddess, many names
> From the centre, all has come
> To the centre, all will go.
>
> One love, many ways,
> One source, many names
> Look within you for the centre
> Feel the oneness of the flow.

We frequently divide the sacred into male and female polarity, the Goddess and the God. Some Pagans consider that these are equal and essential, complementary partners; for some the Goddess is primary and stands alone or is the matrix that holds or gives birth to the God. Branwen would strongly argue that we should never consider different goddesses to be facets or aspects of one Goddess; each is unique with her own name and cultural niche, although groups may share attributes of age or responsibility.

Goddess spirituality, the opportunity to vision the sacred within female bodies like our own, has become terribly important to many women, in both Pagan and Christian paths. Pagans believe that deity is as likely to manifest within a woman as within a man. This Goddess hymn was probably written in the United States:

> Kali, Rhada, Sita, Parvati,
> Mary, full of grace,
> Hannah, Rachel, Kwan Yin, Fatima,
> Let us see your face.
> Bless us, oh mother, sister and lover,
> Take us to your heart.
> Teach us your mercy, strength and compassion,

Hold us in your love.

We borrow myth and imagery from many cultures, including Celtic, Greek, Roman, and Norse. "Hymn to Bridgit" is a Druid invocation to the Irish goddess of fertility, poetic inspiration, smithcraft, and healing, with Gaelic and English verses. It was written by Isaac Bonewits, who leads Ár nDraiocht Féin, North America's largest Druid Fellowship, and by Shenain Bell.

O Bridgit, our heart, O brightest Queen
Cast your blessings unto us.
We are your children and you are our Mother,
So hearken unto us.
You are the cauldron now in our grove,
Wise woman, inspire us,
O fire of love, O fire of light,
Please Bridgit, come to us.

The Pagan God appears independently or as the son and consort of the Goddess. The God may be seen as a symbol of all life: all that which is born, grows, dies, and is reborn; or all that grows, falls, and grows again, like the phallus, like the antlers of deer or crops in their seasons, nourishing both land and people. Hay may also be seen as a solar deity, undergoing birth, maturity, and death with the solstice.

The Goddess moves from youth to age as Maiden, Mother, Crone, and Mystery, but rarely dies except in her aspect of Mother Earth, where she can be harmed. The God, in his ability to experience birth and death, represents ourselves and all life on earth.

Most Pagans acknowledge roots in agricultural cultures and even when they live in cities attempt to maintain a sense of seasonal transformation. The image of the wheel or turning circle covers both the year and the course of our lifetimes. Many Pagans believe in reincarnation either as continuing individuals or into universal energy; some do not. Another common image is the spiral, a circle moving through time.

We try to accept natural change rather than fight it. "The Harvest" is a fall equinox song written by Rick Hamouris, who is associated with the California organization Forever Forests.

Gather the crop we so carefully have tended,
See how fast the basket fills,
And from season to season the days ever turn
On the wheel of the year.

So the Sun King dies, as the corn and the grain
Feel the cool steel scythe of the harvest.
Filled with joy we weep, for the love unknown and missed,
As we reap the seeds we have sown.
. . .

The next set of songs was chosen to portray the concepts of animism and interconnection. We can hear the voices of our deities directly, and how better than in the sound of windswept trees or ocean surges? The Goddess is our Mother and is also the planet herself, apparent if we listen for her. We are truly part of this world, made from its old alchemical elements, earth, air, fire, and matter. All three songs are by unknown authors.

The forests echo with the voices of the Old Ones
And their voices whisper in the wind.
The oceans thunder with the voices of the Old Ones
And their voices sing across the land.

Ancient Mother, I hear you calling
Ancient Mother, I hear your song
Ancient Mother, I share your laughter
Ancient Mother, I taste your tears.

Earth my body, water my blood,
Air my breath and fire my spirit.

Few if any Pagans see this world as a place where we live in order to pass on to a better place after death. Whether we see it as our home and our responsibility, as part of ourselves, as the living body of our Goddess, or as the place to which we will keep returning, we have a vital stake in the planet's health. Many Pagans are urgently committed to peace and ecology activism as part of their spiritual lives, with activities such as anti-nuclear protest as their service for Mother Earth and the observance of their faith in turn nourishing their strength to protest.

"The Burning Times" is by Charlie Murphy, a professional musician in Seattle who writes about personal, political, cultural, and spiritual themes. One verse says this:

Well, the Earth is a Witch and the man still burn her,
Stripping her down with mining and poison of their wars.
Still to us the Earth is a healer, a teacher, a mother,
She's the weaver of the web of life that keeps us all alive.

She gives us the vision to see through the chaos,
She gives us the courage–it is our will to survive.

At times we may think in terms of parental, caring deities. It
is not unusual for a group of Pagans to celebrate a holy day together,
each holding a different but essentially compatible interpretation of
deity. "The Good Earth" seems to grow new verses every year or two
and spans a two-thousand-year vision, from the building of
megalithic sites to space travel. The author is known, but I could not
trace her name at the time of writing.

In days of old, when the world was much younger,
They studied and prayed as the seasons rolled by.
Watching the dance of the moon and the starlight,
They then knew the Lady and Lord of all life.

Around and around and around turns the good earth,
All things must change as the seasons roll by.
We are the children of the Lord and the Lady,
Whose mysteries we'll know, but we'll never know why.
. . .

Now we who reach for the stars in the heavens,
Earning our lives from the meadows and groves,
Still live in the love of the Lord and the Lady,
The greater the circle, the more they love grows.

Many of our best loved songs convey messages of
empowerment; nurturing our courage and unity in work,
particularly in the peace movement, which can numb hope and burn
out its most loyal participants. "Light is returning" is by Charlie
Murphy and is often sung at winter solstice.

Light is returning, even though this is the darkest hour,
No one can hold back the dawn.
Let's keep it burning, let's keep the light of hope alive
Make safe the journey through the storm.
One planet is turning, circling on her path around the sun,
Earth Mother is calling her children home.

The next comes from Greenham Common in England, where
relays of women have camped in continuous protest outside an
American nuclear base for almost fifteen years.

We are the power in everyone.

We are the dance of the moon and sun,
We are the hope that will never hide,
We are the turning of the tide.

The following chant is one of the many created by Reclaiming, an eco-feminist craft tradition based on the writing and teaching of Starhawk. It was written by Rose May Dance and Starhawk.

We are alive as the earth is alive,
We have the power to fight for our freedom,
If we have courage, we can be healers,
Like the sun, we shall rise.

Growing from the ideals of empowerment and self-healing are twelve step programs using Pagan imagery for the "power greater than ourselves" on which we depend. "The Ascent" uses the myth of Persephone as an image of the Goddess that can empower a person during the hard work of recovery. This song was written by Isaac Bonewits; an excerpt follows:

. . .
The road I am walking is high, steep and narrow
And all that surrounds me seems hopeless and grey.
I know far ahead there's a land of bright beauty
But I'll have to get better day by day.
. . .

My Lady, I am told, was an innocent maiden
When first she descended beneath the cold clay.
She returns every spring to bring me her wisdom
I'll have to get better day by day.

Now I walk not alone, for my Lady walks with me,
Her bright shining love keeps the demons at bay,
She lightens the road though she can't walk it for me
I'll have to get better, day by day.
. . .

Pagans drew inspiration from myth, but we live in the real world and take responsibility for our well-being there. We see "magic" as one way of making changes, primarily within ourselves. One saying is that "With the right intent, skill and training, every individual is able to create all the magic that he or she will ever need."

There is a good explanation of that statement in "The Tempered Blade" by Anahita Gula of Ottawa. Anahita is an academic whose current specialty is the ways in which power is manifested in non-traditional religions, such as those native to Africa and North America and in Neo-Paganism.

There's magic in the setting sun, and in the morning dew,
Or in the crashing ocean waves of deepest sparkling blue.
In these are wrapped the mysteries of which our parents spoke,
Not hidden in some arcane words, or underneath a cloak.

The magic's in yourself, my child
The magic's in your soul.
The mystery's your heart, my child
And love shall make you whole.
. . .

I've walked down many twisting paths and fallen on my face
But that's a fact of life, my child, a fact you can't erase.
So learn to take it all in stride and use what e'er you're taught
By earth and water, fire and air, the tempered blade is wrought.

A few of our songs reflect the great pain experienced by Pagans who have come to this path as refugees from abusive home situations (which may have been associated with other spiritual paths), or who have been "burned" by the intolerance of others, which Branwen has described as including harassment, slander, job loss, property damage, death threats, and beatings. For these people, the Inquisition is a living metaphor.

The following song by Isaac Bonewits reflects this from a Druid perspective. A sub-theme is the idea of "old wisdom" that has been hidden, nurtured, and may be regained in new community and spiritual practice.

I watched my parents die 'neath the sword
Because they would not break their word
That they had sworn to the gods above
To sing their songs of joy and love.

I wander now from village to town,
Up each lonely road and down.
I carry naught save a harp and a staff,
A word of faith, a song and a laugh.
. . .

The ancient wisdom, it still lives on.
It lives in a word and a laugh and a song.
Healers, wizards, bards are we,
And we'll walk our rounds till the earth is free.

We wander now from village to town,
Up each lonely road and down.
Each carries naught save a harp and a staff,
A word of hope, a song and a laugh.

Now, in 1992, Pagans are many and diverse. We cannot know exactly what our ancestors did on windy hilltops hundreds or thousands of years ago. We learn from the findings of archaeologists, from the accounts of anthropologists, from observation of other non-Christian cultures, from the writings of folklore and history and myth, from the teachings of the Native peoples willing to share their beliefs with non-Natives, and from the memories of our Elders. We can go to hilltops and discover through experiment and practice what resonates for us–and in our common humanity we may approach the thinking of our ancestors.

When we call on our goddesses and gods we hear and feel them in the winds and in our hearts. We look at each other, different yet alike, and say, "Thou art Goddess; thou art God." We share thoughts and dreams and music. We can support each other and we are determined to guard our precious religious freedom. We must find the courage to talk or sing about our personal beliefs so people can understand them, even though caution may require us to use a post office box while we do so.

In the name of the Goddess: never again the burning.
This excerpt from a song written by Isaac Bonewits says it well:

. . .
You thought that you would silence us,
Make the fires of freedom dim–
But we say No!
Just say No! We say
Never again the burning!
Never again the burning!
Never again the burning!
No!

MUSIC CITED

Bonnie Lockhart. "Who are the Witches?"

Co'Lo'neh. "One." *Children of the Earth Sing Earth Songs and Chants.* Sound cassette. With permission.

Isaac Bonewits. "The Ascent"; "I Wander Now"; "We Just Say No"; and with Shenain Bell, "Hymn to Bridgit." *Be Pagan Once Again.* Sound cassette, published by Ár nDraiocht Féin. With permission.

Rick Hamouris. "The Harvest." *Welcome to Annwfn.* Sound cassette. Published by Nemeton/Forever Forests.

Charlie Murphy. "The Burning Times". *Secret Language.* "Light is Returning". *Canticles of Light.* Sound cassette. Both with permission.

Greenham Common Women. "We are the Power in Everyone."

Rose May Dance and Starhawk. "We are Alive as the Earth is Alive." *Chants,* by Reclaiming Community. Sound cassette. Published by Reclaiming Collective. With permission.

Anahita Gula. "The Tempered Blade." With permission.

Unkown authors. Kali, Rhada; Voices; The Good Earth; Ancient Mother; Earth My Body.

Marcia J. Epstein
Faculty of General Studies
The University of Calgary

Centring the Margins: Of Music, Myth, and Motherhood

To begin: this essay is not a formal academic study. The topic it approaches is too vast for the confines of a single volume, much less a single chapter, and fragmentation is not the path of choice in this instance. What you see here is a cross between a hymn and a report on work in progress. The work in question has several phases: analytical, philosophical, and musical. This essay is simply a portion of the road-map that leads to its realization. The goal of the journey is nothing less than the reintegration of the feminine aspects of deity into Western culture, a journey that many share. The particular path I wish to document is the creation of a new liturgical form: a liturgy of God the Mother. It is modelled on a number of ancient sources—hymns to Inanna and Quan Yin, Gnostic scripture, the medieval Catholic mass, and the infinitely rich cross-cultural tradition of singing as a means of worship. The intention behind it involves a kind of hubris: an assumption that at this point in the history of our culture, neither patriarchal social structures nor patriarchal religions are sufficient (Eisler 1987).

The remedy, of course, is a long, slow, intricate, and wrenching process of restructuring belief systems. The envisioning of God as Mother as well as Father is one small facet of the change, but one that may prove to be crucial to our survival as a species. Our civilization has lost its respect for the Earth and the forces of life, as well as its respect for women. This is no coincidence: the healing of both lies in restoration of a paradigm that has been ignored for thousands of years.

Thus far, most attempts at restoring the feminine side of spirituality have been revivalist in nature. Practiced for the most part by people whose background is urban and secular, they may involve reconstruction of ancient European pagan practices, imitation of Native rituals, or experiments in the traditions of

Wicca. Along with these movements are others within "mainstream" monotheism, which have resulted in renewed attention to the female figures in the history of the more hierarchical religions–in Catholicism to Mary and the female saints and mystics, in Judaism to the mothers of Israel: Sarah, Rachel, Esther, and others whose legends are prominent in the scriptural sources. These may be seen as essentially conservative solutions, looking back in time to what preceded the present system, or focussing on aspects within it.

There is not yet a wholesale attempt to change the paradigm in a way that will give mainstream practitioners direct access to the feminine paradigm. While historical or scriptural study is certainly valuable, it is not the equivalent of a communal worship service, which acts upon the senses, the memory, and the "right brain" as well as the rational mind. The work documented here is a small step in the direction of change. Its mandate is to redefine the traditional anthropomorphic image called "God" in a way that is neither male nor genderless, the usual options we are given for such envisioning). Its purpose is to acknowledge and to define the third, hidden face of that metaphysical being, the female side. It is also designed to attempt the impossible: the uniting of various religions and spiritual traditions, as well as non-believers, into a community of spiritual concord, whether consciously acknowledged or not.

Despite repeated assurances that the Judaeo-Christian God is genderless, the prevailing concept with which most of us in Western culture are most familiar is that of a male entity –patriarch, father, son. Although the deep psychospiritual need for a corresponding feminine image has often been articulated in the recent literature of feminist spirituality, its form is not easy to imagine; God represents ultimate, unbounded power, and the notion of a female with unbounded power is antithetical to our heritage of cultural assumptions. In the standard literature, including that of scriptural traditions, unbounded power in female hands is associated with evil, while goodness in the female is predicated upon her receiving power from a male, or relinquishing power to him. As the work of Simone de Beauvoir first made amply clear, the female is "Other," defined in opposition to the male, not in her own right (de Beauvoir 1956).

How, then, to envision a female deity, a figure of power unique to her gender, in a form suitable to the spiritual needs of the twenty-first century? First, those needs must be examined and defined. In the traditions of scripture, myth, and literature, the male partakes of transcendence, the female of immanence. The essential division is that between Earth-Mother and Sky-Father, a distinction that may be as old as human consciousness. He is up there, she is down here; he is remote, she is close enough to touch; he is spirit, she is matter. Here we have the first clue–the traditional paradigm has assigned transcendent spiritual essence to the male. Step out of the picture for a moment and survey the assumptions inherent in that conclusion, then ask yourself: What are the natures of the Earth-Father and the Sky-Mother? Again, precedent intervenes. The Corn God of ancient European mythology and the sacrificial Harvest King come to mind, along with their echoes in Christian mythology. For the female side, we summon the Egyptian goddess Neter, the self-created, whose menstrual blood held within it the incipient matter of all creation. Egypt also provides the goddess Nut, whose arched body defined the night sky, and her consort Geb, an earth-god whose body strained upward to fertilize her (Walker 1983).

Take the image a step further, and consider the nature of the transcendent feminine: she is the vast complexity of the life force, the potential that begins all being. This quality is exemplified in the Hindu concept of the *Shakti* and the Hebrew *Shekinah*, both representing the energy that manifests potential. In more concrete terms, she is the ocean in which all life found its origins: this association is verified by geological as well as mythological evidence. When science and theology agree, what you have is a powerful paradigm, and this one resonates on many levels. Consider the relation between the medieval Catholic appelation of Mary as *stella maris*, star of the sea, the slow development of the amoeba in its watery cradle on this planet, and the monthly ebb and flow of the female cycle. Consider, without much need for rational analysis, and you may find your memory reaching back to recall the face of the Mother-God.

Her nature is also that of the protector, coming to the defense of new life. She is the ferocity of the mother bear whose cubs are threatened, and the heart-stopping courage of the mother bird who feigns a broken wing to lure predators from her nest. Extrapolate from this quality to the condition of our planet at this time, and you see what may serve as a formula for its necessary healing: the revival, or reconstruction, of a mother-god whose nature is at once infinitely gentle and infinitely fierce.

Again, there is precedent: not only in the Hindu goddesses Kali and Durga, but in Western Christianity. A number of popular devotional songs written in France in the thirteenth century depict Mary as a warrior, coming to the defense of the penitent soul. Written by and for the military aristocrats of the time, the songs equate Mary with sword, shield, lance, hauberc, fortress, and even (in one case) a "defensible dungeon against the damned devil," who snatches souls out of his grasp.[1] This figure is hardly the meek and passive virgin of official church doctrine!

The journey of rediscovery, then, is a process of looking forward to what is missing from our spiritual vocabulary, looking backward to search for models, then forward again to begin living with the assembled cast of personae. The results may be surprising on personal as well as doctrinal levels: during the year of research and preparation that preceded the liturgical project, I discovered levels of emotional strength that had not been accessible earlier, and learned to identify more directly with my own protecting and nurturing qualities. The process is diagrammed in Figure 1, a "roadmap for paradigm change." Pick it up and take it as far as you like, though you may find that it leads you beyond your personal comfort zone. Where it has led me thus far is to the work that is the main focus of this essay, a composition for choir and percussion entitled "*Laudes matris*: A Liturgy for God the Mother."

I completed the piece, which is a five-movement choral cycle, in the summer of 1991, after a year of research and contemplation. The original intention was to write a work with liturgical undertones to commemorate the fourteen women killed in the Montreal massacre."[2] I began with a notion that the texts had to include ancient scriptural references to female deities, and found appropriate ones in the Gnostic scriptures, the Sumerian hymns to Inanna, a Chinese Buddhist litany of Quan Yin, a work of the fourteenth-century anchoress Julian of Norwich, and one modern poem. As soon as the texts were assembled and edited, I began to shuffle them into appropriate order. What emerged bore strong resemblances in structure to the Catholic mass: five sections, composed of a revelatory text, a litany, a creed, a contemplative text, and a commemoration. The focus of the work was thus carried beyond a memorial performance into the perilous realm of ecumenical liturgical reform.

In that light, a few cautionary words are needed. This liturgy is interdenominational and–I hope–applicable to a number of religions as well as to feminists, both female and male, who hold no particular religious beliefs. It is not meant to replace any of the traditional forms, but to supplement them. Nor is it a weapon in the battle of the sexes. Men, too, need and desire a reconnection with the spiritual feminine, and it is hoped that the work will prove attractive and meaningful to both genders. Its intention is not to provoke controversy, but to heal, instruct, and inspire: if the concept of God as Mother also provokes, it is perhaps because we have not yet developed the cultural expectations that give substance to such visioning.

The music of "*Laudes matris*" is also intended to question expectations of the way things are supposed to be. Rather than following the structures inherent in Western tonal music, based on "dominance" of keys and narrative closure, [3] it draws on pre-tonal Western structures from the medieval period and on the rich musical heritages of Eastern Europe, the Orient, and the Middle Eastern regions, where a number of the world's religions began. From the Middle East and the Orient, too, comes the use of percussion instruments—especially small hand-drums –by women to accompany their singing. From Bulgaria comes a vocal technique unique to women, a thrilling dissonant sound used in portions of the piece to emphasize the struggle for recognition. It is this struggle that permeates and shapes the selection of texts, as well as is evident in the first section, an excerpt from an ancient Gnostic poem entitled "Thunder–Perfect Mind," a revelatory text in which a feminine creator-god describes herself and warns of the perils of ignoring her presence.

Revelation

Look upon me, all of you,
and you hearers, hear me.

Give heed to me!
Come forward, you who know me,
Come forward to childhood.

For I am the first and the last,
the honored one and the scorned one,
I am the whore and the holy one,
I am the wife and the virgin,
the mother and the daughter.

Give heed to me!
Come forward, you who know me,
Come forward to childhood.

I am knowledge and ignorance,
I am shame and boldness,
I am strength and I am fear:

Give heed to me!
Come forward, you who know me,
Come forward to childhood. [4]

The musical setting involves canonic phrases,[5] many of which are repeated *ad libitum,* giving an improvisational element to the piece. It begins with three hand-drums and a tambourine in cross-rhythms, then a solo singer, in a low register, enters at

> Look upon me, all of you,
> and you hearers hear me

The choir then goes into canonic passages, alternated with block harmony (homophony). The drums return for the last stanza and refrain . The effect is meant to be dramatic, defiant, and very present: *pay attention!!!* This is the warning call of the Mother-God whose voice has gone unheeded for millennia. It is the warning call of the Earth in peril–Give heed to me!

The second movement is a litany, a descriptive song of praise, set in much gentler tones, with windchimes. The harmonies are delicate and portray the beauty, wisdom, and nurturing aspects of the Buddhist deity Quan Yin.

Litany

> A mind perfected in the four virtues,
> A golden body filled with wisdom,
> Fringes of dangling pearls and jade,
> Scented bracelets set with lustrous gems.
> Her green jade buttons
> and white silk robe
> bathed in holy light;
> Her velvet skirt and golden cords
> wrapped by hallowed air;
> With brows of new moon shape
> and eyes like two bright stars,
> Her jadelike face beams natural joy.
> She disperses the eight woes,
> She redeems the multitude,
> She is great compassion:
> Thus she rules on the mountain
> and dwells at the sea.
> She saves the poor,
> searching for their voices,
> ever heedful, ever wise.
> Her orchid heart delights in green bamboo,
> Her chaste nature loves the wisteria.

She is the merciful ruler of the mountain
from the cave of tidal sound.[6]

The remaining portions of text are a creed, set in the dissonant declamatory style of Bulgarian folk-singing; a contemplation, applying intricate choral polyphony [7] to a fourteenth-century text on the motherhood of God by Julian of Norwich; and a commemoration, in which the style and percussion accompaniment of the first section return. This fifth and final section returns as well to the theme of remembering and re-empowering the feminine aspect of divinity, this time exemplified by the figure of the Sumerian goddess Inanna, whose journey to the underworld at the height of her power carried the risk of oblivion.

Commemoration

From the Great Above
She opened her ear to the Great Below.

Inanna opened her ear to the Great Below.
Inanna set out for the underworld.
Ninshubur her servant went with her.
Inanna spoke to her, saying:

Ninshubur, my constant support,
who gives me wise advice,
my warrior who fights by my side,
If I do not return,
Lament for me by the ruins.
Tear at your eyes, at your mouth, at your thighs.
Go to Nippur, to the temple of Enlil.
When you enter the shrine, cry out:
Do not let your daughter be put to death:
Do not let your silver be covered with dust,
Do not let your precious stone be broken,
Do not let your fragrant boxwood be broken,
Do not let the holy priestess of heaven
be put to death and forgotten.
Inanna continued on her way.
Then she stopped, and said:

Go now, Ninshubur–
Do not forget the words I have commanded you.[8]

The full choir builds in intensity and complexity until the narrative "Inanna continued on her way." At this point, a high soprano soloist declaims Inanna's action quietly over the choral sound. For the words of Inanna, the low contralto soloist of the very beginning returns, admonishing the listeners to remember. The piece ends with windchimes counterpointed by silence.

As the first draft of the piece was completed, I realized that it may be just the first phase of the project. At this point, I plan to write a second liturgy for congregational use, with simple musical lines and texts drawn from more conventional sources. There is also a possibility of adding more liturgical items for mixed choir and perhaps one just for men. Any recommendations for appropriate texts–scriptural or poetic–and for choirs and congregations interested in any aspects of the project would be most welcome as would participants for a conference or network on gender-balanced reform of worship services in any religion.[9] It is time for God the Mother to return from the underworld of neglect and take her place beside her male counterpart.

ROADMAP FOR PARADIGM CHANGE:

Contemplation

    Recognition of definitions & parameters

        Examination of tradition

            Distillation of essential concepts

                New application of concepts

                    New parameters

                        Reflection & absorption

                            New paradigms

REFERENCES

de Beauvoir, S. 1956. *The Second Sex.* Eng.transl. 1989. New York: Vintage Books.

Eisler, R. 1987. *The Chalice and the Blade.* San Francisco: Harper and Row.

Epstein, M. (date TBA). *"Prions en chantant": Devotional Songs of the Trouveres.* Forthcoming from Toronto: University of Toronto Press.

Kinsley, D. 1989. *"The Goddesses' Mirror.* Albany: SUNY Press.

McClary, S. 1991. *Feminine Endings* Minneapolis: University of Minnesota Press.

Robinson, J.M., ed. 1977. *The Nag Hammadi Library in English.* New York: Harper and Row.

Walker, B. 1983. *The Women's Encyclopedia of Myths and Secrets.* San Francisco: Harper and Row.

Wolkenstein, D., and Kramer, S. 1983. *Inanna, Queen of Heaven and Earth.* New York: Harper and Row.

Yu, A.C. 1977. *The Journey to the West.* Chicago: University of Chicago Press.

FOOTNOTES

[1]   The songs are edited and analyzed in my forthcoming *"Prions en chantant": Devotional songs of the Trouveres.*

[2]   The "Montreal massacre" is the term now used for the murder on December 6, 1990, of fourteen female students of engineering at the École polytechnique in Montreal. The women were shot by a man who proclaimed himself an anti-feminist, and the incident sparked a drastic self examination on the part of the Canadian public and the legal system in regard to the issue of endemic violence against women.

[3]   For readers interested in learning more about these concepts and about recent feminist critiques in the field of music, see McClary (1991). Her book, which is both technical and controversial, represents ground-breaking scholarship on a number of issues.

[4]   Excerpted by the author from Robinson 1977, 271 - 77.....

[5]   "Canon" is the technical name for a round–a part-song in which each voice sings the same melody at a different time. An example is "Row, row, rowy your boat."

[6]   Excerpted by the author from Kinsley (1989), 25 - 26. The text is quoted from Yu.

[7]   "Polyphony" is the term used for complex musix made up of several melodic lines played or sung at once, each with different but related configurations. It is one of the foundations of the style that defines Western art music. Examples can be found in any symphony, sonata or concerto.

8   Excerpted by the author from Wolkenstein and Kramer (1983), 52 - 54.

9   The score of *Laudes matris* is available for performance from the author. It was premiered in Calgary in March, 1994, in collaboration with Maenad Theatre Productions, Calgary, Canada.

PART II

INTERPRETIVE DISCOURSES

J.M. Kertzer
Department of English
The University of Calgary

4

Freedom within the Margins: An Ethnic Situation

I want to explore three terms used in the title of the conference—"freedom," "within," and "margins"–to see how they function within what I call an "ethnic situation." I should say first that my approach is primarily literary. It arises from my interest in ethnic literature, in Jewish literature specifically, in Canadian-Jewish literature more specifically, and in English-Canadian-Jewish literature most specifically. This succession of hyphens marks a progressive narrowing of the field that in one way clarifies the situation, but in another makes it seem far too manageable. There is more than one ethnic situation. I am concerned with a particular dramatic and rhetorical dilemma depicted in *The Adventures of Mottel, the Canot's Son*, the final novel by the Yiddish satirist Sholom Aleichem: written in 1916.

> You know that we're looking for a committee in London. Well, looking for a committee in London is like looking for a needle in a haystack. But there's a God in this world. One evening we were walking along Whitechapel. That is, not in the evening, but in the daytime, only in London there is no daytime and no morning. It's always evening. We met a Jew in a short coat and a queer hat. He seemed to be looking for somebody.

> "I could wager that you are Jews," he says to us. Pinney replies, "Naturally! And what Jews—Jews from Jew-land!" (pp.135-36)

For Pinney, who speaks the final words while he is en route to America, "Jew-land" means the land of Yiddish-speaking Jews, that is, Russia and Poland. His situation is ironic in several ways, first because his choice of words is wonderfully inappropriate. Far from being an earthly paradise for Jews, Russia at the turn of the century was cruelly antisemetic, so Pinney's pride is oddly misplaced. At present he is displaced in London, and even as he proclaims himself an authentic Jew, his presence in Whitechapel–a working-class area also associated with Jews–shows he is scorned, homeless, and lost in a fog? In an additional irony that Jewish readers would recognize immediately, the ethnic identity that Pinney carries with him is his real home, and so he is no more (but no less) displaced in England than he will be in America. As if to confirm this point, the English Jew asks Mottel and Pinney to join a *minyan*, the group of ten Jews necessary to hold a religious service. To complicate matters further, later in the book America will undermine their Jewishness by introducing them to a domineering, secular culture; that is, it will offer them a new home only at the expense of their identity. The oddity of the situation is registered by Sholom Aleichem's ironic style, which boldly offers a statement of fact that immediately proves false: "One evening we were walking along Whitechapel. That is, not in the evening, but in the daytime, only in London there is no daytime and no morning." The old joke about the thick London fog expresses Mottel's sense of being placeless. He is cut off from his Yiddish home; adrift in a new land of queer habits; not yet secure in the New World, which will be stranger still.

Mottel's dilemma and the challenge to freedom that it provokes reflect a peculiarly ethnic situation. Sholom Aleichem's mischievous style is one way of expressing its oddity, by which insider and outsider, the queer and the familiar, time and place are continually transposed. Given this shifting configuration, it becomes more and more difficult to locate oneself or to define one's freedom. My point in this paper is that freedom and knowledge require a "situation", and that ethnic literature inevitably dramatizes an unstable cultural and narrative situation. Pinney and Mottel are, in the current term, "deterritorialized."[1]. They are adrift in a fog, yet secure in their Jewishness, which, ironically, makes them insecure wherever they go. Overseeing them is the eye of God, but it is not certain that even God can see through the fog.

Contemporary literary and cultural theory is fascinated with"sites" and "situations," words used to indicate a tendency of thought, a disposition of ideas, an ideology, a "hermeneutical space" (Boelhower 1987: 89), a discourse, and much more. A situation dictates where and how a writer stands in order to survey a given field of inquiry. According to this approach, the "site" provides raw material to be analyzed by historican, economist, anthropologist, or literary critic. But the material under investigation does not simply present itself as an inert fact of nature. It, too, comes already "situated" in accordance with a prior system of selection and judgment, a system that the observer may not have acknowledged but that nevertheless formulates what can be observed and how it can be articulated. Writers about ethnicity are especially sensitive to these problems, which are integral to their discipline. Their job is to explain not just cultural forms, but the ethnic instabilities that beset those forms. Ethnic situations are always volatile, sometimes violently, but also ironically or quizzically. According to Clifford, ethnologists are in a position rather like Mottel's because

> ethnography looks obliquely at all collective arrangements, distant and nearby ... Ethnography is actively situated *between* powerful systems of meaning. It poses its questions at the boundaries of civilizations, cultures, classes, races and genders. Ethnography decodes and recodes, telling the grounds of collective order and diversity, inclusion and exclusion. It describes processes of innovation and structuration, and is itself part of these processes. (1986:2)

Ethnography depends on an oxymoron: systematic disorder. Ethnographers examine rigorously the disruptive forces in what might otherwise be a stable social order. They propose patterns of misrule within the regulation of social behaviour, for instance by emphasizing the ethnic interlopers who upset the *status quo* but also give the *status quo* its sense of solidarity in opposition to the intruders. For an anthropologist like Turner (1974), the paradox of systematic disorder is what makes societies "social". He claims that all social action and awareness depend on a dramatic clash of structure and what he calls "communitas." Structure is orderly, but also divisive, it is "all that holds people apart, defines their differences, and constrains their actions"; communitas is an anti-structural, undifferentiated, and nonrational unity (46 -47). Social order, even the most secure, is always volatile because it consists of a network of forces held in tense balance. A community, no matter how unified, always harbours agents that upset it. Ethnicity, which strains towards particularity and heterogeneity, is a structural agent because it is discordant. It produces order by challenging the undifferentiated sameness of the community.

Boelhower (1987) pushes beyond oxymoron when he treats ethnicity as more than a spirit of misrule or a systematic disorder: as a logical *aporia* in which order, i.e., culture, and disorder, i.e., ethnicity, implicate each other. Culture, he says, is "a way of seeing, doing and structuring things ... a world-building enterprise" (11); whereas ethnicity is the "semiotic abyss" (25) within culture that upsets all that has been seen, done, and structured. Ethnicity "deterritorializes" (133) the conceptual maps drawn by a culture; challenges its assurance in roots, foundations, and origins; and undermines national identity by rendering the "self" multiform and catastrophic (135). In his view, the ethnic situation cannot even be "situated" or fixed in any stable sense, because ethnicity represents the impossibility of defining the ground one stands on. But in that case, ethnicity constantly exposes the powers that both invigorate and disrupt freedom and social identity.

I cite these theorists in order of increasing audacity, in which case the most audacious must be Tyler, (1986) who treats ethnography as, not just writing about culture or the way a culture writes and reads itself, but as poetry. Ethnography, he says, "attempts to recreate textually [the] spiral of poetic and ritual performance ... It has the allegorical import, though not the narrative form, of a vision quest or religious parable" (125 - 26) Sholom Aleichem illustrates how ethnic literature provides ironic insight into the way cultures formulate themselves and each other. Tyler, approaching from the other direction, suggests that social science, when it becomes suitably self-conscious, recognizes how it is literary in its texture and effects. Literary criticism situates itself somewhere between these two approaches, but it, too, will get caught in the "spiral"–Tyler's word of trying to establish one's own bearings. This is a spiral in and out of freedom.

The name of the conference that generated the volume was "Freedom within the Margins," but the preposition "within" reminds us that the situation of freedom is actually more complicated. Freedom involves a number of co-operating and interfering relations that are usually expressed modestly through prepositions, but these prepositions form a signifying network. In one sense, freedom means "freedom *from*: that is, it requires the absence, whether recognized or not, of coercion and constraint. For example, we are free only when we are not in prison, when we are not being oppressed like Mottel and Pinney, or when we are not being manipulated surreptitiously, as with subliminal suggestions in advertising. It is impossible to be free from everything; such a condition is inconceivable. But there are degrees, and situations can be judged comparatively. Pinney and Mottel escape *from* Russia to England, where they encounter an uncertainty that is figured by the foggy streets. Their escape is therefore just the beginning of their quest. Now what are they to do?

Freedom also means "freedom *to*:" that is, it must be exercised by virtue of ability and knowledge. We act freely only when we can use our powers in accordance with effective understanding, and when we can cultivate that understanding. Pinney and Mottel are now free to join in a religious ceremony, something that was dangerous back home. But they would not be free to change a light bulb, or to perform brain surgery, or to analyze a poem, unless they had sufficient experience or could acquire it. Knowledge therefore increases freedom, in keeping with the humanistic maxim "the truth shall set you free." The more you know and the more you can do, the freer you are. But there is an added complication, since knowledge is not just the direct apprehension of truth. Knowledge must be situated within defining conditions. Here we return to the idea of "freedom *within*" and to the margins that separate the inside from the outside.

No freedom is possible except in concert with the conditions by which it operates, conditions that must permit a range of real choices. To limit the range, or to obscure or falsify the choices, is to diminish freedom. The proverbial castaways on a desert island are free *from* virtually everything, but free *to* do very little, because of the impoverished conditions in which they live. They are not free to go see a movie, for instance, because there is no theatre on the island. They are not free to choose effectively even if there is a theatre, but only one: the choice has already been made for them, and they are free only to refuse or to accept what is at hand. Their freedom is limited even if there are a dozen movies available but they all of the same sort, or if they are produced by the same company or intended for the same audience, and so on.

The three prepositions (from, to, and within) indicate that freedom is always multiple, variable, and conflictual–a complex situation that must continually be reinterpreted. Freedom is not a state of being that one just possesses or lacks. Nor is it solely a matter of individual liberty–which is itself never simple–because it depends on a network of varying relations linking the individual to a community and to a group of communities whose relations are themselves continually changing. This shifting network means that freedom is *historical* in nature, in the sense that it gains significance through action, interaction, and change. We understand freedom through the changes effected in our lives. It is *conflictual* because, like culture as described by Turner or Boelhower, it requires a systematic disruption, which will be more or less systematic and more or less disruptive depending on how the network actually works, whether it integrates or disrupts. Choice involves both a power of co-operation that unifies and conserves, and a disruptive power that breaks with the past in unexpected ways.

Mottel's emigration to America acts out both the liberating and conserving impulses of freedom, as he escapes from an oppressive society in order to remain loyal to ancient, religious traditions, only to encounter the transforming challenge of American secular assimilation. Again, there is a spiralling effect. The value of ethnic literature is that it charts this bewildering situation by simplifying it. Although critics nowadays love to talk about indeterminacy and multiplicity, we shouldn't lose sight of the marvelous reductive powers of literature, which permit us not to have to think about everything at once. Literature is blessed with stereotypes. As a final generalization, I would like to suggest that literary works stressing what I called "freedom from," that is, the power that liberates itself from constraint, tend to be heroic and sometimes tragic in their emphasis on resistance or escape. Works that stress what I called "freedom to," that is, powers of accomplishment, tend to become romantic as they exaggerate creative ability until it becomes magical and redemptive. Works that stress the freedom "within" are marked by a double impulse—at once conservative and liberating. On the one hand, they will be comical or nostalgic (the persistent temptation of ethnic literature) if they rely on integrative powers that join people in a vision of social harmony. On the other hand, they will be ironic if they insist on the disruptive energies that set us free by making us different and awkward. The ambiguity of the melting pot image, as it appears in American ethnic literature, illustrates both of these tendencies.[2] It unifies but also destroys; it blends but also betrays it; it frees but also reduces the range and value of choices.

The great advantage of ethnic writing—and this is my final point—is that its remarkable volatility means it is not limited to one of these modes, but condenses them all, and even confuses them. Especially in immigrant literature, as *The Adventures of Mottel* illustrates, the spiral of the ethnic situation twists in subtle ways, finding expression in narrative voice and style as well as in character and setting. Immigrant literature as adventure and departure tends to start in the first category: this is the generation of heroic daring, sacrifice, and loyalty. It then turns into romance: this is the literature of transition and risk, with its dreams of a New World, its fantastic discoveries and transformations.[3] And, finally, almost inevitably, it turns ironic: this is the literature of wry ethnic humour, self-deprecation and absurdity; later it becomes the writing of modernist and post-modern paradox. You might think of individual works that fall into any one of these categories, but you will also find that single works combine all three. Ethnic literature tends to mix genres, because it embodies rival conceptions of freedom. Ethnic literature is impure, but productively so, in the way that a systematic disruption will both generate and challenge understanding.

REFERENCES

Baumgarten, M. 1982. *City Scriptures: Modern Jewish Writing.* Cambridge: Harvard University Press,.

Boelhower, William. 1987, *Through a Glass Darkly: Ethnic Semiosis in American Literature.* New York: Oxford University Press.

Chametzky, Jules. 1986. *Our Decentralized Literature: Cultural Mediations in Selected Jewish and Southern Writers.* Amherst: University of Massachusetts Press.

Clifford, James. 1986. "Introduction: Partial Truths." In *Writing Culture: The Poetics and Politics of Ethnography.* (eds) James Clifford and George E. Marcus. Berkelely: University of California Press, p. 1-26.

Deleuze, Gilles and Félix Guattari. 1986. *Kafka: Toward a Minor Literature.* Trans. Dana Polan. Minneapolis: University of Minneapolis Press.

Sholom, Aleichem. 1961. *The Adventures of Mottel, the Cantor's Son.* Trans. Tamara Kahana. New York: Collier.

Sollers, Werner. 1986. *Beyond Ethnicity: Consent and Descent in American Culture..* New York, Oxford: Oxford University Press.

Turner, Victor. 1974. *Dramas, Fields and Metaphors: Symbolic Action in Human Society.* Ithaca and London: Cornell University Press.

Tyler, Stephen A. 1986. "Post-Modern Ethnography: From Document of the Occult to Occult Document." In *Writing Culture: The Poetics and Politics of Ethnograhy.* (eds) James Clifford and George E. Marcus. Berkelely: University of California Press, p.122-40.

FOOTNOTES

1   The term "deterritorialized" comes from Deleuze and Guattari's account of "minor literature," and is applied to ethnic and American literature by Jules Chametsky (1986).

2   For a discussion of the history and ambiguity of the American melting pot, see Sollers (1986).

3   For a discussion of romance and fantasy as modes of Jewish immigrant literature, see Baumgarnter (1982).

Tamara Palmer Seiler
Canadian Studies
The University of Calgary

5

Celebrating the Margins: Simplicity, Synchronicity, and Abridgement in Annie Magdalene and Various Miracles

Annie Magdalene by Australian writer Barbara Hanrahan (1985) and *Various Miracles* by Canadian writer Carol Shields (1985), can be usefully compared as texts whose celebration of marginal characters (in relation to the centres of social and cultural power) and of the "extraordinary within the ordinary" (Gilbert 1988, 82), though effected in each through very different literary techniques, provides a framework for a post-colonial challenge to imperial paradigms. Or, as Ashcroft, Griffiths, and Tiffin conceptualize it in their book on post-colonial literature, both of these fictions, in valorizing various geographical and social hinterlands, write back to the Empire. Hanrahan challenges the assumption that "ordinary" lives are uninteresting–indeed that they are ordinary at all–and particularly the assumption that a woman can only find love and happiness through a romantic attachment, and ultimately marriage, to a man. She does so through literary techniques– principally" a "faux-naif" narrative voice that draws heavily on oral rather than literary discursive practice. The effect created is what Hanrahan herself has called "a simplicity, a clarity on the surface that masks. . . complexity and mystery" (Gilbert 1988, 66). Shields, on the other hand, uses magic realism to challenge two assumptions embedded in the discourse of the centre: first, that the universe is essentially rational–a clockmaker's world where there is no room for miracles; and second, that only the lives of those at the centre can be truly significant, life on the margins being, ipso facto, trivial.

Annie Magdalene writes back to the empire primarily through its style and structure, its rejection of the conventions of romantic love, and its portrayal of the relationship between individuals and history. Hanrahan skilfully interweaves these three aspects of her text to take up the implied challenge in the following quotation of Virginia Woolf, which she includes as the epigraph of *Annie Magdalene:*

> For all the dinners are cooked; the plates and cups washed; the children sent to school and gone out into the world. Nothing remains of it all. All has vanished. No biography or history has a word to say about it. And the novels, without meaning to, inevitably lie.... All these infinitely obscure lives remain to be recorded.

Hanrahan provides in *Annie Magdalene* the illusion of having "recorded" one of these "obscure lives," or having given voice to the voiceless. The writer's trick hangs on a first person narrator whose voice is sufficiently simple and common to fulfil the expectations already aroused by the Woolf quotation and the title of the text, which invites the reader to expect either biography or autobiography. That Annie speaks to the reader seemingly unmediated is the result of Hanrahan's skilful recreation of orality on the printed page, an effect achieved through simple, at times elliptical; syntax, diction vernacular; and the loose coherence produced by predominantly free-associative rather than causal connections between sentences, as in the following:

> Mum went to the hairdresser on the Beach Road to have her hair tinted–Dad encouraged her because he was still black and she was going grey. My hair was brown with a goldy-red tinge that I supposed I got from Dad's moustache. One day when I was looking in my brother's mirror, I started singing "Silver Threads among the Gold"–I'd found my first white hair. (59).

The text's orality challenges the centre's valorization of the literary over the spoken, highlighting the silencing powers of the former, the vitality of the latter. The reader can see, for example, that Annie's descriptions of her childhood neighbourhood are vivid and interesting precisely because they are (or, rather, seem to be) told in Annie's voice, not through the filters of literary convention. Nor would the reader want the following passage to undergo the manicuring required to make it "literary":

Mrs. Rudd next door had cats and birds. She had a cockatoo that talked and green parrots and a galah. The cocky, Old Bill, didn't like men–if he saw a man he'd chase him; once he took a piece out of Dad's leg. When the old chap up the street walked past in his bowler hat, Old Bill sat out the front on the pagoda and put on an awful turn–swore at him, said "You old bugger". (14)

Further, this orality challenges the notion that an "ordinary" person like Annie is inarticulate; indeed, as Annie herself tells us, "I talked a terrible lot". (16) That her "talking" can hold our attention, and has, paradoxically, been "booked," subverts the notion that only the "great" are sufficiently interesting to deserve such attention. That Annie's telling can captivate, even though her background is working class and, particularly, even though she is a spinster, just another "little old lady," undercuts canonic notions of who is interesting. The structure of *Annie Magdalene* also contributes to this undercutting. Based on a simple kind of writing of the body that moves through four main stages, corresponding to childhood, youth, maturity, and old age, with a gesture towards closure at the end, the text's frame emphasizes the significance and meaningfulness of a life lived on the margins, an "ordinary" life, one that could easily be rendered meaningless by the centre's paradigms (Abel 1982, 17 - 20).

A second major way that *Annie Magdalene* constitutes a writing back to the empire is in its subversion of the conventions of romance. A major article of romantic faith is that a woman can only find fulfilment by connecting with a man, and that a life without sexual activity is a life without love, one that no woman would willingly choose. However, Annie's story overturns this paradigm. First, Annie consciously chooses not to marry, even though she has several chances to do so. "Fancy getting married at seventeen and having a mob of kids," says Annie when she refuses Edmund's offer of marriage (50). Further, Annie is able to live fully, to contribute, to nurture, and to experience joy, all without "the connection business." As Gilbert points out, in Hanrahan's text

Traditional male-female sexual intercourse is demonstrated to be something that Annie could manage without. Love and affection are clearly not reliant upon a sexual coupling, and the cost in terms of loss of independence is too high. Instead, Annie finds obvious delight and sensual satisfaction in gardening, sewing, caring for her animals, cooking, and riding her

Lambretta motor scooter. Annie's work life is presented as full and satisfying. (85)

Indeed, at the end of the text, when Annie is old and ill, her triumph over her present limiting circumstances, as well as over the various constraints and disappointments of her life, is portrayed as stemming from her ability to nurture and to connect with nature, quite literally with the birds and the bees. She is able to "talk to the birds, not in English, but in whistle talk–the same sort of whistle as when they talk quietly to me" (210); and she is able to talk to the bees:

> In summer, when I have short sleeves, the bees sit on my arm. They don't worry me at all, I think they love me; I just let them stay (if you brush them off they get cross), they're only sitting there to have a rest. The bees often come and sit beside me to die. When I pick off the dead flowers from the daisy bushes, I tell the bees they have to put up with me. But you must never talk loud to the bees, you must talk softly. (121)

Annie's "ordinary life" has been extraordinary, as has her ability to make a place for herself, in both society and nature, and to face her death courageously, singing " party songs like "'Look for the Silver Lining'"(119). Hanrahan's text creates this ordinary/extraordinary character by skilfully manipulating the conventions of autobiography, oral history, and fiction, making of their interweaving a memorable challenge to conventional paradigms.

In *Various Miracles* Carol Shields mounts a similar challenge to the empire, but in many ways her approach contrasts sharply with that of Hanrahan. Whereas the power of Hanrahan's text is deeply rooted in the apparent simplicity of a naive orality, that of Shields's fiction is rooted in its highly literary sophistication. *Various Miracles* clearly written in the mode of magic realism, draws its subversive energy from the double discourse that is the essence of this mode. As Stephen Slemon points out:

> The term "magic realism" is an oxymoron, one that suggests a binary opposition between the representational code of realism and that, roughly, of fantasy in a magic realist text; a battle between two oppositional systems takes place, each working toward the creation of a different kind of fictional world from the other. Since the ground rules of these two worlds are incompatible, neither one can fully come into being, and each remains suspended, locked in a

continuous dialectic with the "other," a situation which creates disjunction within each of the separate discursive systems, rending them with gaps, absences and silences. (1988,10).

One can see this "binary opposition," as well as the resulting "gaps, absences and silences," in virtually every story in *Various Miracles*. The title story, for example, is replete with the tension between realistic and fantastic modes. The narrator's recitation of the "several miracles" this year that have "gone unrecorded" moves from the very mundane ("On the morning of January 3, seven women stood in line at a lingerie sale in Palo Alto, California, and by chance, each of these women bore the Christian name Emily" [p.13]) to the increasingly bizarre, mysterious, and fantastic: twin parrots separated by great time and distance die on the very same day; a stolen painting on a wall in Canada falls to the floor at the very moment of the discovery of the place represented in the painting by the young boy (now an adult) who had painted it years before from a postcard sent to him by his father; and finally, a young woman leans over to pick up a paper scattered into her path by the wind and discovers that the words written on it describe her.

This "strange synchronicity" (Thomas 1989, 111) and the questions it raises and leaves unanswered, as well as the absence of any clear attempt at resolution or closure at the end of the story, make it an apt point of departure for the collection as a whole, since these qualities predominate, and are the chief means whereby Shields imbues the ordinary with an aura of the miraculous. This is particularly apparent in the story "Home," in which the omniscient narrator describes a particular airline flight circa 1950 between Toronto and London during which everyone on board achieves, at least for a brief moment, supreme happiness. The result catapults the reader into the world of magic realism, with its uneasy and startling juxtaposition of the rational and the non-rational:

It must have been that the intensity and heat of this gathered happiness produced a sort of gas or ether or alchemic reaction—it's difficult to be precise—but for a moment, perhaps two, the walls of the aircraft, the entire fuselage and wings and tail section became translucent. The layers of steel, the rivets and bracing and ribwork turned first purple, then a pearly pink, and finally metamorphosed to the incandescence of pure light. (p.153)

That this "miraculous" event is witnessed by a twelve-year-old Greenlander boy, Piers, does not provide the comforting closure readers might expect, since it becomes for him "a guilty secret," one that he can't fully share with anyone. When as a young adult he tries to share it with his lover, she leaves him, suggesting he see a psychiatrist. No clear line of causality underpins this story, as it moves in the end to Piers' taking a holiday in Acapulco and to the point of view of a young woman who works in the airport there. Through her eyes we see yet another, but seemingly much more trivial, "miracle": that every tourist but one departing from Piers's plane is wearing blue jeans. The omniscient narrator then tells us that as the individual tourists depart, "they feel lighter than air, they claim, freer than birds, drifting off into their various inventions of paradise as though oblivious to the million invisible filaments of connection, trivial or profound, which bind them one to the other and to the small green planet they call home" (156). One could read this moment as a profoundly significant metonym for the post-colonial moment, in which the old boundaries between centres and margins have been obliterated, replaced with a global vision.

This movement in Shields's fiction out from the centre carried along a discontinuous narrative line, but given a paradoxical foundation by the binary discourse of magic realism, makes the reader at once aware of both the fragmentation and the unity of human experience, a paradoxical insight that is central to both the form and the content of *Various Miracles*. The text's particular harnessing of both centripetal and centrifugal energy, an uneasy synthesis so characteristic of magic realism, is also, I believe, what makes the text so quintessentially post-colonial. In short, there is a clear connection between Shields's marginal positioning as a Canadian female writer and her choice of the magic realist mode. As Slemon suggests, "magic realism as a literary practice seems to be closely linked with a perception of 'living on the margins'" because it encodes "resistance to the massive imperial centre and its totalizing systems" (1988,10). Slemon uses Mikhail Bakhtin to further illuminate the dynamics of this relationship, since Bakhtin sees the novel as a kind of battleground between "a diversity of social speech types," each vying to become the "language of truth" and hence of power.

> This use of language has important consequences in the context of post-colonial cultures. One of the most common assumptions operating in the small, but rapidly growing, body of theory that undertakes comparative analysis across post-colonial cultures is that the act of colonization, whatever its precise form, initiates a kind of double vision

or "metaphysical clash" within the colonial culture, a binary opposition within language that has its roots in the process of either transporting a language to a new land or imposing a foreign language on an indigenous population. (11)

Clearly, one of the central battles in Shields's text is that between the positivist discourse of "pure rationality" and the discourses of non-rationality, since only in the worlds constructed out of the latter can either miracles exist or the idiosyncratic voices from the margins be given voice. Throughout *Various Miracles* Shields challenges the notions of predictability, control, and objectivity inherent in a clockmaker universe. This challenge is often a direct one waged with fantastic coincidences and unexplainable occurrences, as in "Purple Blooms," "Invitations," and "Accidents." But the collection also contains more subtle challenges to rationalist assumptions. For example, in "Mrs. Turner Cutting the Grass," the reader is skilfully lead by an omniscient narrator to an awareness of the elusive quality of absolute, objective knowledge. Shields presents Mrs. Turner from the perspective of the high-school girls who pass by Mrs. Turner's yard and see her as an unsightly old woman who doesn't have the sense to either get rid of or cover up her cellulite-laden thighs; or of her ecologically conscious next-door neighbours who wish she would not spray her yard with chemicals; or of the erudite professor/poet who, seeing her as a loud, philistine tourist in Japan, calls her a "defilement" (25) and asserts that "the things Mrs. Turner doesn't know would...sink a ship...set off a tidal wave, would make her want to kill herself" (19). The reader, however, is also allowed to see a Mrs. Turner who has had a surprisingly adventurous life, who has been deeply loved, and whose unsophisticated experience of the reassuring sameness of human life ("She's never heard the word *commonality*, but is nevertheless fused with its sense" [26]) is at least as significant and valid, if not more so, as the insights gleaned by the professor, who ridicules Mrs. Turner in his poem. And at the end of the story it is the "ordinary," seemingly unknowing Mrs. Turner who, by living her life "the best she could under the circumstances," (22) "...like an ornament...shines". (27)

Shields also uses the doubleness, tensions, and spaces created by magic realism to challenge the centre's hegemony over significance. Like Hanrahan, Shields celebrates life on the margins, suggesting in stories such as "Others", the tragic waste and futility of the sycophantic "colonial" stance. This is displayed in the story by a Canadian couple, particularly the wife, Lila, who continually sees their marriage and their lives in general as lacking when compared to those of an English couple they met by chance on their honeymoon and with whom they have continued to correspond over many years. Similarly, in "Sailors Lost at Sea," Helene's mother, a Canadian poet who goes to France on a Canada Council grant to find her roots, discovers that "...it was not possible at all for them to become part of the community" (37), that her writing suffers as a result, and that her real roots are back in Manitoba. In "Love so Fleeting, Love so Fine," Shields portrays a colonial forever haunted by a seeming absence in his life, which is really his inability to find love in his own circumstances rather than in romantic images from afar.

Perhaps the most profound dimension of Shields's valorization of the margins and her related celebration of the "extraordinary within the ordinary" is her illumination of language itself. *Various Miracles* is a highly metafictional text and, as such, calls attention to language and story as the ultimate miracles, those that link and give meaning to the inexplicable, fragmented "scenes" of experience. As Aritha van Herk puts it in a fictocritical discussion of Shields's text, "...the real miracle is language ...Carol Shields knows this: she writes with one eye on the miracle of language and another on the miracle of miracles" (1989,107,108). This is particularly apparent in the title story, in which the final miracle is the actress discovering herself in the written text that just happens to land at her feet, and in "Accidents," in which the narrator, a professional abridger, seems to be speaking for Shields herself when he discusses the essence of his art, which he plans to use to spare his wife the pain of knowing about the death of the young man who had occupied the hospital bed next to his own:

> It's peculiar profession, I'm the first to admit, but it's one I fell into by accident and that I seem suited for. Abridging requires a kind of inverse creativity. One must have a sharp eye for turning points and a seismic sensitivity for the fragile, indeed invisible, tissue that links one event with another. I'm well-paid for my work, but I sometimes think that the degree of delicacy is not appreciated. There are even times when it's necessary to interfere with the truth of a particular piece, and, for the sake of clarity and balance, exercise a small and inconspicuous act of creativity which is entirely my own. I've never thought of this as dishonesty and never felt that I had tampered with the integrity of a work. (34)

While the above could stand as a description of Shields's technique in *Various Miracles,* it could just as easily be read as a description of Hanrahan's technique in *Annie Magdalene,* despite the obvious and significant differences between fictionalized oral history and magic realism. The complexity that is essential to the celebration of the extraordinary within the ordinary, the miraculous, is, in Shields's text, the product of absences and gaps produced by juxtaposing the two apparently incompatible discourses of fantasy and verisimilitude; the simplicity that is essential to this same celebration in Hanrahan's text is also the product of gaps and absences generated by the juxtaposition of a highly condensed and seemingly ingenuous narration with the reader's awareness of complexity. Both texts are products of the abridger's art, and both challenge the hegemony of the imperial centres.

REFERENCES

Abel, E. 1982. *Writing and sexual differences.* Chicago: University of Chicago Printing.

Ashcroft, B., Griffiths, G., and Tiffin, H. 1989. *The empire writes back : Theory and practice in post colonial literatures.* London: Routledge.

Gilbert, P. 1988. *Contemporary Australian women writers.* London: Pandora Press.

Hanrahan, B. 1985. *Annie Magdalene.* London: Chatto and Windus.

Shields, C. 1985. *Various miracles.* Toronto: General Paperbacks.

Slemon, S. 1988. "Magic realism as post-colonial discourse." *Canadian Literature,* 116: 9 - 28.

Thomas, C. 1988. "A slight parodic edge: Swann: A mystery." *Room of Ones Own,* (Carol Shields issue) 13(1,2):109 - 22.

van Herk, A. 1989. "Extrapolations from miracles." *Room of One's Own* (Carol Shields issue) 13(1,2):99 - 108.

Beverly Rasporich
Faculty of General Studies
The University of Calgary

Byrna Barclay's "Out-Wandering Women" in the Livelong Quartet: New Directions in Canadian Ethnic Fiction

The classification "ethnic literature" in Canadian letters is undoubtedly transitory[1], and clearly tied to the historical evolution of our nation and our concept of national culture. Canada's history, although not its myth, is one of quiet conquest: a continuous story of ever-increasing tribes-in-exodus sparring over rights to primacy in a vast frontier originally inhabited by a native peoples who were the first to suffer defeat. In the aftermath of the British conquest of the French, the Anglo-Celtic majority in English Canada gradually created and canonized their own fictions—often of exile and immigrant experience – with marginal status accorded, if accorded at all, to literature written about ethnic minorities by members of ethnic groups. After the Second World War, however, when the exclusive immigration patterns of the inter-war period that excluded the "lesser breeds" and "lower orders" were altered in favour of "selective restriction,"[2] a new, freer concept of Canada began to evolve that favoured the eventual inclusion of ethnic literature within the literary canon.

To some extent, this development was foreshadowed in the scholarly work of Watson Kirkconnell, a humanist and a Christian, who prior to World War II perceived the forces of racism at work abroad and at home and postulated an ideal concept of a federated Canada that was built not on Anglo-Saxon superiority, but on a blending of the cultures of all immigrants:

> I do not wish to belittle or deny the value of a national culture and a national tradition in giving a warm core of spiritual significance to our Canadian community. I hope for the fullest possible development of such a national culture, blending and cherishing here all the rich legacies of European gifts that are found in the land. (1941, 82)

Canada and her national culture would be a model for a peaceful international "world order" based on "co-operation and justice" (82). Believing in the universal interests and truths of literature, Kirkconnell acknowledged the literary as well as the sociocultural value of the considerable body of writing created by those authors belonging to some two and a half million Canadians of European origin. As a linguist, Kirkconnell contributed to the recognition of what is the most pristine example of what one might define as ethnic literature, that written in languages other than English. His work included Canadian *Overtures: An Anthology of Canadian Poetry Written Originally in Icelandic, Swedish, Hungarian, Italian, German and Ukrainian* (1935), as well as numerous translations and evaluations.

The White Paper of 1966 and the ensuing regulations of 1967 which opened the doors of immigration wider than ever before to all peoples regardless of race, colour, religion, national origin, or sex, saw the politicians recreating the founding myth of the country as a multicultural country, with the original settler cultures, the Anglo-Celtic and the French, still, paradoxically, having authority. The literary canon has, by the 1990s, subsequently absorbed this national dream with more attention paid to the category/categorization of ethnic literature and with a considerable number of writers of politically exiled, or particular immigrant, or ethnic ancestral and cultural, sensibilities acknowledged as chief Canadian storytellers. Joy Kogawa, for example, has been applauded by official culture for *Obasan*, a story of Japanese dispossession in Canada and Josef Skvorecky, a Czech refugee, won the Governor General's Award *The Engineer of Human Souls*. Interestingly, it may be said that this shift in 1984 placed Canadian writing in the mainstream intellectual movement of postmodern thought and writing in the Western world. As Linda Hutcheon (1988) explains, one of the major thrusts of the postmodern writer is to query the so-called universal truths of the liberal-humanist tradition and to write from a marginal or ex-centrix position with regard to the dominant culture. In a postmodern context, in fact, the emphasis in literary valuing on "the different and the diverse, in opposition to the uniform and the unified" (Hutcheon 1988, 19) is an attitude that accords well with what is now a dominant Canadian self-image.

Postmodern culture in Canada, which espouses new models based on "contingency, multiplicity, fragmentation, discontinuity," is also largely expressed, as Hutcheon points out, "in new forms that embody ethnicity and the female" (18 - 19). In response to feminism and immigration patterns, these new forms, which are expressions from the borders of cultural power, are beginning to reshape our canonized literature. One writer who is a part of postmodern female and ethnic fiction-making is Byrna Barclay. Her *Livelong Quartet*, a series, to date, of three novels, *Summer of the Hungry Pup* (1981), *The Last Echo* (1985), and *Winter of the White Wolf* (1988), is an extraordinary epic exploration of female generation and tribe played out as immigrant myth on the prairies, and as an ethnofictive reflection of the new Canadian pluralistic nationalism.

Female authors must perforce reject or alter established literary forms because of their male-centredness. Thus, in the hands of Alice Munro the *Kunstlerroman*, a novelistic form that shows the development of the artist from childhood to maturity (traditionally male) evolves as female genre in *Lives of Girls and Women*; (1971) and Aritha van Herk creates a contemporary feminist picaroon in her picaresque-parody *No Fixed Address* (1986). Similarly, Byrna Barclay in *The Livelong Quartet*, drawing upon her Swedish ancestry, re-visions a variant of the epic and Norse sagas as female-centred immigrant odyssey. Rejecting patrilinear fictional chronology in her *Quartet*, Barclay begins her first novel, *Summer of the Hungry Pup,* at the fictional centre of her story cycle with a narrative focus on the story of an *aboriginal* Old Woman, a Cree medicine woman, whose tale of exodus/exile across the forty-ninth parallel and return to the Saskatchewan prairies is that of the Cree people after the North West Rebellion of 1885. This tale is filtered through the responses of a contemporary woman, Annika, of third-generation Swedish ancestry on the prairies, who is the spiritual granddaughter of Old Woman, Annika, and who also relates Old Woman's blood-sister relationship to her own Swedish grandmother and *original* immigrant, Johanna of Hannas. Barclay begins at the beginning with the story of Johanna of Hannas in Sweden before emigration, and in the third novel, *Winter of the White Wolf*, postmodern complexity allows for multiple texts: the story of Annika, an artist figure, in contemporary dis-settlement in Livelong, Saskatchewan; her grandmother Johanna's tale of early settlement there; autobiographical points of view of subsequent family members; and the return odyssey of Annika to Sweden, both as questing metafictional artist and the ethnic dispossessed. There is no closure in this trilogy, only the wanderings of heroines who circulate bravely in the epic tradition, longing for home, and in the case of the contemporary Annika, searching for artistic inspiration in a vision quest that also resists finalities: *"Begin again, as late in the story as possible ... We resist change and finalities. Even a story-song does not want its last verse." (1988, 151).*

The nature of the epic in its original oral, poetic form broadly speaking is that of the heroic story incorporating myth, legend, folk tale, history. *The Livelong Quartet,* which is largely prose narrative, has the richness of these elements as well as the celebration of tribe and heroic character that is characteristically epic. Richard Dorson points out that "heroic epics and sagas have enthralled audiences with their tribal and nationalistic appeal" as the listeners identify with a hero of their blood, cast in their mold" (1978, 1). In Barclay's contemporary epic, however, there is a re/vision of the masculine ethos of the genre; tribe is not patrilinear, but authoritatively matricircular. Annika, who is both contemporary artist and ancient skaldic bard, is poeticizing the deeds not of male heroes but of a genealogy of championing women, with her grandmother as the whole and centre. In *Winter of the White Wolf,* Annika envisions: "On her quilt and etched into the central beam, four women danced now, weaving in and out of each other, separate and yet tied up together until they became, in the grey light, Johanna of Hannas".

The ancient heroic epic was as much a cultural as a literary phenomenon: "Epic poems grew out of appropriate cultural conditions, the so-called Heroic Age bridging nomadic and sedentary stages of civilization, a preliterate era when bards celebrated the deeds of great warriors." (Dorson 1978, p.2). This phase of transition between nomadic and sedentary culture is approximated by Barclay and presented as immigrant dilemma of some distress to her out-wandering Swedish women, who shift their allegiances between old country and new. This is particularly marked in the émigré Johanna of Hannas:

"[Johanna] cannot know: a half century of building on the wrong plan in the new land, of tending to one man and his children and loving his brother will cut deep and leave an empty place in her like the hollow left by an unearthed cavestone. She will be an out-wandering woman, running thither and yon, forth and back from homeland to new land, back and forth from the new world to the old. (29)

At the same time, the nomadic way is preferable for the heroic woman as quester who is entrapped by the masculine conceptualization of home/land and by a wrong-headed notion of land/holding on the prairies. Barclay suggests that such a conceptualization is indeed, contrary to an Aboriginal and successful nomadic existence. As Annika explains, "It is not unusual for an Indian to move from place to place" (1981, 31).

In *Summer of the Hungry Pup*, the Aboriginal Old Woman is, in effect, mentoring woman and inspirational nomadic female muse. Her story runs parallel to Johanna's and is told in an oral-literate way in the first person, with old Woman herself as poetic bard, situated in a folk frame of orality as she recounts her life story to Annika. In both Old Woman's and Johanna's life histories, men initiate love and war and exodus. Women wait and follow. Johanna's emigration is occasioned by her romantic love for Arvid, the Northlander who marries another and whom Johanna unsuspectingly follows to Saskatchewan, only to conveniently marry his brother Bjorn as a means of surviving on the prairies, as well as to discover the mistake in her idea that "where Arvid is, there is home" (1988, 136). Similarly, Old Woman the first wife of Horse-Dance-Leader is led through periods of famine and extreme physical hardships in flight across the forty-ninth parallel by the remaining Indian leaders, Lucky Man, Little Poplar, and Little Bear, after the Cree surrender at Battleford, and is later captured with her tribe and driven back to Saskatchewan by the American army and the redcoats.

What Old Woman encompasses, firstly, is the understanding of the Real People, the Prairie People, of "man's" relationship to the land. It is she who frees Johanna of Hannas from her fear of open prairie spaces and not knowing "how to live well" (1981, 204). It is the *white man* who builds "on the wrong plan" on the prairies with his squared-off visions, with "dots for towns, triangles for farmhouses, and rectangles for grain elevators" and "squared off farmer's fields" (1981, 50). It is the white imagination that draws up the "dividing line" of artificial national borders, in the failure to understand that "Earth is Only Mother and She is the same on That Side of dividing-line as She is on This Side" (1981, 50). Keeping the Indians *in line*, it is the white man who fails to comprehend the circular unity of creation and ensures his own dispossession on the prairies.

In this geometrification of country, Barclay is also true to a non-native Canadian literary vision. As Gaile McGregor explains in *The Wacousta Syndrome*, one of the "Canadian's tools for arranging his conceptual world—in this case for exploring the posture of the self with relation to its field of action—is the graphic analogy. In particular, loaded references to lines and circles abound throughout the corpus, dragging in their wake a complicated vision of alternate and possibly antithetic philosophies of life." (1985, 349). In *The Temptations of Big Bear* by Rudy Wiebe (an author with whom Barclay studied), for example, as in Barclay's fiction, white men are line oriented and the "natives" are "identified with the circle of the seasons, the all-embracing curve of earth and sky" (McGregor, 350). In Barclay's work, however, the circle-line analogy is also a battle plan for the female as adventuring "hero" and creatrix. When the medicine woman is about to have her first baby, she burrows into the ashes, "My toes press against stones circling fireplace. My body curves into earth. I will make a grey nest to have my child in" (1981, 49); but she is rudely uprooted by her mother, Too-Much-Woman, Bear Woman, who, a larger-than-life epic character, will herself later rush into the male battleground and disrupt battle conventions and the seriousness of war. Bear Woman pushes her daughter into a vertical position, insisting that she "Walk! Walk Far!" behind the wagons in exodus to Montana, with the daughter becoming in the process a striking heroic vertical figure and creative life-force in a circular landscape divided artificially by the white man's forty-ninth parallel:

> Now I understand why my mother make me walk behind wagon. I walk through darkness of night, through all my pain, and I know there will be light of new day and new child on other side of it. I walk. Soul of a person must walk through wind on night of coming into life. I walk my child ... I do not know what circle of prairie holds for him on other side of dividing-line (1981, 52 - 53).

For the Swedish-ethnic women, for Johanna and Annika, the concept of settlement in a new home/land boxes them in as much as it does the Natives who are put on "left-over-land" (reserves). They, too, become "looked-after-persons" in a patriarchal system of ownership where there is little communication between the sexes: men are obsessively driven to work and possess the land and women are locked into homesteads as home-makers. In this system, farm women, peasant immigrants, "are workhorses and breeding mares" (Barclay 1988, 45). For the contemporary third-generation ethnic woman, for the young Annika contemplating marriage to a young Arvid, grandson of the lost lover of her grandmother (romantic love) Johanna's lost possibility also is no answer. With the young Arvid, "a quiet life in the country" will "chain [Annika] to the stove and diaper pail" (1988, 46).

In the history of agrarian settler fiction on the prairies, as Tamara Palmer has pointed out, a central theme has been a "preoccupation with work" in a hostile landscape.

> There are no traces of the generosity born of paradisiacal abundance in the elemental landscape that is portrayed in novels about ethnic experience on the Prairies: nothing that would create a languorous sense of well-being in those who dwell there. Rather, the landscape engenders a profound insecurity, and the price it exacts for lessening this insecurity is endless toil to eke sustenance from its stern expanses (1987, 56).

As Johanna the emigrant reckons as she leaves Sweden, "Canada, I said, I am for that place, knowing that learning how to live well anywhere has to be got by task (1988, 3). Writing in retrospect, from the perspective of the third generation, however, Barclay moves the mythology of prairie immigrant fiction in a new direction. Rejecting the faith of the Swedish grandparents, and the mythology of an earlier fiction that hard work brings its ultimate rewards (Palmer 1987, 70), and that home/land is desirable and possible, Barclay substitutes an allegiance to ethnic and female tribe, not squared-off place, as a pattern for living with authority, independence, and creative power.

One of the functions of Old Woman is that of female artistic and spiritual muse. Hers is a shamanic tutorship of Annika. Following the tradition of much earlier female Canadian non-Native writers (Barbara Godard explains that Frances Brooke has her character Arabella admire "the beauty of movement of the squaw" [1986, 88]), Barclay discovers in the image and example of the Native woman, a means to empowerment and creative freedom. By having Old Woman adopt Annika as granddaughter in the Native way and initiate her into tribal wisdom, Barclay acknowledges the Native idea that the nature of storytelling is communal and that the art of fiction-making itself is a sacred trust, transmitted through a female shamanic society. The lessons of Old Woman are clear. Consideration of tribe, the Real People, is foremost for the female leader and artist. When her first child dies, she acknowledges the obligation of female-creator to the tribe: "My first born belonged to People before she was my child ... I am only visiting here" (1981, 181). With milk from her breasts she feeds the children of other mothers, and in the situation of polygamous marriage she assists and leads the female community of her

husband's other wives. Most important, hers is the capacity to
dream and receive visions that provide new customs and
spirituality for tribal women. In her first vision, Man-of-all-Songs
comes to her saddened because the old customs are dying, but
empowering her with the creative capacity to begin anew.

My granddaughter,
            You are protected
            I will show you how to make new
Dance. I will show you where to find medicine.
I will show you how to make feast.
            Where you go, you are protected.
            I will give you power of words. But
I do not give you song of your own. I give you
Song-of-women. You must sing it for them and teach[3] [3]
them new words. Song is for women and for children
of children.
            Where you go, you are protected. (1981, 61)

As an initiate into this world of female tribe, Annika discovers
home in the native philosophy of the unity of all things, and her own
skaldic power to recreate ancestral history, to *originate* her Swedish
grandmother's story, whose very naming—*Johanna* of Hannas—is
a linguistic echo of unified being.

What Old Woman said was true: Johanna was part of me,
and now apart. Also, I then felt the calm that only comes
with the feeling of knowing that all things are joined
inside and outside, of finding a reflection of my inner
world in the outside world: miyopayiwin, the unity of all
things under the sky.
I had come home (1981, 225).

Annika also joins the ranks of "other heroines in Canadian
novels" who "in their search for empowerment, in quest of spiritual
insight and creative expression ... enthusiastically follow the
example of Native women and discover a new intersubjective
relationship with nature and the cosmos as well as a greater
originality in their art" (Godard 1986, 88).

Old Woman, then, in *Summer of the Hungry Pup*, clarifies the
aesthetic need for Barclay and her alter ego, Annika, to centre on
gender and ethnic-tribal affiliations. With an epic sensibility
derived from the oral, folkloristic forms of Scandinavian
ancestors, from the likes of the Poetic Edda, the Rig-Veda hymns,

the Icelandic Sagas (Barclay 1985, 95) Barclay goes on to champion the female adventuring of Swedish tribe. The saga of Johanna of Hannas in the new world, alluded to in episodes in *Summer of the Hungry Pup* , is more fully developed in *Winter of the White Wolf*. A heroic epic of perilous adventure and womanly daring is recounted in Johanna's isolated emigration, her steerage voyage across the ocean, and her lonely trek across the prairies by oxen. Heading west, on an old trail without markers or farmsteads,

> she lifts her head: a crossing. Which way? North to Bjorn's quartersection, *eja* Arvid can forget about that, she's not a bride for stealing or trading. She hasn't lost command of herself ... She's Johanna, daughter of a soap-boiling woman and she will never forget it (154).

Unlike the shamanistic heroine Old Woman, however, who is the magic centre of her own story cycle, Johanna is a more realistic epic heroine who, without the benefit of tribe, which she alone must engender on the prairies, is superior above all for her fortitude and endurance. When she begins to lose heart on the prairies, and her own centrality ("She is held at the center of the turning century but is pushed towards its ending. She is lost, undone, castaway by her own out-wandering" *[1988, 108]*), in the style of the epic-odyssey she stumbles upon the wizard-like Hembrow, an Englishman situated in vagabond comfort on the vast prairie, whose dance for her and whose song, "Beautiful Dreamer Waken to Me" enchant her into forbearance, under the mythic symbol of female life, the moon.

> The moon turns, it slides away from the earth. On the rim of that golden globe, a young woman dances, twirling and spinning, the skirts of her festival dance swishing and whirling. Yellow ribbons twine down her bronzed hair. She dances dances, dances off the edge of the moon and falls falls, falls towards the earth (1988, 110).

Johanna of Hannas and Old Woman both, like their author-artist, are faced with the dilemma of reoriginating culture and tribal custom that are about to vanish in the Canadian context. Annika inherits the wisdom of her grandmothers and her mission as an artist becomes this very re-creation, a mission that Barclay builds into *Summer of the Hungry Pup* as subtext and *Winter of the White Wolff* as metafictional inquiry. In the former, when Old Woman dies Annika is visited with a native vision of creation, and in the latter, she returns to Sweden, the homeland of her ancestors, in quest of family and Swedish legend, folklore, and myth, becoming in the process an epic, and ethnic Canadian, skaldic heroine. Hers is a fictional skald saga, a mimic of that ancient Icelandic genre that paid tribute to the poet-hero (Dorson 1978, 149). The female artist figure who emerges here is one of Viking ambition. In the last lines of *Summer of the Hungry Pup* she is invested through Man-of-all-Songs with the poetic knowledge of "the words to all the songs" (303) and in *Winter of the White Wolf*, in Sweden, she is the out-wandering poetess who will be the wordsmiter, medium, artistic interpreter, and myth-maker of transcontinental tribal history in her reverse exodus to the land of her forbears. In fragmented self-talk, Annika the artist considers the nature of her art, and her quest for artistic and tribal wholeness:

> Livelong was my childhood home ... Landscape become wordscope. There is no wordescape. In Hannas and in Molltorp I found two halves of the original homeplace; and through the movement from south to north I brought them together....All the myths are now true. Re-vision will be swift and easy ... There are ways of bringing metaphor to metaphor, or imposing illusion upon reality upon dream, of superimposing landscape upon landscape and words of one language upon another. It all joins now (1988, 211).

In *The Livelong Quartet*, the very title of which suggests a bardic lay, Annika's, and Barclay's, aesthetic manifesto is one of epochal magnitude and broad circular sweep as she weaves her fictions backward and forward in time and around places and continents. If the first instrument is Old Woman, the second is Johanna, who in *The Last Echo* is brought back to her own tribal roots and the beginnings of the family saga and genealogical lineage that develops as one feature of the author's tribute to Swedish ethnicity in these novels. At the heart of *The Last Echo* is family myth. Barclay explains in private correspondence:

> Rather than focus on recorded myths, I turned to snatches of story told to me by my grandmother and mother. For example, I was told that my great-grandfather, a carpenter, fell from the church steeple. He also wore a rag tied around his thumb. That became the basis of the character Per Lundahl. The rest I imagined. I never knew my great-grandmother, nothing was ever said about her, but my grandmother made her own soap and candles, and the soap-boiling woman came from my memory of that lost art ... My focus was family myth, which I believe

to be a universal characteristic of all Europeans who settled in Canada. (letter to author, July 19, 1986)

The family myth of Per Lundahl becomes in *The Last Echo* the folkloristic tale of "The Woodcarver's Fall" in which the elfish paterfamilias, who is dominated by his round, strong, and combustible soap-boiling wife, falls from the church steeple, only to revive as he is being prepared for burial. After his wife has shaved his skull for the bone fragments from a dead man that, according to Swedish folk remedy, she needs to cure her daughter's epilepsy, he awakens "berserk" (34) to a scene of comic ribaldry that is a tongue-in-cheek parody of male epic exploit. (In Norse mythology a beserker was a fierce warrior who fought in battle with frenzied violence and fury.) The "family fiction" of *The Last Echo* told within the larger framework of an immigrant female genealogical saga in the *Quartet*, is a richly sensuous tableau of larger-than-life peasant character, psychology, custom, and superstition with all of its old-world folk magic. This is a legendary world of Midsummer's Eve custom, of forest trolls, of pickled herring and oyster soup, rye krisp, potatoes boiled with their jackets on, "*kottbullar, vitabord* and *kram* pudding" (27), a world where skaldic poems are still sung:

> Arvid told ... that the shield was the ship of the vegetation demon who comes on land in the spring and leaves in the fall. In the north, he said, shields were covered with leather, painted not carved. Not for war, the giving of the shield obliged the recipient to pay with a poem, the Ninth Spell of Odin, and he sang of *night hags sporting* (122).

Here, too, the artistic magic of *renaming* primitive tribe is conveyed, as it is in *Summer of the Hungry Pup*, through Barclay's use of a poetic diction and a kind of imagery that is a salient characteristic of Old Norse poetry (see Hallberg 1985). Kennings, or "naming" symbols, are compounded metaphorical expressions, such as those used by the author here: "Guest-giving house," "soap-boiling woman," "stay-sail," "heart-grief," "giftbag," "proudflesh," "priestyard," "windflag." Typically, as in the heroic lays of the Poetic Edda, kennings add descriptive colour, and to the ambiance of poetic grandeur.

Clearly, in *The Last Echo*, Barclay succeeds in imaginatively recovering and reviewing both ethnic familial ancestry and ethnic tribe. In the *Quartet*, and most explicitly in *The Last Echo*, the metaphor that links the two, that is family and tribe, is that of the family tree that branches into the mythological Scandinavian world tree. In the new world, Bjorn will build a home for Johanna beginning with a carefully chosen log that will be the "guardian tree of their new home" (Wolf, 194), an act that echoes the larger Scandinavian myth. Johanna speculates on Bjorn's choice:

> "Of all the trees you might have chosen" Why that one?"
> ... Arvid would say because the gods live in its uppermost branches, the earth is its middle, and the underworld its root. The Eagle lives at its top, the serpent curls around its base, and the trickster squirrel running up and down the trunk carries insulting messages from one to the other. He would go on to tell her that Ask and Embla, the first man and woman, were created by gods from trees on the seashore, the man from ashen spar, the woman from a piece of elm (1988, 194).

Family myth is also woven together with the larger Nordic myth of the World Tree (the great tree that holds up the universe and is a symbol of life) in the mythic meeting of Arvid, Johanna's lover, with the Olding, the mysterious and ancient nomadic Laplander, who provides him with a prehistoric forest horse, a symbolic source of cultural knowledge: "Only the forest horse knows about the serpent coiled around the roots of the great tree, about the eagle's watch in its upper-most branches, about the chittering squirrel carrying insulting messages from one to the other" (1988, 78). When Arvid leaves his family and leaves his horse to venture into the new world, he loses the mythology of his Scanian world, which has been carefully preserved, even between Nordic tribes, to go on to build on the wrong plan on the prairies. As the Olding explains to Arvid, "I got her [the horse] from a Norwegian who got her from a Finn who got her from an Icelander who got her from a Gotlander" (93) and "never sell or trade her" for "if you do, your life will be altered for the worse" (94).

A dominant theme in *The Livelong Quartet* is that of the loss of original culture, as symbolized by Arvid's abandonment of the prehistoric forest horse in *The Last Echo*. Yet Barclay manages to re-invent the horse in the new world by reconstructing the history and pre-history of Swedish settlement in Saskatchewan, and as a Swedish Canadian female skald, by mythologizing blood-sisters in two continents. Her invention of tribe and tribal history is inspired by Native character, an inspiration that is constant in the literature of western Canada, where the Indian is designed by both male and female non-native writers such as Margaret Laurence, Rudy Wiebe, Robert Kroetsch, and Andy Suknaski, as a totemic first ancestor in a prairie landscape. On one level, the appeal of the iconic Indian is to tribe and to the nomadic condition, and an affirmation of the immigrant's first motivation: to leave the home/land behind and to become the out-wandering adventurer of the epic myth. At the same time, as Terry Goldie points out, the indigene in Canada is the very "symbol of national essence" (1989, 216) and, as such, symbolizes for these writers the paradoxical desire for a national culture, one that combines the old-world ethnic tribe with that of the aboriginal. As ethnic writers in western Canada have melded a variety of ethnic and religious heritages with Aboriginal ancestry—for instance, Suknaski, the Ukrainian Catholic; Wiebe, the German Mennonite; Laurence, the Scottish Presbyterian; and Barclay, the Swedish Lutheran -- they may appear to be at the margins of the contemporary national vision in Canada that currently espouses multiculturalism and female place, yet in practice asserts English, French, male dominance; but they can also be seen to be at the centre. In postmodern culture, which argues for speaking authoritatively from the borders, marginality may soon be fully equated with national identity, certainly on the "home" front, and perhaps even internationally. Linda Hutcheon speculates, "Since the periphery or the margin might also describe Canada's perceived position in international terms, perhaps the postmodern ex-centrix is very much a part of the identity of the nation" (1988, 3).

Although Byrna Barclay in *The Livelong Quartet* is a part of the larger tradition of ethnic fiction writing in the West, she is also quite clearly establishing a new direction. In choosing to create tribal allegiance by rejecting the idea of a land-based national culture in favour of a philosophical and metaphysical concept of the "unity of all things," she is, in part, exercising a womanly prerogative. The concept of home/land is one that has restricted the female, that has made her the passive agent in the marriage *plot*, and that has disallowed her from being the skald or heroic protagonist. The history of women-in-exile also has always been occasioned by male rule, forcing the female to carry her home within: *miyopayiwin*. As the exiled Latin American writer Marjorie Agosin suggests," I carry a country within myself. Like all women, I carry my home in my hair and carry love in my body full of spirits and pilgrimages" (1989, 26). Thus, in *The Livelong Quartet*, Barclay and her heroines reverse the male order of Ulysses-unbound. They are out-wandering women, with she and her heroine Annika giving poetic voice to the tribal exploits and history of women, singing the songs-of-women in the epic style. By so doing, they begin to move themselves as artists and as women from the margins to the circular centre.

REFERENCES

Agosin, M. 1989. *Women of smoke*. Stratford: Williams-Wallace.

Barclay, B. 1981. *Summer of the hungry pup*. Edmonton: NeWest Press.

Barclay, B. 1985. *The last echo*. Edmonton: NeWest Press.

Barclay, B. 1988. *Winter of the white wolf.* Edmonton: NeWest Press.

Department of the Secretary of State. 1979. *The Canadian family tree*. Don Mills, ON: Corpus.

Dorson, R. 1978. "Introduction." In *Heroic epic and saga*, ed. F.J. Oinas. Bloomington: Indiana University Press.

Godard, B. 1986. "Voicing difference: The literary production of Native women." In *A/Mazing/Space,* ed. S. Neuman and S. Kamboureli. Edmonton: Longspoon/NeWest Press.

Goldie, T. 1989. *Fear and temptation: The image of the indigene in Canadian, Australian and New Zealand literatures.* Kingston: McGill-Queen's University Press.

Hallberg, P. 1985. "Elements of imagery in the Edda." In *Edda: a collection of essays,* ed. R.J. Glendinning and H. Bessason. Winnipeg: University of Manitoba Press.

Hutchoon, L. 1988. *The Canadian postmodern.* Toronto: Oxford University Press.

Kirkconnell, W. 1935. *Canadian overtures: An anthology of Canadian poetry written originally in Icelandic, Swedish, Hungarian, Italian, German and Ukrainian.* Winnipeg: Columbia Press.

Kirkconnell, W. 1941. *Twilight of liberty.* London: Oxford University Press.

McGregor, G. 1985. *The Wacousta syndrome.* Toronto: University of Toronto Press.

Munro, A. 1971. *Lives of girls and women.* Scarborough, ON: McGraw-Hill Ryerson.

Palmer, T. 1987. "Ethnic response to the Canadian prairies, 1900-1950: A literary perspective on perceptions of the physical and social environment." *Prairie Forum.* Spring. 50 - 73.

Palmer, T.J. and Rasporich, B.J. 1985. "S.V. Ethnic literature." *The new Canadian encyclopedia.* Edmonton: Hurtig.

van Herk, A. 1986. *No fixed address.* Toronto: McClelland Stewart.

FOOTNOTES

1   For a general definition of ethnic literature, see Palmer and Rasporich (1985). This definition includes "emigre writing both in the nonofficial languages and in translation; literataure by writers who perceive themselves as belonging to an ethnic minority and write from this perspective (usually in English or French); and works that deal with immigrant or ethnic experience but are not necessarily written by a member of the group portrayed." This article points out that "the relationship between ethnic literature and mainstream writing is very much in flux" and "the latter is increasingly defined in the light of Canada's ethnic diversity."

2   In the interwar period, for example, the Chinese were completely excluded by the Chinese Immigration Act of 1923. Eastern and southern Europeans were restricted, and xenophobia swept across Canada and the United States. See Department of the Secretary of State (1979).

Michael Taft
Department of Culture and Recreation
Edmonton

Use of Ethnic Traditions: A Family in Crisis

The folklorist's task is to attempt to place the role of creativity within its social framework. That all human society is creative is beyond debate. Narratives, songs, dance and music, games, rituals, material arts and crafts, the clever use of language–all are a part of the ongoing expressiveness of all people in all groups. While we might rightly stand in awe of our own artistry, folklorists explore the reasons why people use specific forms of creativity in specific situations: how does a narrative or piece of artwork–to pick two examples–function for those who perform, create, re-create, or observe these expressive forms?

The idea of "function" pervades modern folkloristic scholarship; at least since the works of Malinowski and Radcliffe-Brown, functionalism has been one of the leading schools of thought among folklorists. Yet, as American folklorist Elliott Oring (1976) pointed out almost two decades ago, there are logical pitfalls in applying functionalist methodologies to folklore. Briefly, the more general a functionalist explanation is, the more likely it is to be useless in understanding the role of folklore in a given culture, or even in a given situation.

Let us consider an example of the dangers of a generalized functionalist approach. Too often, folklorists have glibly asserted that the function of this or that bit of folklore is to maintain the social cohesiveness of a group of people. Folklore as the glue of social bonding is an alluring idea; it makes us feel warm and comfortable–it allows us to think of "the folk" as striving together towards some utopia devoid of conflict and dissension. Certainly, the maintenance of social cohesion is a constant struggle among people who form a group, and elements of folklore certainly assist in this struggle. But there is also a large body of traditions that work against social cohesion; schoolyard taunts, ethnic jokes, narrative gossip and rumour, rituals of humiliation, and the fashioning and use of weaponry might all be seen as forces of disunity and disruption within society. Yet they, too, are forms of folklore.

My intent, however, is not to set up a dichotomy between unifying and disunifying forces in folklore, but to examine the necessity of this entire line of reasoning. Must folklore always be seen as functioning in these ways? Do folklore performances in fact have the power to maintain *anything*–cohesive or otherwise–in the everyday lives of people? Especially in academic investigations of the folklore of Canadian ethnic groups, researchers have tended to apply the kind of cheery and optimistic functionalism I have described. How do these groups maintain their ethnic identity: singing and dancing, of course; foodways and costuming, of course.

My unease with such functionalist analyses of ethnic folklore stems from the fact that, while the overt and festive forms of folklore usually associated with ethnic groups might foster ethnic identity, there is a large body of traditions that cannot claim this function but nonetheless remain a part of ethnic expressiveness. As well, all the singing, dancing, and eating in the world will not maintain cohesion in an ethnic group if social, psychological and economic forces are working against cohesion. To come back to an earlier point, does folkloristic expression have the power to maintain *anything*?

To illustrate the points I have raised, I will describe the ethnic traditions of a Flemish-Canadian family, a family that, at the time I interviewed them, was undergoing a series of crises stemming from psychological, social, and economic pressures. Claude and Renate Maertens were both born in the 1920s in small Flemish-Canadian villages in southwest Manitoba. Their parents had emigrated from Belgium in the early part of the century. Thus, they grew up in Flemish-speaking households, but their schooling was in English, and many of their neighbours were "English" or "Canadian"–that is, non-Flemish. They met and married in the 1940s and had three children: Sue and Donald, born in the early 1950s, and Peter, born in the early 1960s.

Claude was a mechanic and farm labourer whose work was seasonal, depending as it did almost entirely on the agricultural year, and involved a lot of travelling. By their own count, they moved their household between ten and fifteen times while Claude looked for work, and he often had to leave Renate in Manitoba to tend the children and look after the house while he travelled as far as Peace River country in search of employment. I first met them in June 1981, after they had moved from Dauphin, Manitoba, to northern Saskatchewan. They had bought some land on the outskirts of town and had moved their two small, wooden houses from Manitoba to this property.

Claude and Renate lived in one of the houses and Donald, his wife, and four-year-old child lived in the other. Sue had married and was living in town, and Peter attended the University of Saskatchewan. The land they had bought was swampy and not at all suitable for the farming they had hoped to do. The houses were considerably the worse for wear after their move from Manitoba, and lacked plumbing and electricity. The property was strewn with bits of machinery upon which the Maertons' men tinkered, and they kept goats for their own use. Except for Renate, the entire family—even Peter, when he wasn't at university—worked part time at an alfalfa dehydrating plant. Otherwise, Claude and Donald fixed machinery and sharpened discs for farmers in the area. But clearly, they were not making a go of it, and whatever dreams they had when they bought their Saskatchewan property were far from being fulfilled.

Claude and Renate are fluent in Flemish and speak English with a Flemish accent; their children have varying degrees of proficiency in Flemish. Family members are all short and stocky; the men are full bearded and dress in somewhat makeshift clothing. As newcomers to the community, the Maertens' appearance, behaviour, and "foreign-ness", as well as the state of their homestead, made them marginal characters; they were cruelly branded "hillbillies" by the locals and were undoubtedly the butt of jokes among the more established townsfolk.

When I first met them, they were undergoing considerable economic and social stress, although they were most hospitable towards me and appeared cheerful and even optimistic about their condition. I had gone to interview them specifically about Renate's skill at making Belgian lace, a craft she had learned from an elder in her village and that had all but died out among the Flemish-Canadians she knew. As it turned out, the entire family contributed to this craft in one way or another, and I learned much from them about lace-making. They gave me more than I had bargained for, however, in that I became a willing audience for their performances of various Flemish traditions: sayings, rhymes, songs, narratives, religious beliefs and rituals, and games—all related to the old-world Flemish culture of Belgium. They expressed these traditions with pride and enthusiasm, and that evening a good time was had by all.

Their purpose, I think, in regaling me with these Flemish traditions was to display their ethnicity to an interested guest, for their identity as a family was certainly tied up with their sense of Flemishness, and they were intent on explaining themselves to me. At the same time, they seemed genuinely to enjoy their own performances, and I understood that—without television or the proper light to do much reading—these ethnic traditions were a continual source of entertainment for the family.

These traditions, although shared by all the family members, alienated the Maertenses from the rest of the world, and not only the non-Flemish world, but also the world of their Belgian and Belgian Canadian confrères. They had moved away from those Manitoba communities where other Flemish Canadians lived, but in their own perceptions of their ethnicity, they had also distanced themselves from the Flemish Canadian community as a whole. For example, because they had not been born in Belgium, and had never visited that country, their feelings about their European homeland were ambivalent. They took a great interest in Flemish customs and were quite knowledgeable about Belgian history and geography, but their overall sense of Belgium was that it was a place of danger and social discomfort. For instance, they stressed the linguistic disunity of Belgium—not between the Flemings and Walloons, but within Flemish society. In explaining how each Flemish community spoke its own dialect of the language, and how these dialects made for mutual misunderstandings, Donald said, "Every little frog stayed in his own little well and they were happy there, you know." In other words, from the Maertens's perspective the communities of Belgium were exclusive and unfriendly places, where outsiders were imperilled.

They saw Belgium as a kind of city-state—an urban environment with all the crime and alienation that rural people associate with the city. In their descriptions of the old country, they stressed violence, thievery, and drunkenness. For example, Claude said, "You take actually in Belgium: you'll get punished more for shooting a jackrabbit than you will for killing a person." In short, the Maertenses expressed none of the nostalgic or romantic attitudes towards their European motherland that one sometimes finds among ethnic groups in Canada. They directed some of this attitude towards their fellow Flemish Canadians. While Claude and Renate had good things to say about the Flemish neighbours of their childhood villages, they saw other Flemish Canadians—whom they met in their travels around Manitoba—as strangers who spoke unintelligible Flemish dialects and, perhaps, as people who were not as well-versed in Flemish traditions as were they.

Their negative, or at least ambivalent, attitudes towards Belgium and towards any solidarity with other Flemish Canadians were revealed in how they expressed some of their traditions. For example, Renate took great pride in being one of the last of the authentic Belgian lacemakers, yet in several ways she consciously diverged from the tradition as practised in the old country. What was a cottage industry in Belgium was, for Renate, no more than a hobby; although in Belgium the different parts of the lace-making process were carried out by specialists (those who made the netting as opposed to those who filled in the design), Renate took pride in being an expert in all aspects of the process. She made Belgian lace, but not in a Belgian way.

Although she learned her craft in the traditional manner–she apprenticed herself to an immigrant, Flemish neighbour–and although her first designs were traditional to Belgian lace– decorative geometric figures and floral patterns–she soon diverged from this tradition. Many of the designs she now uses come out of North American popular culture, taken from crocheting magazines, for example, the "Home Sweet Home"; domestic, rather kitschy designs of cats and dogs; and elaborate treatments of the words "Mother" and "Father." Obviously, Renate has turned away from symbols of ethnic significance and towards symbols of the family and domesticity.

Another genre in her repertoire of designs deals with Canadian history and patriotism. She has made lace wall-hangings of the ensignia for Canada's centennial and for Saskatchewan's seventy-fifth anniversary. She honoured Manitoba's centennial with a hooked rug, since that ensignia did not fit her lace-making aesthetic. Here again, we see a European tradition affected by what is clearly a new world sensibility. The syncretism that Renate displays in her craft expresses what she also says in words: "Now we're not Belgians. We're Canadian born."

This same syncretism, this same conscious breaking away from the authority of old world or conservative traditions is evident in Claude's stories and songs. He knows a number of tales that have analogues in early medieval European tradition, especially fables and bawdy tales of the type that Chaucer would have appreciated. He learned these stories from his father, which meant he learned them in Flemish, and while he can and does tell them in Flemish, he is quite at ease relating them in English. His Flemish songs, because of the nature of poetry, he necessarily sings in Flemish: songs that range from international ballads such as "The Soldier's Deck of Cards" to locally composed ballads of murders and mishaps in Belgium to an anti-English song dating from the Boer War. Yet he readily gives English summaries of these songs and even managed to sing a verse of a Flemish song in English, maintaining the rhyme in his translation. As well, he and Renate serenaded me with a Canadian-composed song that was macaronic: made up of lines in Flemish, French, and English.

For the Maertenses, then, there is nothing sacred about their Flemish traditions; they have no sense of maintaining some

European authenticity in their performances. Their concern, rather, is to reshape these traditions to meet the needs of their new-world situation, and more specifically the needs of their immediate family. One might see the traditions not so much as ethnic folklore, but as family folklore. In this sense, these Flemish traditions work to alienate and separate the Maertenses from their roots, as well as from their non-Flemish neighbours. Do these traditions, however, function to maintain the Maertenses as a cohesive family group? It seems not.

As I mentioned earlier, the Maertenses were undergoing hard times and their hold on their land, as well as on their internal cohesion, was tenuous. Economic forces and the outside world had already loosened the bonds: Sue was married and living away from the family compound, Peter spent most of his time at university and would soon marry and permanently leave home. While these flights from the nest were expected, other family problems were not. Shortly after I interviewed the Maertenses, they did indeed lose their land and their part-time jobs at the alfalfa plant. Claude and Renate, Donald, his wife, and their child moved to Saskatoon, where they lived in a trailer park and were without work. Donald's marriage broke up amidst charges of wife-beating, and when last I saw him on the street, he seemed to have degenerated considerably. I need not go into further detail. Crisis had turned into tragedy, and all the Flemish songs and stories, all the games and crafts, could not have prevented what happened.

If the Maertens's Flemish traditions failed to prevent this series of disasters—if these traditions, in fact, were never meant to function as a preventative—what role did this ethnic folklore play in their lives? Certainly it was a form of entertainment, and this function should not be ignored in the analysis of any form of folklore; telling stories, singing songs, and engaging in hobbies diverts us from our troubles. But the Maertens's use of their Flemish traditions went beyond diversion. By using them as a means of entertaining and enlightening me, and through me, outsiders and strangers, the Maertenses were certainly expressing their pride in their own achievements, abilities, as well as their peculiarities. Nor was I the only outsider whom they impressed.

Although Renate never marketed her lace-making, she did enter her pieces in craft contests at local fairs, where she invariably won prizes. In this way, the family achieved some social status, or at least some positive recognition from an outside world that, in other respects, worked against their best interests. As well, through her expertise in lace-making, Renate (and her family) were able to establish some kind of control, however symbolic, in a world that generally left them disempowered. Renate's public display of her craft, then, was a palliative to the social pressures the family faced, but of course it was no cure. In effect, her public success with lace-making countered, in a purely artistic and aesthetic way, the many failures of the family.

Similarly, many of Claude's stories and songs counterbalanced, again in an expressive fashion, the weight of social and economic forces that eventually tore the family apart. Through these folk-literary forms, Claude expressed the relationship of his family to those with authority; but in his narrative world, as opposed to the real world, the disadvantaged hero confounds the authority figure. Most of these stories are some form of trickster tale: the drunken man, wrongly accused of murder by the police, outwits them by claiming to be from the Belgium town of Enghein, said to be a village of idiots and fools incapable of serious crime. Claude told the ancient tale of the priest who opens a closet where a naked maid is hiding to announce to his dignified guests that "here's an old viola I sometimes play." He told the fable of the fox showing the curious wolf what man is; the wolf learns the nature of man through injury and humiliation. He sang a song about a man who dresses as a nun in order to sleep with, and eventually elope with, the dupe's daughter. He told the story of a man who mistook a goat for a ghost and of a clever shoemaker who killed a man pretending to be a corpse: "Those that are dead—bang!—stay dead." He sang the Flemish version of "The Soldier's Deck of Cards" in which a soldier avoids punishment for gambling by relating each playing card to a religious image. He told of how a thief got the better of the rich burgermeister by stealing the nightgown off the back of the burgomaster's wife. And he recounted a tale in which a trickster spies on a priest making love to a woman, and another tale—which can be traced back at least to the twelfth century—about a thief who scares a hypocritical priest.

In all of these stories and songs, the empowered are tricked by the disempowered, except perhaps in Claude's animal fable, where the wise fox lets the stupid wolf be humiliated by the power of man. The relationship of these tales to the Maertens's situation is obvious: they are the expression of a disempowered group who can only win in the upside-down world of folk literature. But more importantly, these traditions are a running commentary on the condition in which this family finds itself, and it is as commentaries that these forms of folklore find their most significant role in the life of the family. Rather than a mechanism for bonding, these traditions are a way of commenting on the strength or weakness of the family's bonds. They are an analysis of the situation, in that they express in various ways the struggle between authority and the individual, between social expectations and personal freedom, but most of all between the wished-for world where the disempowered triumph and the real world where failure is the norm.

These traditions, then, could not help the Maertenses to succeed; they could only mark whatever successes or failures the family experienced. Rather than making the family cohesive, they reviewed the state of that cohesion. I should add, however, that while almost all of the traditions that the Maertenses performed for me that evening related to the themes that I have discussed, there were some stories, songs, rhymes, and games that expressed other concerns. I cannot pretend that the entirety of the Maertens's ethnic folklore was directed towards one set of commentaries. As well, the traditions they chose to share with me represented their state of mind that particular evening and their sense of what I, a stranger, might want to hear, or what they thought I needed to hear.

I do not know what became of the members of this family; I lost contact with them a number of years ago. But I do know that their ethnic traditions—if they still exist at all—could not save them from whatever their individual fates might be.

REFERENCES

Oring, E. 1976. Three functions of folklore: Traditional functionalism as explanation in folkloristics. *Journal of American Folklore* 89: 67 - 80.

PART III

COMMUNITIES OF WOMEN

Jo-Anne Lee
Department of Sociology
The University of Saskatchewan

Community Development With Immigrant Women: Theory and Practice

I write this essay from the margins, looking into the center[1]. It is about my experiences in organizing within an immigrant women's organization in a Prairie city, and the inadequacy of conventional community development theories to help understand and interpret these experiences. It is written in an unconventional style, in part semi-autobiographical and in part as theoretical critique. I begin with the issues, problems, and dynamics that I personally encountered in organizing with "immigrant" women. The voice in which I speak comes not only from the position of an "insider"–a member-participant, as the ethnography texts (Adler and Adler 1987; Fetterman 1989) might describe my "role" as a researcher, but also as a community activist whose membership in the group is authentic and participatory. Yet my two identities as activist and as researcher cannot be clearly distinguished or separated, because they are interconnected and constantly shifting. To isolate a single "voice" in which to write this article would fix me in a temporal slice of time that would subjectify me only as a researcher and objectify my organizing work. Moreover, in written communications the academic research role becomes privileged and my activist-organizer identity seems to shift into a subordinate position. Instinctively, I felt the need to resist this positioning, but how should this act of resistance be realized? The approach I have taken in this essay is to use both the personal and the "objective" voice.

It is important for minority feminist activist/researchers to write from personal, politically engaged perspectives and to ground their theoretical work in their own social reality. Mainstream feminist researchers have demonstrated how male-centred, logocentred logics fail to account for the experiences of white, middle-class women. Minority feminist researchers such as Moraga and

Anzaldua (1983), hooks (1984, 1990) and Mohanty, Russo, and Torres (1991) have made similar points about mainstream feminism's inability to account for the experiences of minority, Third World women. In both these cases, the slogan "The personal is political" remains an important strategy when the production of knowledge is also seen as a site of struggle.

Others might have interpreted events differently or come to different conclusions. But at present such a dialogue over interpretation is not yet possible, since few minority feminists have exposed the nature of conflicts occurring inside so-called multicultural women's organizations. I believe this is now changing (see Resources for Feminist Research 1991). In critiquing orthodox community development theories in light of my experiences, I seek to bring their theoretical presuppositions to a crisis. Spivak (1989, 139) defines "crisis" as the moment at which you feel that your presuppositions about an enterprise are disproved by the enterprise itself. By exposing the blindness of community development to the realities of organizing a multicultural women's group, I want to rupture conventional thinking about community development in order to provide an opening for the subaltern to speak and for the dominant groups to listen.[2] Through my accounting of the internal dynamics of organizing within an immigrant women's community, I hope to challenge and dismantle conventional thinking about community organizing.

This chapter argues that there is a need to rework concepts of "community" in community organizing in order to achieve a more complete understanding of the reality of racialized women's organizing experiences. Orthodox conceptualizations of "community" and "organizing" fail to account for the actual experiences of racialized women[3] organizing for change at the community level. I began to question the assumptions underlying the traditional views of community organizing when it became obvious to me that there was nothing in this literature that spoke to my experiences in organizing. Indeed, revisiting this literature after a long absence while I was simultaneously working with an immigrant women's community group opened my eyes to an entire subtext that was always there, but that I had never before seen or heard.

I begin with a brief background of some of the problems encountered by racialized women trying to form a grass-roots organization, discuss problems with orthodox community organizing literature in light of these experiences, and finally present an alternative conceptualization of community and organizing. In the last section, I re-examine the dynamics of organizing with racialized women within a broadened conceptualization of "community".

THE IMMIGRANT WOMEN'S ORGANIZATION

The Immigrant Women Society (IWS) began in 1984 as a project of the local Open Door Society, an immigrant settlement agency. With a federal government grant, IWS began as a support group for immigrant women but soon grew into an independent organization with its own bylaws and elected officers. The term "immigrant" in the name is a misnomer because IWS membership includes "visible minority," "refugee," "white," foreign-born, and Canadian-born women who support the goals of the organization. The membership is extremely diverse in terms of English-language skills, educational levels, work experience, length of time in Canada, political ideologies, age, and other characteristics.

The organization is part of a larger provincial structure consisting of four regional chapters that differ in size and orientation. In the past, responsibilities were divided between the provincial organization and the local chapters: the provincial organization took responsibility for advocating on behalf of immigrant and visible minority women on broad social concerns, and the local chapters provided social support and services. As a grass-roots organization, IWS struggles to survive on volunteer labour and project grants. It is managed by an elected board of directors, receives no core funding, and, like other grass-roots women's organizations, it is only as strong as the women who support it.

When I first became involved, IWS was going through difficult and demoralizing times. The presidency had changed hands three times in one year. There had been charges of financial misconduct, including the use of organizational monies for personal advantage; favouritism; racism; and power grabs. Membership had fallen off drastically, with fewer than twenty women attending the previous general meetings. The organization also faced no funding for the upcoming year. Owing to internal chaos and a lack of decision-making, the organization had depleted its savings, by renting large, costly premises when there was only one staff person working fewer than ten hours per week and no programs being offered.

The personal relationships among board members were extremely fragile. At the first few board meetings I attended, the group dynamics were so hostile and acrimonious that the meetings would end in tears, shouting, and accusations. In this divisive climate, the annual elections were being planned. Information was withheld because one ethnic group did not want another ethnic group "to take over." This situation did not occur overnight; the board had not been working together for quite some time. Different factions in the board accused each other of bringing this about.

Prior to the resignation of two presidents in the same year, the previous president had served for three terms and worked extremely hard for the organization. She was a highly trained professional woman from an upper-class Pakistani family background. Certainly, her willingness to help the organization needs to be acknowledged. But as president, she tended to consult only with staff and a small, inner circle of supporters in making decisions. This style of leadership was to have serious consequences for the organization.

Because IWS was a multi-racial, multi-lingual women's organization, English was used as the common language. This meant that women who came from English-speaking countries or who were well educated and spoke English fluently tended to become actively involved in decision-making processes. Increasingly, women from ex-British colonies, primarily India and Pakistan, began to dominate the board. The impression was created that the organization was not really open to all immigrant and visible minority women. Interest began to wane as more and more women perceived the organization to be unresponsive and irrelevant to their experiences. In recognition of the lack of participation from other groups, one of the main concerns during the time the elections were being planned was how to involve more Chinese, Vietnamese, and African women.

The organization had received grants over three successive years from Canada Employment and Immigration for a Canadian Jobs Strategy Training Program aimed at job re-entry training for immigrant women. As a result of these relatively large grants, and the president's leadership style, the organization focused mainly upon the administration of this job-training program. It began to function as though it were a formal service agency. The organization became increasingly bureaucratized as the board became involved with policy, management, and administration of the job-training program to the exclusion of other concerns. As with other community-based women's organizations, diminishing involvement by members was closely associated with acceptance of government funding. Rather than being member driven, the organization became staff driven.

When IWS lost its job re-entry program funding, it also lost its staff. In addition, the newly elected incoming president had just resigned. Immediately, the frailty of the organization was exposed.

Because information and decision-making had not been shared, the remaining board members had no idea how to manage the organization administratively, financially, and organizationally. Underlying class, ethnic, and language tensions that had remained submerged and veiled suddenly exploded into a flurry of accusations of financial mismanagement, racism, favouritism, and egotism. All the conflict was personalized and individualized since no one had been able to move to overall analysis.

The underlying disputes came to a head when the organization's annual general meeting was held in May 1991. Few members had seen the bylaws and constitution and even fewer could understand them, especially since there were several versions in circulation. A Secretary of State official who attended the meeting intervened and began interpreting the organization's bylaws to the members. According to her, she was the only person present who knew the history of the organization and was "neutral," but in fact she spoke up defending the actions of one of the board members. Frustrated and dissatisfied with the existing board and the chaotic meeting, members elected a relative newcomer as president. As a volunteer appointed to fill a vacant board position two months earlier, I was concerned that the organization was on the verge of collapse. Because I felt strongly that IWS was too important a "voice" for racialized women to be destroyed by personal divisions, I spoke out at the general meeting. I must have struck a sympathetic chord among members, who elected me president by acclamation.

On reflecting about the underlying dynamics operating within the organization at the time, I began to see that the problems encountered did not fit the pattern offered by conventional theories of community organizing. The actual dynamics could not be characterized simply as the ebb and flow of organizational development (Roberts 1979), nor were they a result of lack of leadership and organizational ability on the part of immigrant and visible minority women.[4] Many members were highly educated and skilled in political activism in their home countries and in Canada. The problems could not be attributed to a lack of ability or will. I saw the process shot through and through with the complex dynamics of language, race, and class. More and more, I saw the divisions, conflicts, and tensions in the organization as a struggle over the politics of representation and identity. The organization did not represent a group of "immigrant" women who shared a common identity that could be the basis for building "community." Instead, it represented a diverse group of women who differed in complex ways.

In the next section, I discuss why traditional concepts of community in community organizing are problematic for organizing ethnically, racially, and linguistically diverse women.

TRADITIONAL VIEWS: ESSENTIALIZING OF COMMUNITY

In returning to the traditional literature on community organizing,[5] the difficulties with traditional views of community and community organizing we throw into greater relief when we consider the actual community-organizing experiences of racialized women. One main problem stems from traditional notions of community that hold as fundamental a common referent, such as location, need, or interest (Rothman 1974; Sanders 1983; Warren 1963). But these traditional accounts pay no attention to those whom Vandana Shiva (1991) describes as having been uprooted from organic communities through war and "development" of various types. What is community's referent in a society populated by dislocated people who have been uprooted to new lands either by choice or by necessity? What need or interest is held in common? How do categories of representations formulated and imposed on racialized women affect community organizing?

Orthodox views of community, whether based on geographic location, felt need, interests, or common identity, provide few answers to these questions. For example, orthodox views have not examined critically the state's role in constituting categories of representation (Ng, Muller, and Walker 1990). The definitional and classificatory approaches customarily employed as theory in community development (see especially Rothman 1974) are of little use in understanding the complexity of relationships involved in empowering racialized women. Although community organizing may result in oppositional strategies and empowerment, the practice of organizing can also further reproduce gender, class, race, and language inequalities and maintain ethnocentric hierarchies under the guise of building "community." Even Kuyek's (1990, 10) recent definition of community as "the name we give a geographically-based human relationship between a number of people who know each other quite well, share a sense of purpose and values, and interact in their work, play and family, and share power to shape their lives" (1990, 10) does not permit us to see community in contradictory and emergent ways. Community as spirit and location must be seen as an outcome of struggle that does not remain fixed in time and space and follows no predetermined logic of development.

I stand with Ng and her collaborators (1990), who have raised concerns about the inadequacy of traditional frameworks to account for the diversity of people's lived experiences and forms of community organizing. If racialized women's lives are to be accorded their rightful significance and full stature, it is urgent to take apart notions of community so that the underlying assumptions that limit recognition and understanding of the reality of women organizing at the community level can be revealed. Several notions about community and community organizing seem especially problematic; these are discussed below.

THE MYTH OF A COMMON TRANSCENDING IDENTITY

Despite the ambiguity in the concept of community, a fundamental assumption of community organizing is that individuals may be organized on the basis of some commonly shared identity, whether that be based on a locale, need, or interest (Roberts 1979; Minar and Greer 1969; Carey 1973). No matter what definitional approach is taken, people are thought to identify and share something in common. In a recent volume, community is defined as "people that live within a geographically bounded area who are involved in social interaction and have one or more psychological ties with each other and with the place in which they live" (Christenson and Robinson, Jr. 1989, 9). In the orthodox versions of community development theories, citizens/individuals/human beings are taken as universal, homogeneous subjects who can be brought together on the basis of some objective, pre-existing social identity (Cox et al 1974). When race, ethnicity, gender, language, or class are raised, rarely are they analyzed as dynamic interrelationships; more often they are taken up singly and added together, or taken as biologically or culturally fixed determinants of group identity (see Kuyek 1990; Rivera and Erlich 1984).

Even if differences are acknowledged, the possibility of a unitary, transcending identity as the basis for community is still a fundamental assumption underlying all traditional accounts of community organizing. What seems basic to popularly held notions of community organizing, is that they accept as *a priori*, a common community identity as the basis for forming community. There is an underlying historicism in these conceptualizations; community is and will always be. The task of strengthening and building on such an identification becomes the responsibility of the organizer who brings "strategies, techniques and tactics" (Cox, et al, 1984) to the group.

THE OBJECTIFICATION AND REIFICATION OF COMMUNITY.

In the orthodox literature, community is reified as a fixed social entity existing as objective reality "out there." It is seen as an eternally pre-existing form outside of the people whom it supposedly encloses. The literature talks of community building, where actors supposedly work towards reclaiming or rebuilding a form of social relationship that, although abstractly conceived, is still perceived to be objectively knowable. Thus, this view reifies community which is taken to exist in some pure, idealized form against which communities may be measured against. The Hobbesian notion of people coming together naturally to serve their own self-interest has tended to dominate orthodox understandings of community.

Community is often endowed with agency. It is treated as an aggregate of individuals that somehow takes on a life of its own beyond the agency of its constituents. We talk of the community doing this and that, and we use the noun "community" as a form of shorthand to refer to a conglomeration of individuals, but this leads to thinking about community as a unified, conscious subject. The limitation of this kind of thinking is that once community is reified as a monolithic acting entity, it is no longer possible to interrogate its internal constitution.

THE DICHOTOMOUS POLARIZATION OF COMMUNITY.

Traditional approaches to community organizing have also been limited by a normative dualism that has been set up opposing categories of community: rural/urban, *Gemeinschaft / Gesellschaft*, modern/traditional. These oppositional categores have tended to preclude thinking about community as emergent social relationships that take different forms at different historical conjunctures. One result of polarized, dichotomous thinking about community is a functionalism in community that leads to normative and instrumental logic.

Here the term "normative" refers to the way in which different types of community are seen as desirable while others are not. This is especially true of the modern/traditional oppositional form, via which a traditional form of community life is idealized and modern, technologically driven community life is considered alienating and individualizing.

Instrumental logic, in this instance, is manifest in the way community development is presented as a somewhat benign process that may be utilized in dual ways: either as a tool of modernization or as a tool to resist change and modernization. For example, Blakely (1979) goes so far as to describe community development as an applied behavioural science. Moreover, the professions of social work, adult education and planning tend to see community organizing as a field of practice. In these fields, community is usually objectified as a site or group where the community organizer, as a professional practitioner, intervenes as a conscious agent[6] :

Community development work is primarily concerned with helping people where they live, and it depends for its success on the worker winning the people's confidence and willing cooperation. Hence he [sic] cannot direct or control them in detailed conformity to a national program. He has to stimulate and educate them in relation to their own local needs and interests. (Batten 1962, 13).

Following from this assumption is a fourth, the uncritical conceptualization of the state and of power relations in community organizing.

STATE AND POWER IN COMMUNITY ORGANIZING

Orthodox views of community have not examined critically the state's role in constituting categories of representation in community (Ng, Muller, and Walker 1990). In traditional accounts, power is seen to rest outside of the community, usually in the hands of the state. Power is seen as a quantity and a resource. The state, as the holder of greater power, is seen as a monolith and separate from the community, which typically has less power. The construction of dichotomous, mutually exclusive categories precludes thinking about dynamic relationships that might exist among state, economy, and community. In some orthodox Marxist accounts, the state is viewed as an oppressive power operating over and above the community in the interest of the dominant groups. In liberal pluralist accounts, the neutral state is thought to respond in the common good to pressure from pluralistic community interest groups. More recently, theories of the state have suggested that the state is not a monolithic entity operating over and above community, but is itself a terrain of struggle (Poulantzas 1978) and an important actor in constituting community and allocating status, legitimacy, and resources (Offe 1984).

ANDROCENTRISM IN COMMUNITY

The concept of citizen participation appears to be neutral, but in fact "citizen" is understood from a male position and this experience is generalized to everyone else (see Spiegel 1968). The supposed gender-neutral language in social science literature has been critically challenged by feminist researchers (Harding 1987). The traditional community-organizing literature is no exception to this critique. Orthodox literature has tended to generalize and universalize from a limited frame of reference. This ignores the different interacting realities of language, gender, class, age, and race. The Alinski (1971) model acknowledges class and power differences but subsumes other forms of identity such as race and gender, under these dynamics. Christenson and Rubenson's (1989) recent book on community development fails to address race and gender as issues for community development. Such gender- and race-blindness is typical of the universalizing, generalizing language of much of the orthodox literature. Despite the progress made through feminist critiques, with few recent exceptions there is still a failure to acknowledge the complexity and contradictions of the diversity of racialized women's experiences in community organizing.

ETHNOCENTRISM IN COMMUNITY

The community development literature reflects a strong middle-class, Eurocentric bias. The poor, ethnic minorities, blacks, in fact, all non-Anglo groups were thought to be culturally distinct and unable to work collaboratively in organizing their communities.

Communities differ in their ability to incorporate the loyalties and energies of their members...people of different background also differ considerably in their ability to construct local communities that are rewarding. Catholics seem especially able to do so; blacks far less so. (Ahlbrandt, Jr. 1984, 4)

The early literature saw community development workers as necessary technologists in helping communities to adjust to social change. Here, social change did not mean change defined by the community, but change brought about by outside forces, such as modernization or necessary economic development: "to help people to adapt their way of life to the changes they accept, or have had imposed upon them" (Batten 1957, 6). The orthodox literature is characteristically modern and Eurocentric in its underlying assumptions. Perhaps these influences in traditional accounts help to explain recent criticisms that community development practices have been "co-opted" by government and big business. Given the inherent biases in traditional accounts perhaps community organizing has always been the method par excellence of dominant groups, and the co-optation has been from the direction of those resisting domination.

COMMUNITY DEVELOPMENT AS A COLONIZING PRACTICE

The preceding points bring me to comment on the colonial history of the practice of community development/organizing (Batten 1957). We need to remember that community organizing as a distinct field of practice and scholarly inquiry originated in the colonial administration of colonized peoples. Batten quoted a conference of colonial administrators meeting in 1948 who defined community development as "a movement to promote better living for the whole community, with the active participation and if possible on the initiative of the community, but if this initiative is not forthcoming, by the use of techniques for arousing and stimulating it in order to secure its active and enthusiastic response to the movement (1975, 1). The kind of theories and knowledge that are produced about community organizing cannot be taken as objective, eternal truths but need to be subjected to critical deconstruction. If community development began as a technique of social management, then these values and ideologies will be reflected in the kinds of explanatory frameworks that have been developed. As Foucault (1980) has pointed out, truth and power come together in forms of knowledge.

To conclude, there are major problems in orthodox accounts of community development. Given the assumptions underlying this literature, it may be necessary to consider a major reformulation of its basic concepts, one that allows for the specific conjunctures, material conditions, processes, and activities under which various forms of community organizing occur. To move towards such an analysis, I would argue that is necessary to utilize a more open, dynamic conceptualization of community. I address this problem in the remaining portion of this essay.

TOWARDS ALTERNATIVE VIEWS OF COMMUNITY ORGANIZING

In my view, community organizing with immigrant and other racialized women needs to be seen as a contingent and emergent process, that to a large extent depends on the complex interplay of representational categories. Organizing "community" within these groups is necessarily dependent on the outcomes of the micropolitics of representation and identity that involve class, race, language, and gender within an arena circumscribed by the state and the economy. By "representation," I mean discursive and material practices, both cultural and political, by which people–in this case racialized women–come to see themselves, are seen by others, and are inserted into specific social categories by others (see hooks 1990; Mohanty, Ranty, and Torres 1991; Spivak 1987). How one represents oneself, how others are represented to one, and how one is forced to be represented publicly are dynamic and interrelated phenomenon. Each of these dimensions has a constitutive effect on the other dimensions. For example, Ng (1988) argues that the social category of "immigrant" woman is a category that one enters upon arriving in Canada. Until she emigrates to Canada, a woman does not see herself, nor do others see her, as an immigrant. It is only upon her arrival in the adopted country that she finds herself publicly represented in this way. Because the category of "immigrant women" is materially reinforced through laws and state administrative policy, she begins to represent herself as "immigrant" in order to survive . Her self-identification and her identification by others are in the category of immigrant, and she is continually reinserted into this category in everyday life.

As there are multiple ways by which racialized women have been represented, and multiple overlapping categories of representation and self-identification, community organizing is necessarily messy and contradictory. Analyzing the dynamics surrounding the politics of representation provides an entry point into understanding community organizing with racialized women. While there are common elements, such an understanding can only be partial and specific to particular historical conjunctures.

In the unfolding of hierarchical relations between people, representational categories played an important part. For example, the members of IWS accepted the representation of the president who served three terms as a well-educated, professional woman who knew best. She, in turn, behaved as though she did know best. The social relations that developed within the organization, especially among the president, staff, and members, developed out of reciprocal expectations regarding what was "proper." Non-English-speaking working-class members were seen as "clients," and they behaved in a dependent, client-like manner, while professional, English-speaking-women were seen as "leaders." "Leaders" were identified on the basis of certain characteristics, such as articulate English-language skills, a professional occupation, and a high level of education. Women who displayed these attributes fitted a socially constructed category of "leader" and were thought suitable to publicly represent IWS. Hierarchical social relationships derived from the complex interplay of representational politics and socially constructed identities underlay many of the conflicts in the organization. This was just one example, but I hope it was sufficient to illustrate my argument that traditional concepts of community organizing have failed to address the actual, real-life experiences of organizing with racialized women. The voices and faces of these women have rarely been encountered in the literature.[7]

To begin a rethinking of community development, it is necessary to rethink the basic concept, of "community." An alternative way of conceptualizing community is available that sees community not as pre-existing, essential, and eternal, but as a social formation that is culturally and socially constructed. Benedict Anderson's (1983) formulation of "imagined community" provides a non-essentialist view of community as always in the process of being imagined. Marxist historian Eric Hobsbawm (1983) saw nation and community emerging from invented traditions, while Bhabha (1990) suggests that "community" is a cultural space for the creation of peoplehood, one step on the way to mythical nationhood. hooks's (1990) notion of "yearning" lends a poignancy to community that is missing in other formulations.

The idea of an imagined or yearned-for community rejects essentialism and offers the opportunity to view community as an outcome of political struggles. Community can now be seen as an emergent social form rather than as an idealized, romanticized longing for an invented and imposed past. The idealized Gemeinschaft-type of community may be a cultural invention popularized to serve the purpose of nation-state formation.[8]

Second, community development requires a theory of the subject. Post-structuralist concepts of discourse, language, deferral, difference, and subjectivity can help to move us away from a preoccupation with a single unifying identity as the basis for community. Because the meaning system underlying language is continually shifting, and because consciousness is linked to meaning, it is possible for individuals to hold several identity positions or subjectivities (Weedon 1987). Lacanian psychoanalysis offers another insight into the construction of subject identities. Although certain subject positions may be privileged and others repressed through discursive networks of power, individuals cannot be made into wholly homogeneous subjects because of processes of difference and deferral (Weedon 1987). Hence, the possibility for resistance is always present through submerged and deferred identity positions. Feminist theory has used discourse theory to show how the experiences of men cannot be generalized to women, and racialized women have argued, similarly, that the experiences of white, middle-class women cannot be generalized to the experiences of women of colour (hooks 1984)

The implication of post-structuralist theories of the subject for community organizing is that there can never be one single, transcending identity that forms the basis of community. Community organizing must face the reality of multiple identities in every individual that have the potential to generate contradiction and conflict in community organizations. Commonality must be seen as temporal, strategic, and fragile. Even if women stand in political solidarity against oppression, they must be seen to do so only in a tactical sense that remains open and contingent. Accordingly, fractious disputes within community groups can be seen as a normal development, not as some incompetence on the part of group members. Moreover, there can be no necessary or predetermined logic governing community organizing. If the process of organizing is constantly developing and contingent on the outcomes of specific struggles—over representations of social actors, among other things—prespecified progression/development is not to be expected.

In order to contextualize community organizing, we need a broadened conception of state/economy/community relations. Poulantzas (1978), Gramsci, and Laclau and Mouffe have all contributed to a more open and relational view of the state. The state is not seen as a separate monolithic structure operating outside of the community and the economy. Post-Marxism, as this perspective has been called (Jessop 1991), sees the state as constitutive of community, as community is constitutive of the state. Moreover, the determinacy of the economy is no longer primary, but also constitutive and constituted through community and state interactions. Thus, the analytical distinctions between state, community, and economy become blurred. This perspective helps to broaden our theoretical understanding of the dynamic interactions that exist among social actors shaping community, economy, and state. It undermines the privileged position of class determinacy as the basis of social transformation.

Alternative conceptions of power, such as that found in Foucauldian analysis, do not see power as necessarily repressive and unidimensional. Rather, power is seen as relational and embedded in institutional networks and personal relations. Power is everywhere present and always resisted. It is seen to operate through the body and through discourse; the challenge in community organizing is to specify which bodies and which discourses. In attempts to understand the actual experiences of organizing, power differentials among various actors at the level of community no longer need to be juxtaposed against those actors "outside" of the community. All forms of community are conflict ridden, since power invades all social relationship. Power as it actually operates in community organizing can be analyzed as a relation that shifts strategically among variously represented categories of social actors.

Post-structuralist theory draws attention to the need to view the constitution of community itself as problematic. If community is no longer taken as natural or automatic, community organizing may be seen as a selective process of incorporating certain subject positions in community while excluding others. In other words, participation in various forms of community organizing can be seen as an outcome of struggle over representation and identity in "community."

A culturally, racially, and linguistically diverse women's organization is not a naturally occurring entity in Canadian society.[9] Such an organization is a construction of the state. Government policies and agents have constructed an invented community of immigrant and visible minority women who are then perceived publicly as a homogeneous group sharing a unifying immigrant experience. Under the federal government Women's Program funding guidelines (Secretary of State, n.d.,), uni-ethnic women's organizations are not eligible for government funding. The federal multicultural community participation and support program requires ethnic community groups to serve several ethnic communities. Whether intentionally or not, selective funding by the state of community-based multicultural women's organizations helps to construct the public representation of racialized women. This is not to say that state interventions necessarily result in containment and control of immigrant, ethnic, and racial minority women. State intervention has contradictory effects, since the outcomes of state funding are contingent upon the interaction of other forces, including the capacity of the so-called immigrant women to take action.

The contradictory effects of state funding may be shown by examining dynamics around language in the immigrant woman's organization. Language segregated women into those who had a voice because they were able to communicate effectively in English, and those silenced because they were unable to communicate effectively. Although translation and interpretation services were available to facilitate non-English-speaking women's participation, their voices remained muted and indirect. The effect of these multiple factors was to make non-English-speaking women more invisible and less powerful than English speakers.

In a multi-ethnic, multilingual, multiracial, and multicultural women's organization, I found that using the familiar mantra of race, gender, language and class on a one-at-a-time basis did not help to further an understanding of community organizing, because these very important social relationships interacted in complex, contradictory, and entirely contingent ways. Because the ability to speak English is related to national, educational, and class backgrounds, the leadership of the immigrant women's organization reflected world capitalist and class hierarchies as well as racialized hierarchies. The organization experienced more contradictions through my involvement as president. Even though I am a third-generation Canadian, because of my physical characteristics I am perceived by the wider community to be an immigrant. This doubled identity works to draw attention to the popular myth, a form of common-sense racism, that all physically distinct people must be "immigrants." The juxtaposition of reality against imposed categories of representation is an effective tool of resistance, even while members insert me into an artificially constructed representation of "leader."

Class/colonial distinctions that many immigrant women experienced in their originating countries were re-enacted inside the immigrant women's organization. Although unintentionally, many women were placed into circumstances reminiscent of class/race-divided organizations in their own country. Those who were poor and non-English-speaking became victims of charity work in their own organization. The well-paid professional staff, who were, incidentally, mainly white women, and the president determined what was "best" for the members. The fact that this situation continued unchallenged for so long reflects the depth of internalization of class, race, and colonial experiences by many immigrant women. These colonized identities were reinforced by the decision-making and power structure of the organization that operated to continue the silencing of the most marginalized. But the space provided by IWS for racialized women to speak, to validate their experiences, and to gain confidence in organizing should not be discounted. Even though power relations within the organization were employed in a non-empowering manner for a period of time, members did resist silencing and employed democratic measures to bring in new leadership. Lack of English does not stop critical thinking in one's own language, although others often misinterpret passivity and silence as ignorance.

Despite the fact that one main goal for this community-based immigrant women's organization is to provide a voice for all immigrant and visible minority women, its inherent contradictions often worked to reinforce an existing hierarchy of racialisation based on language and ethnic background and a state-constructed "public" representation of a universal immigrant women's organization. Beyond questioning the conceptual basis of orthodox views on community, we may also ask, Whose interests are being represented in any community, and why? Why are immigrant women publicly represented in this way, and why is this representation privileged by the state? It is beyond the scope of this essay to probe these questions, but questions concerning the politics surrounding categories of representation as they affect community organizing must be addressed by critical feminist organizers working with minority women.

CONCLUSION

The "myth of community" in the organizing literature is based on an a priori assumption of commonality. One of the main agents involved in perpetrating this myth is the state whose policies, regulations, and official statements establish the limits for community struggle. This essay identified several ontological difficulties in the orthodox community development literature that help to explain why this literature is not very useful in understanding diversity and conflicts in community-based organizing with racialized women. Although I discussed the particular case of immigrant women organizing, there are wider implications for community development. I challenged the orthodox literature on the basis of its inability to account for the dynamics of race, class, gender, and language in community organizing. The absence of these structuring dynamics reproduces male-centred, Eurocentric assumptions of community to the exclusion of other realities.

Those organizing with racialized groups must first recognize how the imposition of externally defined representational identities functions to mediate social relations among members. Such imposition, however, is not a straightforward matter. For example, immigrant women continually struggle over government attempts to regulate their representation. At times this struggle amounts to no more than passive acceptance in order to survive, but the potential for resistance through submerged identity positions always remains. In the IWS organization, members eventually challenged the actions and views of staff and the past president towards non-English-speaking members. We need to pay attention to the micropolitics of representation and the politics of identity formation in community for two reasons: First, representations of women are important in constituting meaning and identity. Second, these representational positions guide and orient action.

A reconceptualization of community organizing is therefore needed to break the silence about the real-life experiences of marginalized women's groups in society. Using feminist and post-structuralist social theory, it is possible to refuse the closure of community, reveal Eurocentric, male biases in community organizing, and reclaim possibilities of resistance to domination through community organizing. Thus, community should not be seen as a fixed social form, but as a contested terrain of social relationships that is constantly in the process of emergence. Homi Bhabha described the nation as "more hybrid in the articulation of cultural differences and identifications—gender, race or class—than can be represented in any hierarchical or binary structuring of social antagonism" (1990, 292). This description holds true for community as well. Community needs to be seen as always in the process of being formed; it is more than a physical site of face-to-face interaction, more than a form of identity; it is above all a place of struggle. Existing concepts of community in the community-organizing literature must be reformulated to account for the actual experiences of organizing with racialized women. This reformulation must move community beyond universal generalities to greater concrete specificity; it must account for power differentials between actors, acknowledge the micropolitics of representation and identity, and contextualize community organizing within broader state and economic relations.

REFERENCES

Adler, P.A. and Adler P. 1987. *Membership roles in field research.* Newbury Park, CA: Sage.

Ahlbrandt, R.S. Jr. 1984. *Neighbourhoods, people and community.* New York: Plenum Press.

Alinski, S.D. 1971. *Rules for radicals..* New York: Random House.

Anderson, B. 1983. *Imagined communities.* London: Verso.

Batten, T.R. 1957. *Communities and their development.* London: Oxford University Press.

Batten, T.R. 1962. *Training for community development.* London: Oxford University Press.

Bhabha, H., K. 1990. "DessemiNation: time, narrative, and the margins of the modern nation." In *Nation and narration,* ed. H.K. Bhabha. London: Routledge.

Blakely, E.J., ed. 1979. *Community development research: concepts, issues and strategies.* New York: Human Sciences Press.

Carty, L., and Brand, D. 1988. "Visible Minority" women–A creation of the Canadian state. *Resources For Feminist Research* 17:39 - 42.

Cary, L.J. ed. 1983. *Community development as a process.* Columbia: University of Missouri Press.

Chekki, D., ed. 1979. *Community development: theory and method of planned change.* New Delhi: Vicas.

Christenson, J.A. and J.W. Robinson Jr., ed. 1989. *Community Development in Perspective.* Ames, Iowa, Iowa State University Press.

Cox, F.M., Erlich, J.L., Rothman, J., and Tropman, J.E., eds. 1974. *Strategies of community organization.* Itasca, Ill: F.E. Peacock.

Cox, F.M., Erlick, J.L., Rothman, J., and Tropman, J.E., eds. 1984. *Tactics and techniques of community practice.* (2ded.) Itasca, IL: F.E. Peacock.

Edelston, H. C. and Kolodner, F.K., 1968. "Are the poor capable of planning for themselves?" In *Citizen participation in urban development vol. I: Concepts and Issues, ed. H.B.C. Spiegel.* Washington, DC: NTL Institute for Applied Behavioural Science.

Egan, C., Gardner, L.L., and Persad, J.V. 1988. "Politics of transformation." In *Social movements/social change* ed. F. Cunningham, S. Findlay, M. Kadar, A. Lennon, and E. Siva. Toronto: Between the Lines, Winnipeg: Society for Socialist Studies.

Fetterman, D. 1989. *Ethnography step by step,* Applied social research methods series, vol. 17. Newbury Park, CA: Sage.

Foucault, M. 1980. "Truth and power." In *Power/knowledge: Selected interviews and other writings* 1972 - 1977. ed. C. Gordon. New York: Pantheon.

Harding, S. ed. 1987. *Feminism and methodology.* Bloomington: Indianna University Press.

Hobsbawm, E. 1983. "Introduction: Inventing traditions." In *The invention of tradition. ed. E. Hobsbawm and T. Ranger.* Cambridge: Cambridge University Press.

hooks, b. 1984 *Feminist theory: from margin to center.* Boston: South End Press.

hooks, b. 1990. *Yearning race, gender, and cultural politics..* Toronto: Between the Lines Press.

Jessop, B. 1991. *State theory.* Cambridge, MA: Polity Press.

Kuyek, J. 1990 *Fighting for hope.* Montreal: Black Rose Books.

Miles, R. 1989. *Racism.* London: Routledge.

Minar, D., and Greer, S., eds. 1969. *The concept of community.* Chicago: Aldine.

Mohanty, C., Russo, A., and Torres, L., eds. 1991. *Third world women and the politics of feminism.* Bloomington: Indiana University Press.

Moraga, C., and Anzaldua, G., eds. 1983. *This bridge called my back.* New York: Kitchen Table/Women of Colour Press.

Ng, R. 1988. *The politics of community services.* Toronto: Garamond Press.

Ng, R., Muller, J. and Walker. G., eds. 1990. *Community organization and the Canadian state.* Toronto: Garamond Press.

Offe, C. 1984. *Contradictions of the welfare state.* Cambridge, MA: MIT Press.

Poulantzas, N. 1978 *State, power, socialism.* London: Verso.

Resources For Feminist Research. 1991. *Transforming knowledge and politics*. (3,4).

Rivera, F., and Erlich, J. 1984. "An assessment framework for organizing in emerging minority communities." In *Tactics and techniques of community practice*. ed. Cox et al. Itasca, IL: F.E. Peacock.

Roberts, H. 1979. *Community development learning and action*. Toronto: University of Toronto Press.

Rothman, J. 1974. "Three models of community organization practice." In *Strategies of community organization*. ed. Cox et al. Itasca, IL: F.E. Peacock Publishers.

Sanders, I.T. 1983. "The concept of community development. " In *Community development as a process*. ed. L.J. Carey Columbia: University of Missouri Press.

Shiva, V. 1991. "Time is out of joint." *Resurgence* 142: 22 - 27.

Spiegel, H.B.C., ed. 1968. *Citizen participation in urban development, vol. I: Concepts and issues*. Washington, DC: NTL Institute for Applied Behavioural Science.

Spivak, G. 1987. *In other worlds: Essays in cultural politics*. New York: Methuen.

Spivak, G. 1989. In *The post colonial critic: Interviews, strategies, dialogues*. Harasym, S., ed. New York: Routledge.

Warren, R. L. 1963. *The community in America*. Chicago: Rand McNally.

Weedon, C. 1987. *Feminist practice and poststructuralist theory*. Oxford: Basil Blackwell.

FOOTNOTES

1   hooks (1984) writes about being on the margin in feminist theory and practice.
2   Spivak (1989, 141) describes the term "the subaltern" originating as a military rank. Gramsci, under censorship, called Marxism "monism" and used "subaltern" to describe the proletariat. Spivak uses the term to describe everything that doesn't fall into class analysis. "Subaltern" is a code word used to describe a multitude of oppositions, but according to Spivak it lacks theoretical rigour, which is part of its attractiveness.

3   In order not to take categories such as "immigrant women" as representative of any objective truth, Miles (1989) has employed the concept of racialization to name the process by which certain groups of people are placed into different social categories on the basis of signifying racial characteristics. I use the term "Racialized women" to name the process by which women, for example, immigrant, visible minority, and non-English-speaking women, are separated out for differential treatment on the basis of language, race, religion, culture, and ethnic origin. Following Miles, I use the term "racism" to describe negative, subordinating practices of the dominant groups. Because the label "immigrant women" has been accepted in everyday language to name women who have been racialized, and because the group of women I have been working with call themselves by this name, I will use this term when referring specifically to this group.

4   Edelston and Kolodner concluded that the "inability of uneducated poor people to conceptualize and their tendency to individualize all problems cast doubt upon the likelihood that the process itself can produce innovative ideas" (1968, 238). We find the same sentiment expressed two decades later, but the category of "poor people" has been replaced by the category "people of different races and cultures." Writing from the perspective of a white, middle-class activist, Kuyek writes, "when we work with other races, we need to be rigorously honest with ourselves, having a sense of humour about our 'white mistakes,'" ... The success that middle-class whites enjoy for following the rules and being reasonable often leads them to think that these are also good strategies for non-white/poor people to follow. In fact, most non-white/poor people can only use these tactics if they have 'acceptable' white, educated people to do it for them". (1990, 91 - 92). Both statements reveal assumptions that "the poor" and "non-whites" are somehow culturally distinct and are incapable of participating in community organizations in the same way as white, middle-class people.

5   I recognize that there is a growing literature that has departed from the "orthodox" approach to understanding community development, but in this essay, I am limiting my comments to the literature in the field of adult education that is considered foundational and whose line of reasoning is following in contemporary writing.

6   Among the many examples are Roberts 1979, Cox et al 1984, Batten 1957, and Chekki 1979).

7   There are a few notable exceptions, but generally these perspectives are not found in the community-organizing literature. See, for example, Egan, Gardner, and Persad (1985).

8   Although Tonnies' purpose was more to draw attention to the disorganizing and dehumanizing aspects of capitalist development.

9   By this I mean that ordinary social relations among women, particularly among members of the immigrant, non-English-speaking population, would normally be with those sharing at least a common language.

Multicultural women's organizations are not organic entities; instead, they must be seen as outcomes of government multicultural and immigration policies. Carty and Brand (1987) have argued that the Nationaly Organization for Immigrant and Visible Minority Women (NOIVM) did not grow out of grass-roots demand, but from a series of government-sponsored conferences where bureaucrats, state-funded consultants, and advisors played a significant role in shaping the conferences' agenda and selecting participants.

Poverty and Native Women

INTRODUCTION

Native women of the Plains have come to realize that Canada has a mosaic that is stratified according to class, race, and gender. This type of classification causes grave problems for women of colour, other minority groups, and especially Native women, who appear lowest on the hierarchy. The Plains Indian women of western Canada, with specific concentration in the Alberta region, exemplify their low position of this stratified society with low incomes, poor education, and minimal political authority. Such a system of classifying groups has numerous ramifications, as it limits growth and change in the lives of the affected individuals (Jamieson 1978, 5; Porter, 1965, 20).

The Canadian Constitution and Bill C-31 have called attention to racism, discrimination, and lack of education and employment among Indian women in Canada, which all lead to poverty. I examine the reasons why Native women have struggled and are struggling to overcome racism, poverty, and the stigma of not being considered as valuable as, and equal with the rest of Canadian society. The most effective way for Indian women to counteract these social problems is to formally educate themselves to understand how to deal with racism, oppression, and inequality. Native women indicate that they are becoming increasingly aware of their rights and strengths, first as human beings, but also as Native women.

The Indian Act, the prime reason for and contribution to the poverty of Native women, is said to have been amended. Bill C-31 was passed by Parliament in 1985, and since that time has raised awareness among Canadian people regarding the differences between them and Native people. Research shows that the bill has caused numerous divisions and dilemmas for Native women. Then, the Canadian Constitution brought about another problem of equality for Native women-- the fear of not having their rights and freedoms met.

According to Porter (1965), Native women are ranked lower than most Canadian groups within the vertically stratified Canadian class system (Lautard 1972,304; Porter, 1965). One reason why Native women are in a class below Canadians is the fiduciary relationship of Native persons and the federal government of Canada. This relationship, plus the ranking order, have resulted in oppression and lack of self-determination. The government's Indian policies have caused oppression by denying Native people their right to make choices and decisions concerning their lives and those of their children. Oppression teaches the oppressed no other life-style but to become oppressors. This type of influence and teaching has caused Native leaders to become dehumanized and in turn to dehumanize. Freire (1987) explains it as follows:

> The oppressed suffer from the duality which has established itself in their innermost being. They discover that without freedom they cannot exist authentically. Yet, although they desire authentic existence, they fear it. They are at one and the same time themselves and the oppressor whose consciousness they have minimized (p. 32).

THE INDIAN ACT AND ITS IMPACT ON INDIAN WOMEN.

The first time that Native people had a limited amount of influence in creating an amendment to the *Indian Act* was when Parliament amended sections of the *Act* which discriminated against Indian women. Native women were the influenced the greatest by that amendment. A group of Native women who lost their rights as treaty Indian women lobbied the Canadian government to make changes. These women also lobbied the United Nations until amendments were made to the Indian Act. The *Indian Act*, in the past, has been amended numerous times, but always without consultation with Native people, e.g., in 1869, Native women lost the right to remain Indian once married to non-treaty men. The assimilation policy was passed by the government in the same year (Jamieson, 1978, 30; Getty and Lussier, 1988, 43).

Bill C.31 and the Canadian Constitution have created levels of power, control, and authority that allow Native leaders to choose to become door-openers or door-closers for Native women. The bill and Constitution have created class levels among Native people. The power and authority invested in Native people is apportioned by the federal government, which holds institutionalized power and authority over Native groups in Canada.

An example of the struggle for self-determination among Native women in Canada is their fight to implement Bill C-31 which is long overdue. It is clear that there is a difference between the Canadian women and Indian women in terms of self-determination of ones life. In 1977, one hundred years after the signing of the last treaty in western Canada, Jeannette Lavell, who had lost her treaty status by marrying a man without such status, charged the federal government (Department of Indian Affairs) with discrimination. Lavell took her case, which protested her loss of treaty status, to court. The courts decided against her, saying that all Native women were to be treated the same; her case was no different from that of other Canadian Indian women who had married non-treaty, status men and had consequently lost their own treaty status (Jamieson 1978, 12; Selman 1987, 188).

Native women across Canada became aware their loss of treaty rights was unfair and caused them to be on the periphery of both Native and Canadian society. Indian women began to become aware of the impoverished state in which they were required to live. They also became aware of their lack of education and knowledge of their rights as women, and most of all as treaty Indian women who were penalized for marrying outside their own domain.

During the mid-1970s, various Indian women across Canada slowly became aware of the sexist and racist discriminatory acts they were encountering as Indian women. This awareness evoked the need to organize themselves, not only as women, but also as Indian women who had lost treaty status by marrying non-status men. Most of the relevant organizations were influenced by Indian women who were returning to their respective reserves to ask for reinstatement of band and treaty status. Many of these women were amazed when they realized that the chiefs and councils on some reserves not only would not, but sometimes could not, reinstate them (Selman, 1987, 21, 33, 108). They began to realize that they had lost their treaty status when they married white men and, furthermore, that white women who had married Indian men had gained treaty status. They began to realize that other Canadian women did not have to live in poverty and without an education, and could return to their place of birth if they married outside of it. They soon realized their living conditions were below the poverty line.

The Tabique Indian women's group was instrumental in changing the law. Most of these women were on welfare, but that did not stop them from pooling their money to lobby for justice at selected political conferences across Canada. Their strength, courage, and commitment enabled them to bring about a change and to advance a step closer to justice, equality, and freedom for Canadian Indian women. Their effort in going to the United Nations caused Canada to bring the Indian Act into parallel with the Charter of Rights and Freedoms. Although these women had very few dollars with which to accomplish a tremendous, against-all-odds, they were successful. Changes began to occur. In order to bring the Indian Act into accord with the Charter, the government added Section 35 to the *Charter of Rights and Freedoms.*

the Tabique women organized and carried out a walk to Ottawa from New Brunswick to demand equality and justice for Native women, to raise public consciousness, and to pressure the government to make changes in the Indian Act and address non-Native racist actions across Canada. The walk also addressed housing problems and poverty on reserves. These women wanted the public to become angry that such conditions should exist in this day and age and in Canada (Selman, 1987, 152). A certain group of Native leaders tried to stop the women's walk, but the women ignored the road blocks and continued their march, which became larger and stronger. In the end, the women staff members of Native leaders joined the walk (Selman, 1987, 159, 161). Not many Indian people supported these women who were demanding and fighting for their treaty rights, because of they lacked knowledge about the Indian Act versus treaty rights. Fear of losing their own treaty rights caused people to hesitate to become involved. During the walk, those from nearby Indian reserves questioned the need to fight, what the fight was about, and what justice was being sought. Many non-Indian people, including women's groups, came out and walked with the Tabique women in support of their cause, and for justice. These non-Indian people were able to support the march because they had a better understanding of the government and the role it plays in Canadian society: perhaps some of them had a better understanding of the *Indian Act* than some of the Native people themselves.

Upon reaching Ottawa, the Tabique women met with Prime Minister Trudeau. The meeting with the prime minister and with Indian Affairs officials revealed the bottom line: that the Indian women's male leaders were themselves working to prevent any change to the sexually discriminatory Section 12(1)(*b*) of the *Indian Act*. Native leaders saw the changing of the *Indian Act* as disruptive to all Native people across Canada; it would create chaos and separation.

Because these Indian women united and fought hard and long, other Native people benefitted. People used to live three and four families to a house; now more housing money was made available. Others lived in any vacant, condemned building or old schoolhouse. One woman put it thus: "I will not have to live in the jail any more. I can stop going to jail. We will have inside toilets and running water in all houses" (Selman, 1987, 165-66). These conditions of living had applied for many years. One of the women said, "Nowadays we should not have to live in those impoverished, deplorable conditions because we are Indian, and because we are women" (Selman, 1987, 146).

Once the walk took place, more Indian women across the country began to organize themselves and came together to support each other in strong lobbying groups. This networking became powerful and was in place for about ten years until Bill C-31 was made final in 1987 (Selman, 1987). However, today Native women continue fighting the system for their rights and freedoms.

Many determined Indian women who fought, and continue to fight to overcome poverty, were part of this walk for justice and equality. These women's children were a part of the touching ordeal and of the walk for equality and justice to Ottawa. At the end of the walk, the group gained more support than they ever envisioned. It was the Year of the Child, July 1987, when these women arrived on Parliament Hill, tears running down their faces, dirty, sweaty, grubby, tired, and with all their children and a few welfare dollars in their pockets. This was their first activist experience and their first time ever in Ottawa (Selman,1987, 165). This was not their last activist experience. The walk was only the beginning for Native women who continue to fight for equality, freedom and justice.

REFERENCES

Freire, P. 1970. *Pedagogy of the Oppressed*, The Continuum Publishing Corp., New York, New York.

Getty, A. and A. Lussier. 1988. *As Long as the Sunshine and the Water Flow*, University of British Columbia Press, Vancouver.

Jamieson, K. 1978. *Indian Women and the Law in Canada*, Minister of Supply and Services, Ottawa.

Lautard, H. 1971. "Occupational Segregation and Inequality Between Native and non-Native Indians", *Canadian Journal of Native Studies*, 2:2,302-312.

Porter, J. 1965. *The Vertical Mosaic: An Analysis of Social Class and Power in Canada,* University of Toronto Press, Toronto.

Selman, J. 1987. *Enough is Enough*, The Women's Press, Toronto.

PART IV

HEALTH ISSUES

Wilfreda E. Thurston and Anne McGrath
Canadian Mental Health Asociation,
Alberta South Centreal Region
Southern Occupational Health Resource Service
Department of Community Health Sciences,
The University of Calgary

10

Health Promotion for Women: The Need for a Global Analysis in Local Programs

Our recognition of the issue of global analysis/local action has been heightened recently because we are conducting a research project to assess the mental and workplace health promotion needs of immigrants in our city. Our interest in this project is both professional and personal. We have some personal experience with immigration. One of us immigrated from Ireland almost thirty years ago and the other is a fourth-generation Canadian who recently migrated to one of the wealthiest provinces of western Canada after having spent all of her life in the "Third World provinces" of Atlantic Canada. However, we are very conscious of the fact that we are two white women conducting this project and that we have benefitted from that and from having English as our first language.

The project began because we were given a mandate by our respective organizations to assist in designing health promotion programs for the previously under-served population of immigrants. Health promotion is receiving greater attention from our organizations because of many initiatives that are occurring at many levels: international, national, provincial, and local. This is the first example of how global action has had an impact on local programs. And we know that the immigrant population is under-served in our organizations because, despite the fact that one in five Calgarians was born in a country other than Canada (Corbett 1990), we see few immigrant clients in our programs. This is the second example of how global policy affects local need and, in some cases, action.

The objectives of our research project are:

1. assess the mental health service needs of immigrants in Calgary, with particular attention to the workplace;
2. propose a health promotion project or projects that would address specific needs; and
3. evaluate the organizational capacity of the sponsoring bodies to deliver health promotion programs to immigrant populations.

We are trying to fulfil our mandate and to reach these objectives within a health promotion framework. In other words, we are trying to use a process that makes the themes of enabling and empowerment a part of our research and program planning and evaluation.

How are we doing this? First, we have an advisory committee that includes people who can speak with authority, personal and professional, about the immigrant community. Second, through the needs analysis we will attempt to give individual immigrants, and agencies serving immigrants, a voice. The report of the Canadian Task Force on Mental Health Issues Affecting Immigrants and Refugees (1988) clearly and comprehensively described the many barriers facing this population. Although we use this report as a framework, we are trying to proceed based on expressed concerns of immigrants in our city. We believe this will make any program recommendations more relevant to local needs and increase the chances that collaboration and co-operation will occur in any new services. For instance, although we could have skipped a needs assessment and recommended "special" services for immigrants in our respective organizations, immigrant agencies have been telling us, both directly and in published literature, that "special" services often become "ghetto-ized" services that disempower all involved. Take, for example, the case where one counsellor is expected to deal with all immigrant clients and, therefore, with all of their problems. This can disempower in at least three ways. First, the issues of reducing inequities in access are addressed in a minimal way. There is no way that one person can provide equity in quality of service to all types of clients. Second, the counsellor is disempowered by the isolation experienced in the workplace and the unrealistic expectations of performance. She or he may even be criticized for not being sensitive to all cultures. Finally, if everyone in the agency or program does not examine their ethnocentricity, the social and political environment in the community may not be made healthier overall.

We are aware that we are taking a risk as individuals because there are no guarantees that the organizations that gave us our mandate will respond to the voice of immigrants. We are conscious of the politics surrounding organizations' utilization of research (Palumbo 1987; Schaefer 1987). However, we are willing to take this risk because we intend our research to become a resource for immigrants in our community, and in the long term, this will meet our goal of operating in a health promotion framework.

In addition to trying to give local people a voice, we are trying to ensure that consciousness and analysis of global issues runs throughout our research and its outcome. There are two reasons that such an analysis is important: first, policy and program decisions made locally in the name of health promotion can have an impact on the lives of people in other countries (local action, global vision); second, in order to provide health promotion locally to multicultural groups, we need a sensitivity to cultural differences in values, beliefs, and experiences (global vision, local action). We will discuss both of these points, but first we will clarify what we mean by health and health promotion.

HEALTH, HEALTH PROMOTION, AND PREVENTION

We hold specific beliefs about health and health promotion. The World Health Organization (1986, 246) and the federal government of Canada (Epp 1986 6) define health promotion as "the process of enabling people to increase control over and to improve their health." Health, in our view, is multidimensional and should be viewed as a dynamic system with two components: health balance and health potential (figure 1). In health balance, the physical, psychological, social, and spiritual aspects of our health interact to create a state of well-being (Noack 1987). At any given time, we may be at a high or a low level of health balance. An equally important part of our health is our health potential, or the resources we have to maintain our health balance or to restore its equilibrium when that is upset. These resources can include such things as genetic predispositions to wellness or illness, e.g., fitness or whether we experience menstrual pain or not or skills that are acquired, e.g., coping skills or assertiveness. One strength of this conceptualization of health is that it can be applied to communities as well as to individuals. This conceptualization represents a "global", i.e., holistic, view of health.

FIGURE 1. A CONCEPT OF HEALTH

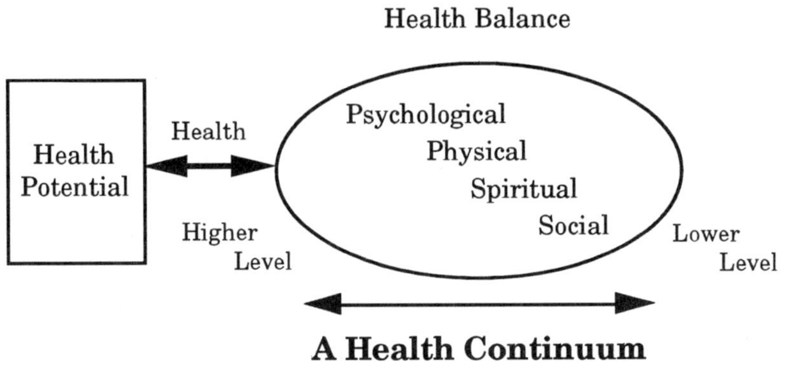

Health Balance

A Health Continuum

Health promotion is a relatively new field. It is not synonymous with prevention, which is primarily focused on problems, dysfunctions, or diseases; but there is no consensus about the relationship between the fields. There are three levels of prevention. Primary prevention focuses on the prevention of the occurrence of problems; secondary prevention is directed at early detection of problems in order to halt their progress; and tertiary prevention is aimed at stopping the development of complications, usually described as treatment (Last 1987). We believe that health promotion, as defined above, can be distinguished from prevention by its focus on health potential, or increasing people's health resources. The three levels of prevention are primarily directed at restoring health balance. Given that, health promotion must also play a co-ordinating role with the three levels of prevention.

Figure 2 illustrates these relationships and provides examples of programs that would promote women's health relevant to the field of addictions (Thurston and Bowhay 1991 p. 9). The degree of linkage between health promotion and prevention depends, by definition, on the actual program objectives, activities, and projected outcomes; however, the implication is that people involved in health promotion or prevention must adopt a more global perspective and look at broader implications of their program activities.

FIGURE 2. HEALTH PROMOTION AND PREVENTION:
THEIR RELATIONSHIP TO HEALTH, WITH PROGRAM
EXAMPLES

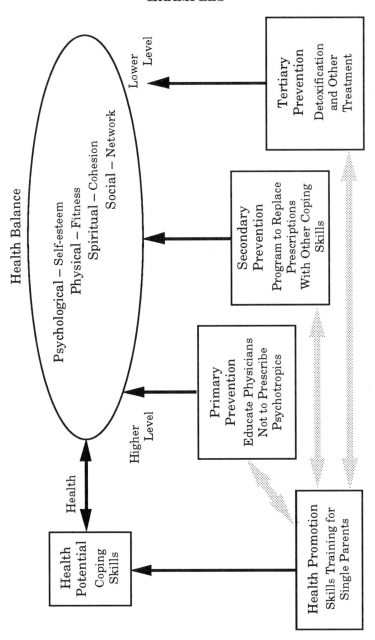

LOCAL ACTION, GLOBAL VISION

"Global" means "pertaining to or involving the whole world" (Funk and Wagnalls Standard College Dictionary Canadian Ed.) Sometimes we behave as though our whole world is one village, one town, one city, and so on. We think that people must begin to move their vision outward to the next community, the whole province, the next province, in ever-widening circles. This is not to imply that everyone must be active in all of these circles, but it does mean a continuous recognition of our ties. There are many examples of how local policies and programs have an impact on the lives of people in other communities, who may also sometimes be in other countries. Canadian women have felt the impact of the policies of multinational corporations that control grain prices (Buchan 1991). There have been many negative effects on the health of people on farms in Canada, and farm women are doubly affected because of the economic and social policies of the provincial and federal governments, which set policy that treats them as secondary players. At the same time as economic stress has exacerbated and increased social problems, services to rural areas are decreasing (Dyach 1991). A decrease in service doubly affects women, who are traditionally the guardians of family health (Heller 1986).

In the area of prevention of alcohol and tobacco problems, evidence exists that the North American alcohol industry has been sophisticated and powerful in countering preventive policies with marketing strategies (Morgan 1988; Mosher and Jernigan 1989). International economic and trade policies have meant that women in other countries are being exposed to marketing that intends to increase their alcohol consumption levels (Grant 1985; Moser 1985). As regards tobacco, the International Network of Women Against Tobacco was formed in response to a perceived lack of attention to the special needs of women in the existing public health networks. A sister organization, the Latin American Women's Association for Tobacco Control (AMALTA), was created to decrease tobacco consumption by Latin American women (McLellan 1991). The tobacco industry, partially in response to the success of anti-tobacco policies in North America, has targeted markets in developing countries. The marketing campaigns, which should be familiar to us all, attempt to link independence, wealth, thinness, and sex appeal to smoking, in order to increase the appeal of smoking among women who lack other, more health enhancing sources of personal power.

GLOBAL ANALYSIS, LOCAL ACTION

In developing local programs that will reduce inequities, increase prevention, and enhance coping, program planners need an analysis of multicultural needs. In Calgary, for instance, one in five citizens was born in a country other than Canada. There are several special agencies that provide settlement services to immigrants in the first year of their residence, and several agencies provide training in English as a second language. Many people recognize however, that there are large gaps in services to immigrants. This perception motivates the needs' assessment we are undertaking. There are few services in the areas of mental health and occupational health that have programs designed to increase access for immigrants.

Global analysis is necessary in order to recognize the diversity among immigrants. First, immigrants who are refugees have very special needs, strengths, and vulnerabilities. Refugees did not choose to leave their countries of origin, and may have been victims of torture. Refugee women may be at a triple disadvantage: "first, they are women, second, they are poor, and third, they lack support of other immigrants" (Sellens 1991 p. 41). Second, immigrants from one country are not all the same. There is not, for example, one "Chinese community", or one "African community". Similarly, there is not one group of aboriginal people in our country. In Alberta, there are several tribes with distinct cultural characteristics. Third, women within ethnic communities may be torn between loyalty to that community and recognition of the discrimination against women within that community. Each of us must decide which political group we will work with at any given time; however, this may be more complicated for the immigrant woman; for instance, a lesbian may have to decide whether to focus her political activity on racism or homophobia.

HEALTHY PUBLIC POLICY

Global analysis in local programs, therefore, requires co-ordination of knowledge as well as of action at several levels. This includes co-ordination of policies so that they work together to promote health both locally and globally. When one is designing local programs, it is important to be aware of the possible barriers to co-ordinating healthy public policy. Pederson et al (1988) have identified five barriers: (1) lack of experience in working together among groups and agencies; (2) conflicting or competing interests, or unwillingness to share power among interest groups; (3) underdeveloped mechanisms for increasing participation; (4) weak political will (although it is difficult to clarify this); and (5) conflicts over which approach to implementation should be taken (top-down or bottom-up). Additionally, little is known about how to facilitate collaboration between various government jurisdictions that affect health.

CONCLUSION

We have briefly discussed our experience in applying the theme of global vision/local action in our work to improve access to mental and other occupational services in one city. We believe that the process of health promotion research and program development should be health promoting. In addition, we have found that two perspectives are necessary. Programs must be examined for their potential impact on other communities, possibly in other countries, and they must be examined for cultural sensitivity and reduction of barriers to access at the local level. This global analysis necessitates creation of healthy public policies, and there are a number of barriers to overcome.

REFERENCES

Buchanan, C. 1991. *Report: The economics of poverty,* (Workshop by R. Rose, N. Weibe and R. Neil presented at ninth biennial conference of the National Association of Women and the Law, Toronto). *Jurisfemme* 11: 27 - 29.

Canadian Task Force on Mental Health Issues Affecting Immigrants and Refugees. 1988. *After the door has been opened: Mental health issues affecting immigrants and refugees in Canada.* Ottawa: Supply and Services.

Corbett, B. 1990. "Immigrants: Adding to our workforce." *Calgary Commerce* 22: 35 - 38.

Dyach, M. 1991. *Report: Regional disparities* (Workshop by N. Johns, K. Foristall, and L. Stimpson presented at ninth biennial conference of the National Association of Women and the Law, Toronto. *Jurisfemme* 11: 25 - 27.

Epp, J. 1986. *Achieving health for all: A framework for health promotion.* Ottawa: Health and Welfare Canada.

Grant, M. 1985. *Alcohol policies.* Copenhagen: World Health Organization.

Heller, A.F. 1986. *Health and home: Women as health guardians.* Ottawa: Canadian Advisory Council on the Status of Women.

Last, J. M. 1987. *Public health and human ecology.* East Norwalk, CT: Appleton and Lange.

McLellan, D. 1991. International network of women against tobacco. *World Smoking and Health*: 15 - 16.

Morgan, P. A. 1988. "Power, politics and public health: The political power of the alcohol beverage industry." *Journal of Public Health Policy*, Summer: 177-179.

Moser, J. 1985. *Alcohol policies in national health and development planning.* Geneva: World Health Organization.

Mosher, J. F., and Jernigan, D. H. 1989. "New directions in alcohol policy." *Annual Review of Public Health 10:* 245 - 279.

Noack, H. 1987. "Concepts of health and health promotion." In *Measurement in health promotion and protection,* ed. T. Abelin, Z. J. Brzezinski, and V. D. L. Carstairs. Copenhagen: World Health Organization.

Palumbo, D. J. ed. 1987. *The politics of program evaluation.* Newbury Park, CA: Sage.

Pederson, A. P., Edwards, R. K., Kelner, M., Marshall, V. S. and Allison, K. R. 1988. *Coordinating healthy public policy: An analytic literature review and bibliography.* Ottawa: Health Promotion Directorate, Health and Welfare Canada.

Schaefer, M. 1987. *Implementing change in service programs: Project planning and management..* Newbury Park, CA: Sage.

Sellens, S. 1991. Family and forced poverty (workshop by Z. Ali, A. K. Moorthy, and S. Jwazeia presented at ninth biennial conference of the National Association of Women and the Law, Toronto). *Jurisfemme,* 11: 41.

Thurston, W. E. 1991. Development and formative evaluation of a decision-management health promotion program on healthy weights for women. Ph.D. The University of Calgary.

Thurston, W. E. and Bowhay, C. L. 1991. *Healthy public policy on women and substance use: A discussion paper.* (Submitted to the National Alcohol and Drug Study, Women's Project, Health Promotion Directorate, Health and Welfare Canada, Ottawa).

World Health Organization. 1986. "Health promotion: A discussion document on the concept and principles." *Public Health Reviews* 14: 245-253.

Marja J. Verhoef
Department of Health Sciences
The University of Calgary

Women's Social Roles as Barriers to Their Health and Health Behaviours

The number and type of social roles women have, including employment, marriage, and parenthood, is related to their mental and physical health status. Women who have multiple roles are usually in better mental and physical health than those who have only a few of these roles, provided that women experience their roles as satisfying. However, the health benefit of multiple-role involvement for women seems to be primarily due to the paid worker role. Women's social roles have also been found to be related to their health behaviours, such as exercise participation.

A large-scale survey of 1,113 randomly selected Calgarian women aged twenty to forty-nine, done in 1990-91, showed that parenthood as well as being married were negatively related to exercise participation. However, multivariate analysis, adjusting for age and education, showed that parenthood was the most important barrier to exercise participation. Feelings of role overload due to role obligations were also a barrier to exercise participation. These feelings were more important than the more objective number of hours spent on daily activities. These findings indicate that women with traditional, non-workplace roles seem to be in a disadvantaged position with respect to their health and health behaviours. Therefore, health promotion efforts should be programmed differently for women in different social contexts.

Many women face widely varying interpersonal and structural barriers to good health and positive health behaviours, such as lack of information, lack of support, poverty, membership in a minority group e.g., disabled women, immigrant women, racism, and sexism. There is considerable evidence that the number and type of social roles women occupy e.g., employment, marriage, and parenthood can also be such a barrier. These social roles are intricately related to many of the above factors, as they are embedded in the broader structure and culture of society.

Even though men and women occupy the same roles, these take on a different meaning for women than they do for men. Men tend to have better jobs than women and to be the provider, while women are much more likely to hold part-time jobs and be primarily responsible for childcare and homemaking. Deeply embedded cultural values regarding the role of a male as breadwinner and the role of a female as the family "nurturer" support the differences between men's and women's social roles. Social roles not only contribute to differences between women's and men's health and health behaviours, but also to differences among women with different combinations of roles (such as employed married mothers, unemployed single mothers). My focus in this work will be on health and exercise participation of women only. In the first part I describe the effects of social roles on women's physical and mental health, based on a review of the literature, and in the second part I will focus on the effect of women's roles on their health behaviours, in particular on exercise participation, based on the results of a large-scale study conducted in Calgary in 1990–91.

THE CONCEPT OF "SOCIAL ROLES"

The term "social role" is used to refer to either a social position, the behaviour associated with a position, or a set of expectations belonging to a social position (Heiss 1981). Most commonly, a social role (such as parent, spouse, employee) refers to the rights, obligations, and normatively approved patterns of behaviour for the occupants of a given position or status.

Roles are social, because it is not possible to consider a position without at least implicit reference to other persons or positions (Stryker and Statham 1985). For example, there can be no mother without children. The role of a mother not only has the child role as a counterpart but, usually, many others, such as that of the child's father or the child's teacher. The array of reciprocal role relationships that is associated with each social position is called a role-set (Merton 1968).

Social roles specify how individuals occupying a particular status should act towards members of the role set. As points of convergence between the sociocultural system and the individual, roles are the translation of abstract cultural values into specific prescribed ways of acting. Individuals enact social roles–in particular, major roles such as employment, marriage, and parenthood–because roles provide the opportunity and means to achieve important internalized life goals. Problems arising within and around roles, then, pose a threat both to the functioning of the social system and to the well-being of the individual (Aneshensel and Pearlin 1987).

Role occupancy is also important because it determines the range of potential stressful experiences. Role occupancy increases the chances of exposure to some stressors and precludes the presence of others. For example, only an employed mother can be exposed to feelings of guilt towards her children because she works outside of the home. In addition, a woman's social roles, that is, whether she is employed, lives in a stable relationship, or has children, are closely related to her life-style, indicating how she lives, what her beliefs and interests are, and how she behaves.

WOMEN'S SOCIAL ROLES AND HEALTH STATUS

The interest in the effects of women's social roles, and in particular, of multiple roles e.g., employed married mothers on their well-being started when mothers increasingly entered the workforce. The first studies focused on the number of roles women occupied. On the one hand, it has been hypothesized that the more roles a woman has, the more stress or strain she will experience (Goode 1960). Role strain may be due to role overload (constraints imposed by time) or role conflict (discrepant expectations) or both. According to this hypothesis, as the number of roles increases, so does the potential for role strain, ultimately leading to a deterioration of physical and mental health (Coser 1974; Slater 1963). This hypothesis was challenged by Gove and Tudor's (1973) suggestion that men's mental health advantage over women could be explained by their involvement in both work and family roles, and it was hypothesized that the more roles a woman has the better her health will be. By providing linkages to other persons and resources, having multiple roles brings rewards, such as privileges, status security, self-esteem, personality enrichment, and social relationships, which outweigh role strain (Marks 1977; Sieber 1974; Thoits 1983). Empirical evidence has suggested that involvement in multiple roles yields a net gain of benefits over costs with respect to both physical and mental health (Gove and Zeiss 1987; Kandel, Davies, and Raveis 1985; Sorensen and Verbrugge, 1987; Verbrugge 1983). Multiple roles have a positive effect on health, because greater social involvement and feelings of personal achievement may offer large emotional benefits and resources, which in turn may enhance physical well-being. However, social selection (the selection of women into and out of roles because of their health) may be operating as well. Healthy women are better able to participate in job and family roles. One study has shown that health may be a strong selection factor for women's employment (Waldron et al 1982), but Froberg, Gjerdingen, and Preston (1986) indicate that social selection does not explain all the research results thus far obtained.

The initial focus in the research literature on number of roles is now widening to include the consideration of the effects of specific types of roles, of role constellations, and of role characteristics. Research has shown that social roles are not interchangeable in their impact on health status. The health benefits of multiple role involvements for women primarily out of the paid worker role (Baruch and Barnett 1985). The association between health status and marital status is usually positive but weak, and the evidence regarding parenthood is inconsistent (Baruch and Barnett, 1985; Gore and Mangione 1983). Several studies have addressed the negative effects of women's non-workplace roles, such as homemaker, mother, and wife, on health status (Aneshensel and Pearlin 1987; Froberg, Gjerdinger, and Preston 1986), and concluded that these roles, especially that of mother, "are generally low in control and high in demands, that is, high-strain roles, that are particularly problematic with respect to stress-related outcomes" (Barnett and Baruch 1987). Gove and Hughes (1979) have suggested that women's poorer health, as compared to men's, may be due to their being confronted with more nurturant role demands— demands that interfere with their ability to care properly for their own mental and physical health. This was called the nurturant role hypothesis. The degree of nurturing in social roles helps to explain why women with only non-workplace roles tend to be in less good health than women occupying work as well as family roles (Verbrugge 1983).

Studies that have included more or less objective role characteristics e.g., number and ages of children, type of work as well as role experiences (the broad range of feelings and experiences that people may have in their roles) have concluded that role experiences are more strongly related to well-being than the more objective role characteristics (Baruch and Barnett 1985; Verbrugge,1986). These studies also found that although occupying multiple roles was associated with good health, this did not deny the existence of role strain. However, role strain may be more related to the type and quality of roles than to the number of roles (Froberg Gjerdingen, and Preston 1986).

Although more research is needed to identify ways in which rewards and stresses within each role interact to produce health outcomes, there is clear evidence of the importance of the number and types of roles women occupy.

WOMEN'S SOCIAL ROLES AND HEALTH BEHAVIOUR

An often-used definition of health behaviour is, "any activity undertaken by a person believing him or herself to be healthy, for the purpose of preventing disease, or detecting it in an asymptomatic stage, (Kasl and Cobb 1966). Examples of health behaviours are exercising, abstaining from smoking, consuming low levels of alcohol and following a healthy diet. Health behaviours have or are believed to have an effect on mental and physical health. In her review of women's health behaviours, Graham (1990) concludes that there is evidence of a causal relationship between smoking and diet and cardiovascular health, that the relationship between exercising and cardiovascular health is "probably causal", and that the relationship between alcohol consumption and cardiovascular health is largely correlational.

During the past two decades there has been a strong emphasis, supported by the government (Lalonde 1974) on personal behaviours as determinants of health and well-being. However, these behaviours take place in a social context, and the emphasis on individual life-styles should not ignore the fact that a woman's social situation may pose a barrier to positive health behaviours. Given the evidence that health status is affected by women's roles and role obligations, researchers should also investigate whether health behaviours are affected by social roles. Several relationships between each of the roles and certain health behaviours have been observed, but very few studies have addressed what the relative importance of each social role and of role combinations is.

Before discussing social roles and exercise participation, I will provide a few examples with respect to other health behaviours. Although some studies have indicated that increases in women's employment have contributed to increases in women's smoking, there is evidence that a woman's employment has little direct effect on whether she becomes a smoker (Waldron 1988). A study in the UK has shown that among women in lower socioeconomic groups, smoking is most common in those women with traditional roles such as wife, mother, and homemaker (Graham 1987). This seems to be consistent with the negative effect on women's health of occupying only non-workplace roles. Wilsnack and Cheloha (1987) have found that women's problem-drinking is related to role combinations. Problem-drinking increases with the lack or loss of marital, employment, and parental roles. The demands of multiple roles did not appear to be a major cause of women's problem-drinking at any age.

WOMEN'S SOCIAL ROLES AND EXERCISING

The major difference between health behaviour and health status is that the first is a voluntarily undertaken activity whereas the second is much more beyond personal control. In addition, exercising is time- consuming, and therefore it is questionable whether women with multiple roles, who are most likely to be healthy, are also the ones who exercise most. Given that many women report that exercising makes them feel better (Bouchard et al 1990), one could also hypothesize that women with stressful role combinations are more likely to exercise.

Some studies have found that marital status and parenthood have a negative effect on women's exercise participation (Smith 1987; Woodward, Green and Hebron 1989), and others have found that employed women exercise more than non-employed women, although the differences were small (Canada Fitness Survey 1984). However, in most of these studies the social roles were not studied in combination with each other, controlling for potential confounding variables. Therefore, a cross-sectional study was undertaken in 1990–91, of Calgarian women, aged twenty to forty-nine, who were not pregnant and not immediately post-partum and who were willing to respond to a mailed questionnaire. Random digit dialing was used to select a sample from the Calgary population. Of the 1,417 eligible women who were contacted 1,261 (89 per cent) accepted the questionnaire. Of these, 1,118 women (89 per cent) returned the completed questionnaire.

Exercise was defined as leisure-time physical activity. Women were classified into three categories: Very active were women who over the past six months had exercised strenuously for at least thirty minutes at a time, at least three times per week. Moderately active were women who satisfied two of the preceding conditions and were moderately active during the past six months. Inactive were women who satisfied only one condition or did not exercise at all. These categories are based on instruments developed by Godin and Shephard (1985) and Godin Jobin, and Bouillon (1986).

In the analysis two dependent variables were used: "exercising," which was dichotomized into "inactive" and "active" (moderately as well as very active); and for women who are exercising, "the amount of exercise," which was dichotomized into "moderately active" and "very active." The rationale for using two dependent variables rather than combining them lies in the suggestion that increasing the number of women exercising and upgrading women's performance are two different issues (Clark and Haag,1988).

TABLE 1. EFFECTS OF PARENTHOOD, MARITAL STATUS, EMPLOYMENT STATUS AND NUMBER OF ROLES ON EXERCISING

Variable		Exercising		χ^2-test
		n/$\underline{N}$*	%	p-value
Parenthood	Parent	307/626	49.0	<.001
	Non-parent	301/487	61.8	
Marital status	Married	432/820	52.7	.030
	Prev. married	64/117	54.7	
	Single	112/176	63.6	
Employment status	Employed	477/872	54.7	.509
	Unemployed	22/47	46.8	
	Non-employed	109/194	56.2	
Number of roles	0 or 1	159/258	61.6	.001
	2	279/491	56.8	
	3	170/364	46.7	

Note: n/$\underline{N}$ - Number of women exercising/total number of women in each group.

Parenthood and marital status were significantly related to exercising (table 1). The proportion of mothers exercising was lower than the proportion of women without children. The proportion of married women who exercise was not very different from the proportion of previously married women who exercise, but was much lower than the proportion of single women who exercise. For women exercising, parenthood and marital status were also related to the amount of exercise (table 2). Employment status was related only to the amount of exercise and not to exercising. The proportion of very active non-employed women was lowest, followed by employed women, and the proportion of very active women was highest among unemployed women. However, this relationship may be due to the fact that the last group was very small.

TABLE 2. THE EFFECTS OF PARENTHOOD, MARITAL
STATUS, EMPLOYMENT STATUS AND NUMBER OF ROLES
ON THE AMOUNT OF EXERCISE

Variable		Very Active		X^2-test
		n/$\underline{N}$*	%	p-value
Parenthood	Parent	64/307	20.8	<.001
	Non-parent	112/310	37.2	
Marital	Married	117/432	27.1	.023
status	Prev. married	15/64	23.4	
	Single	44/112	39.3	
Employment	Employed	146/477	30.6	.028
status	Unemployed	9/22	44.9	
	Non-employed	21/109	19.3	
Number of	0 or 1	62/159	39.0	.005
roles	2	71/279	25.4	
	3	43/170	25.3	

Note: n/$\underline{N}$ - Number of women who are very active/total
number of women in each group.

As a woman's total social context is important, and not each
role in itself, the relationship between the number and combination
of roles and exercise participation was studied. Women with fewer
roles were more likely to exercise or to be very active than women
with more roles (see tables 1 and 2). Table 3 shows the relationship
between role combinations and exercising. The proportion of
exercisers was lowest in the group of women who occupied three
roles. Table 3 also shows that the four combinations that include
parenthood ranked lowest. Table 4 shows the relationship between
role combinations and the amount of exercise. Again, the role
combinations that include parenthood ranked lowest.

In order to study which role is most important with respect to
women's exercise participation, we applied multi-variable analysis
(multiple logistic regression), adjusting for the effect of the potential
confounding variables of age, education, and health status. With
respect to exercising as well as to amount of exercise, the results of
this analysis showed that, taking all three roles into account, only
parenthood had a significant effect on exercising and on the amount
of exercise. No interaction effects between the three roles were
found.

TABLE 3. ROLE COMBINATION BY PROPORTION OF
WOMEN EXERCISING

Role combination	Total group	% Exercising	Rank order
Not married, not employed, no children	14	78.6	1
Employed, not married, no children	202	62.4	2
Married, employed, no children	241	61.4	3
Married, not employed, no children	30	53.3	4
Married, parent, not employed	185	53.0	5
Employed, parent, not married	65	50.8	6
Parent, not married, not employed	12	50.0	7
Married, employed, parent	364	46.7	8
Total	1113		

TABLE 4. ROLE COMBINATION BY PROPORTION OF
WOMEN WHO ARE VERY ACTIVE

Role combination	Total group	% Very active	Rank order
Not married, not employed, no children	11	54.5	1
Married, not employed, no children	16	43.8	2
Employed, not married, no children	126	38.1	3
Married, employed, no children	148	34.5	4
Married, employed, parent	170	25.3	5
Parent, not married, not employed	6	16.7	6
Married, parent, not employed	98	16.3	7
Employed, parent, not married	33	12.1	8
Total	608		

Multiple logistic regression analysis was also applied to determine the importance of feelings of role overload, which means strain resulting from having too much to do and not enough time to do it (Bird and Bird 1986), as compared to the more or less objective number of hours that women spend on their daily activities, adjusted for confounding variables. This analysis showed that feelings of role overload were a more important determinant of not exercising, or not being very active, than the number of hours spent on daily activities (data not shown). Not surprisingly, mothers experienced significantly more strain due to overload than women without children.

DISCUSSION

The previous results have shown that for the analysis of barriers to women's health and their health behaviours, in particular exercising, social roles are an important factor. Empirical evidence has supported the claim that women who occupy several roles are healthier than those with fewer roles. However, types of roles, role combinations, and attributes of these roles also need to be considered. Women occupying family roles only have been found to be in a disadvantaged position with respect to their physical and mental health, compared to women who occupy the employment role as well.

The results with respect to exercising are slightly different and show that one family role in particular, namely parenthood, is a barrier to women's exercise participation, disregarding women's employment status.

At present there is still strong societal pressure on many women to overperform in family roles. It will be to women's health benefit to bring about structural and individual changes, which will allow more and more women to combine job and family roles, and to do so more easily. Public education and policy efforts should be aimed at reducing sex discrimination in income and employment opportunities and providing adequate day care at low cost, maternity leave benefits, and flexible work schedules without income penalties. Health education should focus on social support and coping skills for women with heavy family responsibilities.

Exercise promotion should focus on employed as well as non employed mothers. Different approaches are needed for these two groups of women. For employed women it is important that employers and spouses encourage and support women with multiple roles. In the exercise study, lack of support from spouses as well as from peers was considered a major barrier to exercising (Verhoef 1992). The importance of feelings of role overload with respect to exercising indicates the importance of coping skills. For example time management, should be an important focus in exercise promotion programs. For mothers who are at home, exercise promotion could include the development of safe and beneficial home exercising, flexible class structuring, and provision of on-site child care or concurrent programming.

The exercise study has also shown that many women perceive exercise as important for reasons other than physical or mental health benefits. Exercise functions as a social activity, a recreational activity, and a stress management technique. This information can be used to put exercise participation in a broader context and to make it easier for women to relate to the usefulness of exercising.

In conclusion, in planning health programs for women, one must taken into account the entire context of women's social and biological life experience. Women themselves should be brought into the planning process, and not remain passive recipients of health promotion and education efforts.

REFERENCES

Aneshensel, C.S., and Pearlin, L.I. 1987. "Structural contexts of sex differences in stress." In *Gender and stress,* R.C. Barnett, L. Biener and G.K. Baruch. ed. New York: Free Press.

Barnett, R.C., and Baruch, G.K. 1987. "Social roles, gender, and psychological distress." In *Gender and Stress*R.C. Barnett, L. Biener and G.K. Baruch. ed. New York: Free Press.

Baruch, G.K., and Barnett, R.C. 1985. "Role quality, multiple role involvement, and psychological well-being in midlife women." *Journal of Personality and Social Psychology 51*: 571 - 585.

Bird, G.W., and Bird, G.A. 1986. "Strategies for reducing role strain among dual-career couples." *International Journal of Sociology of the Family 16,*: 83 - 94.

Bouchard, C., Shephard, R.J., Stephens, T., Sutton, J.R., and McPherson, B. 1990. "Exercise, fitness and health: The consensus statement." In *Exercise, fitness, and health.: A consensus of current knowledge* C. Bouchard, R.J. Shephard, T. Stephens, J.R. Sutton and B. McPherson ed. Champaign, IL: Human Kinetics Books.

Canada Fitness Survey. 1984. "Women's Program and Canada Fitness Survey." *Changing Times: Women and Physical Activity.* Ottawa: Fitness and Amateur Sport.

Clark, A., and Haag, K. 1988. "Exercise participation among working women." *New Zealand Journal of Health, Physical Education and Recreation 21*: 5 - 8.

Coser, L. (with R.L. Coser). 1974. "Sex differences in psychological distress among marrier people." *Journal of Health and Social Behaviour 24*: 111 - 21.

Froberg, D.G., Gjerdingen, D., and Preston, M. 1986. "Effects of multiple roles on women's mental and physical health: What have we learned?" *Women and Health 11*: 79 - 96.

Godin, G., Jobin, J., and Bouillon, J. 1986. "Assessment of leisure time exercise behavior by self-report: A concurrent study." *Canadian Journal of Public Health* 77: 359 - 62.

Godin, G., and Shephard, R.J. 1985. "A simple method to assess exercise behavior in the community." *Canadian Journal of Applied Sport Sciences 10*: 141 - 46.

Goode, W.J. 1960. "A theory of role-strain." *American Sociological Review 25*: 483 - 96.

Gore, S., and Mangione, T.W. 1983. "Social roles, sex roles and psychological distress: Additive and interactive models of sex differences." *Journal of Health and Social Behavior 24*: 300 - 312.

Gove, W.R., and Hughes, M. 1979. "Possible causes of the apparent sex differences in physical health: An empirical investigation." *American Sociological Review 44*: 126 - 46.

Gove, W.R., and Tudor, J. 1973. "Adult sex roles and mental illness." *American Journal of Sociology 78*: 812 - 35.

Gove, W.R., and Zeiss, C. 1987. "Multiple roles and happiness." In *Spouse, parent, worker: on gender and multiple roles* F.J. Crosby ed. New Haven, CT: Yale University Press.

Graham, H. 1987. "Women's smoking and family health." *Social Science and Medicine 25*: 47 - 56.

Graham, H. 1990. "Behaving well: Women's health behaviour in context." In*Women's Health Counts* H. Roberts ed. London: Routledge.

Heiss, J. 1981. "Social roles." In *Sociological perspectives on social psychology* M. Rosenberg and R.H. Turner ed. New York: Basic Books.

Kandel, D.B., Davies, M., and Raveis, V.H. 1985. "The stressfulness of daily social roles for women: Marital, occupational and household roles." *Journal of Health and Social Behavior 26*: 64 - 78.

Kasl, S.V., and Cobb, S. 1966. "Health behavior, illness behavior, and sick role behavior." *Archives of Environmental Health 12*,: 246 - 66.

Lalonde, M. 1974. *A new perspective on the health of Canadians: A working document.* Ottawa: Government of Canada.

Marks, S.R. 1977. "Multiple roles and role strain: Some notes on human energy, time and commitment." *American Sociological Review 42*: 921 - 36.

Merton, R.K. 1968. *Social theory and social structure.* New York: Free Press.

Sieber, S.D. 1974. "Toward a theory of role accumulation." *American Sociological Review 39,*: 567 - 78.

Slater, P. 1963. "On social regression." *American Sociological Review 28*: 339 - 64.

Smith, J. 1987. "Men and women at play: Gender, life-cycle and leisure." In *Sport, leisure and social Relations* J. Horne, D. Jary and A. Tomlinson ed. New York: Routledge and Kegan Paul.

Sorenson, G., and Verbrugge, L.M. 1987. "Women, work and health." *Annual Review of Public Health 8*: 235 - 51.

Stryker, S., and Statham, S.A. 1985. "Symbolic interaction and role theory." In *Handbook of social psychology* G. Lindzey and E.C. Aronson ed. New York: Random House.

Thoits, P. 1983. "Multiple identities and social well-being: A reformulation and test of the social isolation hypothesis." *American Sociological Review 48*: 174 - 87.

Verbrugge, L.M. 1986. "Role burdens and physical health of women and men." *Women & Health 11: 47 - 75.*

Verbrugge, L.M. 1983. "Multiple roles and phsyical health of women." *Journal of Health and Social Behavior 24*: 16 - 30.

Verhoef, M.J. 1992. "Women's exercise participation: The relevance of social roles compared to non-role related determinants." *Canadian Journal of Public Health 83*: 367 - 70.

Waldron, I.J. 1988. "Gender and health-related behavior." In *Health behavior: emerging research perspectives,* D.S. Gochman ed. New York: Plenum Press.

Waldron, I.J., Herold, J., Dunn, D., and Staum, R. 1982. "Reciprocal effects of health and labor participation in women: Evidence from two longitudinal studies." *Journal of Occupational Medicine 24*: 126 - 32.

Wilsnack, R.W., and Cheloha, R. 1987. "Women's roles and problem drinking across the life span." *Social Problems 34*: 231-48.

Woodward, D., Green, E., and Hebron, S. 1989. "The sociology of women's leisure and physical recreation: Constraints and opportunities." *International Review for the Sociology of Sport 24*: 121 - 33.

D. Hamm and M. Segall
Department of Community Health Science
The University of Calgary

12

Achieving Workplace Health and Safety within the Margins

Canadian workplaces reflect the growing multiculturalism of Canadian society. How does this cultural diversity affect occupational health and safety? Are we recognizing these health and safety issues among Canadian workers? How should we address occupational multiculturalism in terms of safe and healthy work for all? In Canada these questions have, with only a few exceptions (Bolaria 1988; Hamm and Segall 1992), been ignored, and only a few studies Calgary Society for Immigrant Workers 1989 (Fernandes,1985; Harvey 1987) have considered these issues within Alberta. We offer a framework for considering multicultural aspects of occupational health and safety. These concepts are being developed through our work at the Southern Occupational Health Resource Service in the Department of Community Health Sciences at The University of Calgary in collaboration with multicultural agencies and individuals.

According to Joyce, from the late 1970s there has been a much closer interest in how 'work', 'labor' and 'employment' are in fact culturally defined (1987,11). "Culture" has been called "the collection of beliefs, norms, attitudes, roles, and practices shared within a given social grouping or population" (Pidgeon 1991, 134). It has also been described as "just another term for a mystery factor" (Burnet 1983 238). If we adopt a working definition of "culture" as a set of common characteristics that shape our individual and collective behaviours we can expand the concept of multiculturalism in the workplace beyond racial, ethnic, or linguistic identities to include aspects of "corporate" culture, "safety" culture, social roles, production units, managerial classes, trade categories, professional groups, gender and lifestyle commonalities. We thus have a great many interactive and overlapping cultures in our Canadian workplaces, and this produces complex sets of intersecting multicultural values with potential for conflicting agendas in the workplace.

Within the Canadian workplace, corporate values tend to place priority upon issues of productivity, efficiency, and profitability. Societal values are reflected in provincial employment standards, occupational health and safety regulations, and various other labour codes. (Are public values also reflected in inadequate monitoring of these "rules"?) Union and trades organizations value collective bargaining, accreditation of skills, access to benefits, and binding agreements. Personal or individual values may reflect issues of self-esteem, job satisfaction, skill development, job security, and financial compensation. These interacting agendas can provide common ground for the pursuit of occupational health and safety, but in some cases they may appear mutually exclusive or adversarial.

THE LIMITS OF OUR CURRENT PARADIGMS

In practice, occupational health and safety addresses the dynamic interaction of people, procedures, and hardware within both a physical environment and a managed (social) environment. Safety management has focused on aspects of procedures and hardware, the latter including chemical hazards covered by (the Canadian Workplace Hazardous Materials Information System).

Recently the interaction of people, procedures, and hardware has gained prominence via the study of ergonomics. Attempts to match the task to the worker must consider ergonomic issues, since "the basic assumption of ergonomics is that the selection of objects intended for human use should be based upon human characteristics and capabilities" (Canadian Standards Association 1989 14). Generally, worker characteristics have included anthropometric, biomechanical, and physiological features. More recently, environmental psychology has studied the role of perceptions, cognitions, and attitudes as important worker characteristics. The interplay of cultural factors upon these parameters in the workplace is still virtually unknown and is little discussed in the occupational health and safety literature.

In addition to designing equipment and workspaces appropriate to worker characteristics, matching the worker to his or her tasks includes "fitness to work" assessments, in which medical evaluation of the worker determines his or her ability to carry out a job without danger to the health or safety of the worker or others. Occupational physicians and nurses are involved in this type of evaluation, and also deal with the effects of work and workplace agents on the health of employees. Multiculturally related health issues have been better defined in these more health-oriented disciplines (Donovan 1984; Masi 1988a - c, 1989a - c, 1992; Waxler-Morrison, Anderson, and Richardson 1990). "Ethnicity" has been used as a common operational definition of multiculturalism, although the use of ethnicity as a study variable is fraught with methodological problems (Edwards 1992). Considerable research has also addressed multicultural mental health issues (Canadian Task Force on Mental Health Issues affecting Immigrants and Refugees 1988; Chandrasena, Beddage, and Fernando 1991; Vega and Rumbaut 1991; Williams and Westermeyer 1986), but not enough is yet known about the relationship between occupational multiculturalism and mental health.

The professional approach to occupational health and safety has, with few exceptions (Baker 1987; Friedman-Jimenez 1989, Lee and Wrench 1980; Peel and Clarke 1990), tended to "bracket out" the multicultural issues of the workplace while focusing on the physical environment and its health impacts. Traditional occupational health and safety is almost entirely devoted to physical environmental factors, such as ergonomics, lighting, temperature, humidity, vibration, noise, chemical hazards, ventilation, radiation, personal protective equipment, engineering controls, and exposure monitoring. However, we are coming to recognize the importance of personal factors in worker well-being: beliefs, life-style, gender, ethnicity, social support, perceptions, values, and income. We have also begun to acknowledge the role of organizational factors upon employee health and safety: corporate policies, administrative procedures, management - employee relations, options for communication and decision-making, personal control in work processes, and organizational dynamics and stress.

Several trends outlined below, are now forcing us to face the limitations of a traditional hazard-control model of occupational health and safety.

WORKPLACE "HEALTH" IS INCREASINGLY SUBJECTIVIZED

The World Health Organization's definition of health as "a state of complete physical, mental and social well-being and not merely the absence of disease or infirmity" has encouraged us to think beyond the absence of disease as a basis for conceptualizing our health. Further refinement of this concept views health as a resource for living and includes both individuals and communities in the definition of their own health. In moving our ideal of health to one of ultimate personal well-being we have moved towards a more subjectively defined model.

The rising profile of health promotion has endorsed this paradigm of health and brought it into the workplace. Whereas disease can be considered as the generic definition applied to functional disorders by practitioners of the so-called medical model, illness is the corresponding subjective experience of personal or social dysfunction which uniquely affects the individual. Illness behaviour is the manner in which persons monitor and interpret their dysfunctions and take remedial actions e.g., through self-care, folk care, alternative therapies, or medical care.

Occupational medicine has traditionally adopted the medical model but is now facing issues that require a more comprehensive biopsychosocial paradigm. Today, occupational medicine is grappling with issues that have major subjective definitional parameters, including such conditions as multiple chemical sensitivity, environmental injury, chronic fatigue syndrome, chronic pain syndrome, occupational stress, indoor air quality, and ergonomic injury. Workers compensation boards are attempting to address claims relating to these problems. The conventional hazard-control model seems too restrictive in dealing with such issues. Coming to grips with personalized definitions of health and their implications is going to be one of our greatest challenges in occupational health and safety into the twenty-first century.

HEALTH RISK PERCEPTION IS OF GROWING IMPORTANCE

As workers take personal responsibility for their health, they (and the public) are also voicing increasing concern about perceived risks to their health. Workers judge risks differently depending upon whether those risks are perceived to be voluntary, under personal control, unfair, catastrophic, familiar, natural, dreaded, undetectable, and so on. The health issues revolving around video display terminals illustrate many of these dimensions of risk perception. Subjective issues in risk perception and risk communication ultimately account for many human behaviours in the workplace. To borrow a phrase from Goethe, "What one knows, one sees".

Social science research on risk perception (Covello 1983; Freudenburg 1988; Lee,1986; Short 1984; Slovic 1987; Vaughan and

Nordenstam 1991; Wildavsky and Dake 1990) has identified a set of dimensions that strongly bias people's perceptions of their actual, scientifically determined risks, producing a so-called cognitive distortion of risk. For example, risks perceived as "involuntary", for instance from contaminated air, are considered much less acceptable than "voluntary" risks, such as those from cigarette smoking. Starr (1969) showed that people are generally willing to accept voluntary risks that are about a thousand times greater than involuntary risks.

Risks perceived as not being under one's own personal control e.g., from processes required in the course of a job are less acceptable than risks undertaken under one's personal control e.g., from driving one's own car. Risks that are perceived as "unfair" e.g., from second-hand smoke are less acceptable than those that seem to be "fair" e.g., risks undertaken in recreational pursuits. Risks that are perceived as "unfamiliar" (e.g., from electromagnetic fields are several hundred times less acceptable than those that are "familiar" e.g., from household accidents or hazards.

Risks perceived as "unnatural" or "artificial" e.g., from pesticides are less acceptable than "natural" risks e.g., from routine food products. People tend to think of all chemicals as synthetic and to characterize synthetic chemicals as toxic. However, Ames, Profit, and Gold (1990) have argued that 99.99 per cent by weight of the pesticides in the North American diet are from chemicals that plants produce to defend themselves, and of these "natural" chemicals that have been tested, about half are rodent carcinogens that are present in many of our common foods.

In addition to the above factors, workers also intuitively integrate their perceived benefits of risk-taking, the immediate versus delayed effects of hazards, the perceived trustworthiness of risk communicators, the reliability of risk controls, the impact of risks on vulnerable groups such as children, and the symbolic impact of risks e.g., the public furor over Alar on apples. Many risk perception categories overlap and interact.

In general, the cognitive representation of risk perceptions seems to be structured similarly across cultures but the scalar estimation of specific risks may vary. The role of cultural biases in risk perception and their effects on occupational health and safety have scarcely been adequately addressed.

A PSYCHOSOCIAL ECOLOGY OF WORK IS EMERGING

Until recently, health promotion focused almost entirely on the individual. Attention is now also being directed to the impact of psychosocial factors in the workplace on worker health (Bellingham 1990). The recent work of Robert Karasek and Töres Theorell (1990) illustrates this trend. One of their key concepts is the demand-control-support model of the work environment, adapted in figure 1.

FIGURE 1. THE DEMAND–CONTROL–SUPPORT MODEL OF THE WORK ENVIRONMENT

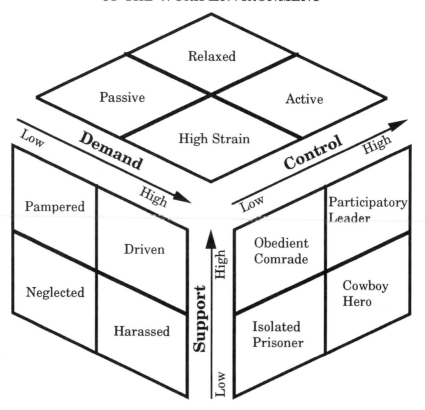

Source: Adapted from Karasek and Theorell (1990).

The foregoing points illustrate the need for a psychosocial ecology of occupational health and safety that encompasses the emerging issues in workplace health and safety. A similar approach is being developed in the field of health promotion (Stokols 1992). Where multicultural variations in exposure to demand, control, and support in the workplace are found, we can expect corresponding health effects.

These authors hold that the relevant aspects of the psychosocial work environment can be described in terms of three dimensions: (a) psychosocial demands both quantitative and qualitative; (b) decision latitude (control), having two components–discretion in using and developing skills with which to enact responses, and authority to decide what to do and how to do it; and social support, from superiors and co-workers.

The interaction of these three dimensions in the workplace has been shown to correlate with workers' symptomatology and their risk of cardiovascular disease. The research in this area is only preliminary, but the demand-control-support model of the work environment offers many possibilities for longitudinal research, including aspects of occupational multiculturalism.

A PSYCHOSOCIAL ECOLOGY OF WORKPLACE HEALTH AND SAFETY

The current models of occupational health and occupational safety are basically the medical model and hazard control model, respectively. These paradigms have played important roles and have enabled gains in workplace health and safety. However, in the light of issues such as those above and in terms of our society's expanding concepts of health and health promotion, these current paradigms will not be adequate for the future. They are particularly inadequate in addressing the multicultural aspects of the workplace. I will consider some of the occupational health and safety concerns of immigrant workers as an illustration of the need for a psychosocial ecology of occupational health and safety.

LOSS OF SUPPORTIVE NETWORKS AMONG NEW IMMIGRANTS

Although some immigrants arrive in Canada with marketable skills and ample resources with which to make a smooth adjustment to a new way of life, for most newcomers the immigration process includes the loss of familiar patterns and supportive networks. Social science research has identified the importance of social supports in personal well-being (Gottlieb 1985; Kuo and Tsai 1986; Lindheim and Syme, 1983). In the case of new immigrants, these supports may be minimal. Moreover, they may also have escaped from political upheaval or persecution with little preparation for a new Canadian identity. Immigrants often experience isolation, nostalgia, a sense of helplessness, frustration, and fatigue as they cope with their new culture. Refugees are likely to have additional stressors owing to the physical hardships, dangers, psychological trauma, and family disruptions preceding their move to Canada.

The immigrant worker's skills may not be accredited in Canada and he or she may have to accept work that is characterized by monotony, a sense of underachievement, and accompanying disillusionment. Immigrants have a strong desire to succeed and will often accept more hazardous work or take risks in order to keep their job. They may not even be aware of recommended work practices, safety regulations, personal protection, or their rights and responsibilities as workers.

More than other employees, the immigrant worker needs the help of his or her co-workers and supervisors in order to learn how the system works. Employers and unions should be aware of the vulnerability of immigrant workers and ensure that they are treated fairly, enabled to work safely, and adequately mentored. Immigrant workers should not be expected to bear a disproportionate burden of risks at work just because they are inexperienced, lack social power, or "don't know better."

Immigrants may also carry a distrust of authorities or even other employees and may be unwilling to complain about unfair treatment for fear of reprisal or loss of work. They may also be unaware of the role or the existence of workers' compensation, government occupational health and safety agencies, and private or corporate occupational health services.

SOCIOECONOMIC BARRIERS TO HEALTHY WORK FOR IMMIGRANTS

Almost all Canadian health and safety information is given only in official languages, and immigrant workers may find this a major difficulty. Moreover, they may not ask for clarification, especially in group settings. It is important not to assume that immigrant workers understand the use and maintenance of safety and protective equipment just because they have received an English-or-French language pamphlet or verbal instruction.

Most workplace health promotion is geared to a white, middle-class culture and takes little account of the multicultural needs of immigrants. Immigrants are often unfamiliar with the Canadian health care system and local social and recreational services. At work, they need to know how to obtain access to the occupational health and safety resources that many Canadians are familiar with and readily use. In some cases provision of this access may involve special measures, such as translated materials or inter-agency collaborative services.

The move to a new country may involve a major loss of income and social status. Immigrants may initially live in substandard or crowded living conditions with possible adverse physical and mental health effects. They may resent being forced to accept work at a relatively low rate of pay in Canada while they learn new skills and a new language and retrain. Immigrant workers may be also be supporting extended family members, such as parents. In some cases, they may be living away from their families in order to find work.

Immigrants may work at more than one job in order to make ends meet, or may hold a job and attend evening classes. Economic constraints may require all members of the family to work, and for some this introduces new issues in family dynamics. Immigrant women may often be disadvantaged in terms of employment owing to their limited opportunities for education and language skills, and they tend to be found in service and unskilled occupations where ergonomic and chemical hazards tend to prevail.

WORKPLACE HAZARDS AND RISKS FACING IMMIGRANT WORKERS

Immigrant workers in unskilled jobs know that they can be readily dismissed and replaced. In their tenuous economic situation, such immigrant workers may be reluctant to question any unsafe work practices or occupational hazards for fear of being fired or demoted. They may also conceal their own health problems in order to keep their job. For example, repetitive strain injuries may be neglected until they become intolerable (and result in prolonged recoveries).

Immigrant workers are often willing to work in hazardous, underpaid, or monotonous conditions (they may have no other employment opportunities). They often work in part-time, seasonal, or temporary jobs with minimal employee benefits. Even where they have trained and worked in certain occupations in their countries of origin, immigrants often find that Canadian equipment and work practices differ significantly. Moreover, workplace expectations may be quite different from those they knew in a family business or farm. Immigrant workers may be unaware of their workplace rights and recourses in what seem to be impersonal organizations, and they lack access to the informal "grapevines" that other employees use.

As a result of the various factors already mentioned, immigrant workers have few points of entry into the formal and informal decision-making structures of their workplace. They lack the understanding of the culturally conditioned clues to corporate behaviour that can simplify their lives on the job. As mentioned earlier, they may perceive workplace health risks differently from their coworkers.

Adequate attention has not yet been given to the multicultural aspects of occupational health and safety, and immigrant workers present a particular illustration of this. Their occupational health and safety needs also demonstrate the limitations of the traditional hazard-control and medical models of occupational health and safety.

TOWARD NEW OCCUPATIONAL HEALTH AND SAFETY PARADIGMS

Traditional occupational health and safety disciplines must broaden their paradigms to include a psychosocial-ecological approach. This need is especially pressing in occupational multiculturalism. While we are beginning to admit that psychosocial parameters can be determinative in occupational health and safety, no consensus model has emerged comparable to that of the hazard-control or the medical model as practised in occupational hygiene/safety and occupational medicine/nursing, respectively.

We must directly address the manner in which people bring their health problems into and out of their workplaces in a dynamic manner and understand how they socially construct their illnesses and sick roles. The workplace is not an independent environment; rather, it is an interdependent component of a larger environment composed of social, psychological, and physical factors embedded in a cultural matrix. Workplaces are intimately linked to their larger social and cultural environments, and we must understand workplace health and safety within this larger (psychosocial-ecological) framework. This global approach to the workplace will require all the skills of the traditional professionals, such as occupational hygienists, epidemiologists, toxicologists, safety engineers, occupational physicians, ergonomists, occupational health nurses, and basic scientists such as molecular biologists and physicists.

The psychosocial-ecological approach to occupational health and safety issues will also call upon new "basic sciences" in occupational health and safety such as cross-cultural psychology, anthropology, social psychology, sociology, behavioural medicine, management sciences, health promotion, environmental design, and educational psychology.

It is important that abundant cross-disciplinary interchange of ideas and concepts be brought to bear on the multifaceted issues of health and safety in the workplace. Although professionals tend to study various workplace conditions in isolation e.g., noise or ventilation and from the viewpoint of their own disciplines e.g., occupational medicine or industrial hygiene from the worker's point of view, environmental factors are intuitively integrated within their own psychosocial ecologies. Indoor-air quality has been an especially fruitful area of interest in terms of psychosocial interactions with physical environments. We can expect further opportunities for such fruitful interdisciplinary collaboration. This is one of the exciting growth areas in occupational health and safety and is absolutely necessary in dealing with occupational multiculturalism.

In developing a psychosocial-ecological model for workplace health and safety, we at the Southern Occupational Health Resource Service, have adapted a model that was first presented in *Achieving Health for All: A framework for health promotion* (Health and Welfare Canada 1986), better known as the Epp Report. We have redefined some of the components of this framework as shown in figure 2. The multicultural aspects of workplace health and safety provide a unique testing ground for this model, and we are currently developing a community-based application of it in Calgary. This modified Epp model enables us to address occupational health and safety issues holistically and in keeping with the current paradigm of health promotion. We are also able to deal with workplace issues on a functional basis rather than as primarily problems in linguistics or ethnicity. We are trying to avoid prematurely resolving occupational multicultural issues into ethnic or linguistic categories until we have determined how such classifications relate to the actual hazards and adverse health effects of work. Our advisors from the multicultural community have highlighted some multicultural workplace issues, such as:

- verbal and non-verbal communication difficulties
- workers' reluctance to admit confusion or ignorance
- hesitation in asking for clarification or instructions
- workers' lack of understanding of rights and due processes
- workers' unwillingness to challenge unsafe work practices

- perceived lack of support for health and safety matters
- limited incentives for employers to address Occupational Health and Safety issues
- failure to understand Canadian Occupational Health and Safety "values"
- limited support for Occupational Health and Safety especially in small businesses
- assumptions that co-workers will "teach the Occupational Health and Safety ropes"
- workers' lack of knowledge of how to constructively address Occupational Health and Safety

Obviously, these problems are not restricted to certain ethnic or linguistic groups. They are generic issues in occupational health and safety that may be magnified by multicultural psychosocial environments.

Some implications of the psychosocial-ecological model presented in figure 2 are illustrated below.

HEALTH AND SAFETY CHALLENGES

"Reducing constraints" on workplace health and safety can involve the provision of understandable information to all workers, either in plain English or French or by translation into other languages that are more readily understood by the workers. Even pictorial signs may need to be translated.

"Increasing prevention" in the workplace may mean mentoring, special training programs, and opportunities for workers to indicate their health and safety needs, among other tactics. More effort should be made to evaluate health and safety training and to make such training ongoing rather than one-shot projects.

"Shared responsibility" could involve establishing fully representative occupational health and safety committees or other organizational structures that are culturally sensitive.

HEALTH AND SAFETY PROMOTION MECHANISMS

"Self efficacy" involves assuming personal responsibility at all levels throughout the workplace for making healthy work within a supportive organizational context a priority. It also includes awareness of rights and responsibilities in the workplace. Self-efficacy includes familiarity with the procedures required for safe work and understanding of the supportive and rehabilitative structures dealing with workplace health and safety.

"Collaborative actions" include effective inter-agency health and safety advocacy and networking for constructive health and safety changes. Workers may also need to obtain access to inter-agency resources dealing with immigration, mental health, health and social services, and so on.

FIGURE 2. A FRAMEWORK FOR WORKPLACE
HEALTH AND SAFETY *

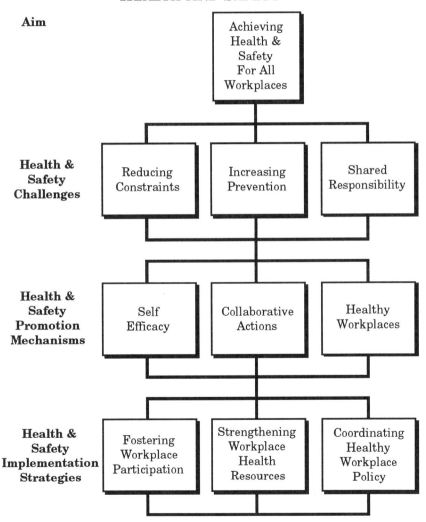

Source: Adapted from Health and Welfare Canada (1986).

"Healthy workplaces" includes obtaining active management support for workplace health and safety at the highest level possible. It also involves adopting health and safety as a corporate "value" that is part of an overall strategy of quality control in the workplace.

HEALTH AND SAFETY IMPLEMENTATION STRATEGIES

"Fostering workplace participation" involves recruiting the participation of all workers in implementing occupational health and safety strategies. It is also necessary to develop a shared health and safety attitude throughout the workplace rather than what some have called a "cowboy attitude". It will be necessary to ensure that employers, supervisors, and managers have adequate health and safety training and knowledge.

"Strengthening workplace health resources" may mean providing practical support for occupational health and safety improvements. Some resources may be offered to small businesses who could otherwise not afford them by specialized centres such as Southern Occupational Health Resource Service and others.

"Coordinating healthy workplace policy" addresses the integrated management of occupational health and safety issues as part of the "corporate culture". All activities of the workplace should be adequately considered for health and safety impact (on both workers and the public). Healthy workplaces do not arise spontaneously; rather, they are the result of intentional and continuous effort by all sectors of the workforce.

CONCLUSION

Occupational multiculturalism is a growing fact of life in our Canadian workplaces, but its implications for occupational health and safety have largely been neglected. This is in part because the traditional disciplines addressing occupational health and safety have lacked the training, orientation, and conceptual models with which to approach such issues. The hazard-control model and medical model have tended to bracket out multiculturalism and have often not considered occupational multiculturalism as a legitimate field of enquiry.

With increasing attention to the psychosocial aspects of work, we are now beginning to address important determinants of workers' health that were previously undefined. The health-promotion paradigm has also taken us towards a new understanding of health in the workplace. At the same time, we are confronting new diseases and dysfunctions that tax the limits of our conventional approaches to occupational health and safety.

As we conclude the twentieth century, we are seeing the rising contribution of the social sciences to the analysis of the multifaceted problems of occupational health and safety. A new psychosocial-ecological paradigm of occupational health and safety will arise from such interdisciplinary collaboration, and we will aquire the tools with which to adequately meet the challenges of occupational health and safety in the margins.

REFERENCES

Ames, B., Profet, M., and Gold, L. 1990. "Dietary pesticides (99.99% all natural)." *Proceedings of the National Academy of Sciences 87*: 7777 - 81.

Baker, C. 1987. "Ethnic differences in accident rates at work." *British Journal of Industrial Medicine 44*: 206 - 11.

Bellingham, R. 1990. "Debunking the myth of individual health promotion." *Occupational Medicine: State of the Art Reviews 5*: 665 - 75.

Bolaria, B. 1988. "The health effects of powerlessness: Women and racial minority immigrant workers." In *Sociology of health care in canada*. B. S. Bolaria and H. D. Dickinson ed. Toronto: Harcourt Brace Jovanovich.

Burnet, J. 1983. "Multiculturalism 10 years later." In *Two nations, many cultures–Ethnic groups in Canada* (2nd ed.) ed. J. L. Elliot. Scarborough: Prentice-Hall Canada.

Calgary Society for Immigrant Workers 1989. *A study of communication skills needs of immigrant workers in selected Calgary industries.* Calgary: Author [(This organization is now called Calgary IDEAS [Immigrant Development and Educational Advancement Society.])

Canadian Standards Association 1989. *A guideline on office ergonomics.* National Standard of Canada CAN/CSA-Z412-M89. Rexdale, ON: Author.

Canadian Task Force on Mental Health Issues affecting Immigrants and Refugees 1988. *After the door has been opened* . Cat. No. Ci96-38/1988E. Ottawa: Supply and Services.

Chandrasena, R., Beddage, V., and Fernando, M. 1991. "Suicide among immigrant psychiatric patients in Canada." *British Journal of Psychiatry 159*: 707 - 9.

Covello, V. 1983. "The perception of technological risks: A literature review." *Technological Forecasting and Social Change 23*: 285 - 97.

Donovan, J. 1984. "Ethnicity and health: A research review." *Social Science and Medicine 19*: 663 - 70.

Edwards, N. 1992. "Important considerations in the use of ethnicity as a study variable." *Canadian Journal of Public Health 83*: 31 - 33.

Fernandes, A. 1985. *Occupational health and safety concerns of new Canadians*. Edmonton: Edmonton Portuguese Media and Communications Society.

Freudenburg, W. 1988. "Perceived risk, real risk: Social science and the art of probabilistic risk assessment." *Science 242*: 44 - 49.

Friedman-Jimenez, G. 1989. "Occupational disease among minority workers." *American Association of Occupational Health Nurses Journal 37*: 64 - 70.

Gottlieb, B. 1985. "Social networks and social support: An overview of research, practice, and policy implications." *Health Education Quarterly 12*: 5 - 22.

Hamm, R. and Segall, M. 1992. "Workplace health and safety for immigrant workers." *At the Centre*, April, 16 - 18. [In French as Santé et sécurité au travail pour les immigrants, *Au Centre*, April:16 - 18.]

Harvey, M. 1987. *Language and literacy problems in Alberta's labour force* File H87-208.1. Edmonton: Research Branch, Occupational Health and Safety Division, Alberta Community and Occupational Health.

Health and Welfare Canada. 1986. *Achieving health for all: A framework for health promotion*. H 39-102/1986E. Ottawa: Author.

Joyce, P. 1987. "The historical meanings of work: An introduction." In *The historical meanings of work* P. Joyce ed. Cambridge: Cambridge University Press.

Karasek, R. and Theorell T. 1990. *Healthy work: Stress, productivity and the reconstruction of working life*. New York: Basic Books.

Kuo, W. and Tsai, Y. 1986. "Social networking, hardiness and immigrants' mental health." *Journal of Health and Social Behavior. 27*: 133 - 49.

Lee, G. and Wrench, J. 1980. "Accident-prone immigrants: An assumption challenged." *Sociology . 14*: 551 - 66.

Lee, T. 1986. "Public attitudes towards chemical hazards." *The Science of the Total Environment. 51*: 125 - 47.

Lindheim, R. and Syme, S. 1983. "Environments, people, and health." *Annual Review of Public Health 4*: 335 - 59.

Masi, R. 1988a. "Multiculturalism, medicine and health–Part I: Multicultural health care." *Canadian Family Physician 34*: 2173 - 77.

Masi, R. 1988b. "Multiculturalism, medicine and health–Part II: Health-related beliefs." *Canadian Family Physician 34*: 2429 - 34.

Masi, R. 1988c. "Multiculturalism, medicine and health–Part III: Health beliefs." *Canadian Family Physician 34*: 2649 - 53.

Masi, R. 1989a. "Multiculturalism, medicine and health–Part IV: Individual considerations." *Canadian Family Physician 34*: 69 - 73.

Masi, R. 1989b. "Multiculturalism, medicine and health–Part V: Community considerations." *Canadian Family Physician 34*: 251 - 54.

Masi, R. 1989c. "Multiculturalism, medicine and health–Part VI: A summary." *Canadian Family Physician 34*: 537 - 39.

Masi, R. 1992. "Communication: Cross-cultural applications of the physician's art." *Canadian Family Physician 38*: 1159 - 65.

Peel, A. and Clarke, M. 1990. "Pregnant women at work: A study of ethnic minority risk in Leicestershire." *British Journal of Industrial Medicine 47*: 649 - 55.

Pidgeon, N. 1991. "Safety culture and risk management in organizations." *Cross-Cultural Psychology 22*: 129 - 40.

Short, J. 1984. "The social fabric at risk: Toward the social transformation of risk analysis." *American Sociological Review 49*: 711 - 25.

Slovic, P. 1987. "Perception of risk." *Science 236*: 280 - 85.

Starr, C. 1969. "Social benefit versus technological risk." *Science 165*: 1232 - 38.

Stokols, D. 1992. "Establishing and maintaining healthy environments– Toward a social ecology of health promotion." *American Psychologist 47*: 6 - 22.

Vaughan, E. and Nordenstam, B. 1991. "The perception of environmental risks among ethnically diverse groups." *Journal of Cross-Cultural Psychology 22*: 29 - 60.

Vega, W. and Rumbaut, R. 1991. "Ethnic minorities and mental health." *Annual Review of Sociology 17*: 351 - 83.

Waxler-Morrison, N., Anderson, J., and Richardson, E. 1990. *Cross cultural caring: A handbook for professionals in Western Canada*. Vancouver: University of British Columbia Press.

Wildavsky, A. and Dake, K. 1990. "Theories of risk perception: Who fears what and why?" *Daedalus 119*: 41 - 60.

Williams, C. and Westermeyer, J. eds. 1986. *Refugee Mental Health in Resettlement Countries*. Washington: Hemisphere Publishing.

PART V

LA COMMUNAUTÊ FRANCOPHONE: IDENTITÊ ET CULTURE

David Millar
Faculté Saint-Jean
The University of Alberta

13

Official Languages or Lip Service? A Comparison of Minority Strategies in the West

There would be
only silence
if you were not here.

(Nowlan, 1969, 86)

L'individu s'oppose à la communauté, mais il s'en nourrit.
Et l'important, c'est bien moins de savoir à quoi il s'oppose
que ce dont il se nourrit.

(Malraux, 1935, 11)

Recent constitutional debates have opposed group to human rights. This opposition has become a cherished myth to many in the West: if we were all unilingual, Canada's identity would be secure. As if there were a fixed fund of human happiness, some assume that rights for minorities must subtract from the rights of the majority.[1] Affirmative action, employment equity, multiculturalism, bilingualism, and even tolerance of difference are seen as granting special privileges. Measures to correct systemic inequality and promote social justice are seen as an interference with the freedom of individuals.

The doctrine of the supremacy of the majority originated with John Locke. Gathering images and assumptions from Adam Smith's market theory and that of the American melting pot, this doctrine was particularly useful to the promoters of Anglo-Saxon dominance in western Canada. First invoked against Native peoples in the Riel rebellions, in the 1890s it justified attacks on schools and other constitutional rights of the French Canadian minority, and in following decades it rationalized assimilation of the new immigrants. Group settlement, schools, language, customs and religion, and other visible manifestations of difference were to be rooted out. Uncritically echoing the unicultural ideology of these past struggles, the Reform Party and others today believe it is an expression of true Canadianism.[2] But the unicultural myth has never accurately described Canadian society. Founded on divergence (from the United States), at its best this country has not merely tolerated but valued diversity. The presence of French Canada, not merely in Quebec but in significant minorities in many regions, puts constant pressure on the federal system for linguistic rights.[3] From this experience there are lessons to be learned. Despite certain weaknesses, the Official Languages Act (OLA) represents a pioneering effort to remedy systemic discrimination, from which those seeking equity for other types of minorities may learn. The ombudsman system of the OLA has been in force for twenty-three years, long enough to distinguish strategies that have been effectively used by the francophone minority in the West.

Like all equity laws, the OLA is resented by some who benefit from the systemic imbalance. Former Premier Don Getty has described language rights as an "irritant." In the civil service, there were those who saw as a form of reverse discrimination the designation of bilingual posts. ("Bilingual" here follows the OLA definition; far from intending to denigrate other language skills, I suggest that we recognize and promote such skills as a positive addition to civil servants' qualifications). There are striking parallels between the stalling of linguistic diversity in federal agencies and the rearguard battle waged by civil service managers against equity for women described by Nicole Morgan (1980). In both cases the goal of reform was equitable representation, as well as service to corresponding segments of the public. Bilingualism is not (as some suppose) a matter of quotas or equal numbers, but of fairness, intended to provide access in proportion to the needs of the minority. In Alberta only about three percent of federal posts are designated bilingual, and even of those many are occupied by anglophones. "Official" language services in the West (despite their importance to francophones) must be seen as a modest corrective rather than a major structural change.

Indeed, the francophone minorities of the West believe their status is still largely unofficial[4] twenty-three years after the passage of the OLA. They blame resistance in federal departments as well as in provincial government. Franco-Albertans still have difficulty securing essential federal services in their language. Their cultural institutions (including school rights restored by section 23 of the 1982 Charter, delayed by Alberta for nine years despite a clear victory by the minority in a Supreme Court challenge) remain under threat to such an extent that their assimilation rate is 75 percent.[5] The provision of essential services (e.g., education, health, welfare) to the linguistic minority by other western provinces has been grudging. By contrast, the rights and services enjoyed by English Quebeckers, or those (far more limited) of New Brunswick Acadians or Franco-Ontarians seem like a dream of paradise. To say that French minorities feel endangered in no way denies that other groups have cogent claims for recognition of collective rights (whether "official" or "designated" or "human"): natives, women, ethnolinguistic minorities, those of different physical ability, religion, or origin.[6] We should also not forget that the collective rights of unionists and the poor have been severely cut back in recent years. Rollback of "official" language rights has been suggested in recent court cases and constitutional negotiations. Not even "official" minorities can afford to neglect political strategies,[7] although the analysis that follows deals only with their administrative strategies in the context of legislated rights.

The administrative procedures of the OLA have been in effect for two decades. In some respects they are stronger than other equity measures, in others weaker. For instance, only in 1988 was the Official Languages ombudsman empowered to take offenders to court. Thus, conciliation and education still take precedence over legal sanctions. What distinguishes the OLA from legislation affecting the private sector, e.g., labour law is that the OLA mandated change by and within the civil service itself. Managers were required by the terms of the law to develop their own plans to remedy systemic discrimination; we now see weaker but similar clauses in the Employment Equity Act. The ombudsman's power to investigate and to require disclosure of internal documents, removes much of the burden of proof from the complainant. But (as in labour and human rights codes) the lion's share of the administrator's workload is conciliation and education. In view of the parallels with other forms of anti-discrimination administration, a study of effective minority strategies under the OLA should interest activists in other areas. What problems and procedures do they have in common? What approaches have failed? What works?

Some specific cases will illustrate the varied needs of a linguistic minority. Security: A gang of rowdies begins threatening your home. You phone the RCMP trying to explain your fears, to give the circumstances, and to obtain help. But in many small towns and rural areas, the receptionist who answers the phone is a municipal employee, who does not speak your language. Health Services: A federal prisoner wants psychiatric services in his mother tongue. Since that language is an "official" one, he believes that this is his right. Information: You need to know why your tax return, UI payment, or pension was cut. A successful appeal may depend on getting a full explanation in your own language and understanding how your circumstances fit the bureaucratic criteria. Access to programmes: A woman with a Quebec grade nine education seeks job training from Employment Canada. She is refused because of low marks on a competency test administered at a community college, in English, though she might have done well in French. The college, in provincial jurisdiction, is not required to offer services in both official languages. The Employment office says it is out of their hands and tells her she is qualified only for washing floors or babysitting.

Five types of strategies may be used in these cases: (1) individual request and negotiation for services, (2) collective request and negotiation, (3) a complaint to the OLA ombudsman, (4) a human rights complaint, and (5) a Privacy Act request for access to personal information. For greater effect, these strategies may be combined.

Individual request and negotiation is assumed by the OLA to be the normal way of obtaining services, because the act itself mandates all federal agencies to comply. The mandate is not always followed, however, and it has clear limits. A citizen's right is only to communication in the official languages (services in non-official languages are offered by a few agencies to improve the efficiency of programs, but not as a right). The act envisages not equal facilities, but a minimum of front-desk services, usually by way of designation of a few bilingual staff or phone lines in key offices. The minority's access is limited by "significant demand" and the "nature of the office," left undefined for twenty years by Treasury Board rules. In practice, this has meant virtual exemption of a number of departments, specialist publications, and services. Even in the better ministries, where bilingual services are designated, notices posted, and staff available, there is often a delay. Since western francophones are usually bilingual, they prefer fast service to waiting. Unfortunately, if a client accepts the use of English in the initial dialogue, or negotiation of the delivery of service, there will be no basis for future complaint. The burden of insistence is on the client. Under new Treasury Board rules, non-insistence may also reduce "significant demand" (see discussion of the Treasury Board's synoptic table below). The burden of offer has now been largely removed from recalcitrant ministries. Even in "key services", the burden of demand on minority clients will be sharply increased.

Collective request and negotiation have been fruitful strategies with departments truly committed to bilingual service, such as Employment Canada. Francophone associations have been able to negotiate directly with regional and local managers. There have been several beneficial results: greater understanding of priorities on each side, reduction of the burden on the individual client, definition of demand in terms of specific needs rather than bureaucratic criteria. Limited at first to correspondence and front-desk information, minority language service was extended to 800-number phone information, community development programs, and applications. Though restricted to areas where francophones were over 5 percent of the population, collective negotiation gave them direct input into the priorities affecting their community (particularly important now that the civil service makes managers responsible for setting their own priorities). A regionwide consultative committee comprising senior managers, respresentatives of designated groups, and front-line staff began to develop better ways of delivering service. For instance, on the 800-lines, direct discussion with an official might be preferred to a recorded message. Proactive negotiation of this sort is an ideal seldom achieved, however. In all the examples above, an unsatisfied individual would be able to lodge a complaint. More usually, the minority receives mere lip service: despite the OLA, and bureaucratic mandates, service is inadequate or nonexistent despite apparent offer in the bilingual signage that so annoys Don Getty and Reformers e.g., at Canada Post. In such cases, the francophone association's strategy has been to gather individual cases, take them to upper management, and when refused, develop a concerted campaign of official complaints. This kind of pressure has had limited local successes. A few branches have been forced to provide bilingual service, particularly since the OLA makes clear that the responsibility for providing it cannot be avoided by privatizing or contracting out by a crown employer.

Complaint to the OLA ombudsman (OCOL: the Office of the Commissioner of Official Languages) is the major remedy to systemic discrimination. By means of a simple phone call, individuals can demand impartial investigation of any infringement of the OLA and have a legal right to take a federal agency to court if unsatisfied. The right is seldom invoked owing to the expense it involves. Under a 1988 amendment to the law, the commissioner may assume the burden of prosecution, a power available to the Canadian Human Rights Commission that was long sought by, and long denied, to the OCOL. Though the ultimate sanction is a court order, complaints are essentially an appeal to the "mandate" of the department concerned.

At the first stage, circumstantial details are carefully recorded and investigated. If the complaint is substantiated, the manager responsible is asked to explain what system they will use to avoid recurrence. To set bilingual quotas or determine the exact means is the responsibility not of OCOL, but of the department. A manager's refusal, or repeated complaints, constitute evidence of systemic inadequacy, whereupon the matter may be carried to the regional or national level for solution. Refusal or long delay at these levels is reported to Parliament in the *OCOL Annual Report*. Usually by the local manager's providing an apology or service to the client, 75 percent of justified complaints are resolved to the client's satisfaction.

The quantity of positive outcomes reported by OCOL is high, but what is their quality? Unsatisfactory or unresolved cases usually involve real services (rather than mere signage or greetings), several levels of management, or the mandate/priorities/funding of an entire department. Qualitative change takes years, as well as political and legal pressure. One of the ways a minority can increase pressure is by concentrating complaints on key areas. Youth, seniors, or others can target a particular office. Multiple complaints with circumstantial details (place, time, dialogue, identification of offending individuals) make it difficult for a manager to get off the hook by blaming the event on a single person or momentary lapse in procedure. And where several kinds of discrimination are involved, complaints may be made to other human rights agencies.

A human rights complaint may be lodged with the Canadian Human Rights Commission (CHRC) or, according to their jurisdiction and mandate, with local, provincial, and even international bodies. Though negotiations and court proceedings may take some time, CHRC agents may be able to judge the strength of a case immediately. CHRC involvement adds greatly to the pressure on a manager to negotiate a satisfactory solution. Provincial agencies should not be ignored: a B.C. Human Rights decision awarded damages on grounds of discrimination, and job reinstatement, to a francophone couple. International proceedings have been launched by women's and Native groups, in order to put pressure on reluctant federal politicians.

Finally, a request may be made under the Privacy Act for access to personal information in a government agency's file. It may be crucial to the success of an OLA or human rights complaint to obtain a full copy of that file (in its unexpurgated state, often with marginal comments). Since privacy and linguistic issues are brought to the attention of regional management, the local official may wish to resolve the matter quickly to the complainant's satisfaction rather than have to explain every note in the dossier to superiors. No one wants a bad evaluation. At very least, a Privacy request ensures that items will not be purged from the file, and allows the pursuit of a complaint in full knowledge of the contents.

However, new Treasury Board rules may severely limit basic language rights and, consequently, the basis of complaints. A detailed draft of regulations in January 1992 was confirmed in April by a publicly issued "Synoptic Table." Its effects on francophone rights in the West include the following:

1. Service to the travelling public involves bilingual signs, security announcements, and counter service in VIA rail stations, planes and airports, and national parks. In parks the "nature of the office" requires all ministry offices and one post office to offer French service, whose absence had been the subject of many complaints since 1968.

2. In large cities such as Vancouver, Winnipeg, Calgary, Edmonton, and Winnipeg, French services will be offered in one office only of each federal agency. This actually reduces service in some departments, and clients will have to travel long distances, especially in the greater Edmonton and Vancouver census areas. At best, phone-in service may improve.

3. In smaller census areas, francophones will be offered six key services in their language: Employment, Post Office, Secretary of State, Public Service Commission, taxes, and security of revenue (pensions and family allowances). Other services may be designated if the minority reaches 30 percent in a rural area or totals 5,000 in a small city or region served by one office. Any bilingual service may be cut if French requests do not reach 5 percent of demand measured over one year.

4. In rural census areas with 5 to 30 percent francophones, key services will be centralized in one office. Only if the minority is over 30 percent will the RCMP and other services be required. Any bilingual services may be cut if French requests do not reach 5 percent of demand.

5. Anomalies: Key services are guaranteed in Whitehorse and Yellowknife, but those offered in similar capitals like Regina and Victoria may be revoked under the 5 percent demand rule. Francophones attached to military bases in the West are excluded (long a source of difficulty for

unilingual families) because they seldom reach the minimum population in a census area. For example, the proportion in rural Comox district is just high enough to ask for key services and RCMP; but not in urban Comox, where the base is located.

6. "Significant demand" is no longer defined by the size of the potential clientele but by its use of the service. It will be very difficult for small minorities in the West to generate the near-universal insistence for French services (often new, little-known, involving delay or difficulty) required to reach the five percent level of demand. The new rule, while appearing to define rights, allows their permanent elimination.[8]

What will be the effect on services in the specific cases previously mentioned? Security: The problem of unilingual receptionists remains. Until now, wherever five percent of the population was francophone, it was RCMP policy that the receptionist try to contact a bilingual constable to call back on radiophone. Even this limited service will now disappear unless the minority is 30 percent and generates significant demand. Health: Bilingual services in federal prisons, however hard to obtain in the past, or desirable for a convict's reformation, will disappear. Like those of military families, prisoners' official language "rights" will cease as soon as they are transferred from bilingual facilities in the East. Information on revenue security will be available as a key service to the minority, subject to the significant demand rule. As noted above, these services are likely to be reduced in the largest cities and may be lost entirely in small cities and rural areas. However, Revenue Canada has for several years provided free 800-line phone service; in a generous interpretation of the rules, such information services could be extended. Access to programmes: Employment programs are included in key services. Qualification problems may still occur. The woman discussed above who was denied training could have considered a complaint under the human rights code as well as the OLA. She requested her file through the Privacy Commission and discussed further action with a legal aid lawyer. It turned out that her OLA complaint and Privacy request were sufficient to put pressure on the local manager to reconsider his position. Her schooling qualifications were recognized and she gained access to four years of re-entry and job-training programs. Not all such cases have such happy endings; and even "key" services may be terminated under the new demand rule. However, this case shows clearly how individual and collective rights can complement each other.

Limited as it is, our analysis suggests some conclusions. "Equitable participation" as defined by the offical language ombudsman[9] is a principle that applies to many anti-discrimination remedies. It implies not the strict equality of individual rights, but fair treatment proportional to need. Charter and constitutional debates have suggested that similar principles can be invoked in support of other historic rights and to correct other kinds of systemic discrimination. Linguistic and other minorities in Canada have given each other mutual support in the recent constitutional round. Further extensions of such a "rainbow alliance" are possible.

The role of the state needs clarification, particularly in comparative study of the winning of different kinds of collective and human rights. A theory of the state should not be monolithic; it needs to examine and account for differences among three levels of government, in their regional and political variations, as well as differences in power at each level of entrenched interests, minority alliances, and public support. An adequate analysis would consider not only the possibility of reform but also negative pressures.

Study of the development of collective rights should include strategies of political action, though the discussion above has been limited to strategies focused on administrative law. Political contextualization is essential, in the comparing of strategies and needs of Native peoples, visible minorities, the handicapped, women, and so on. Many of these groups are still at the lobbying stage. To know how the first legislative gains can be made is as important as avoiding repetition of administrative weaknesses. Both kinds of knowledge are required in order to set realistic goals.

Finally, the question of identity needs to be distinguished from the question of rights. Selfdevelopment goes beyond mere legal rights based on language, race, gender, or other group characteristics, however necessary such entitlements may be to eradicate past discrimination. Majority or minority status, historical exclusion or inclusion, economic, religion, and family differences may lead individuals to identify more freely, or more strictly, with a group claiming certain rights.[10] But any identity will include plural and overlapping centres of affiliation, some given and others chosen. Social anthropology has only begun to disentangle these factors. As the historian E.P. Thompson (1963) observes, identity is not a static structure, but a dynamic and continuing process. Its analysis may also benefit from the concepts of alterity and of polysystem theory.[11] That a minority may legitimately claim linguistic rights should not limit the freedom of an individual member of that group to affirm other memberships and loyalties. Identity's boundaries are additive, not subtractive.

Dans les débats constitutionnels, comme dans beaucoup des théories politiques, on a tendance à opposer les droits individuels aux droits des collectivités.[12] Cette théorie, qui prend racine dans certaines thèses de John Locke, était soigneusement élaborée par les américains lors de leur grande assimilation des immigrants, et que certains canadiens-anglais (surtout dans l'Ouest) ont adaptée pour justifier un régime uniculturel depuis 1890.[13] C'est un mythe de l'Ouest, cher au parti Réforme, que pour être égal on doit perdre toute identité particulière, tout droit collectif. Ce mythe n'a jamais collé à la réalité canadienne, que même les américains l'ont abandonné dans le droit syndical (où il s'agit, d'abord et avant tout, de la reconnaissance d'une collectivité) et dans les remèdes contre la discrimination. L'administration de nos lois canadiens linguistiques, démontre concrètement comment le droit individuel peut soutenir et renforcer le droit collectif des minorités.

Parce que la loi sur les langues officielles est plus développée que la plupart des autres lois pour assurer l'égalité, il y a des leçons à y apprendre. Cinq stratégies minoritaires sous cette loi peuvent se distinguer. On verra ensuite l'effet du nouveau règlement proposé par le gouvernement fédéral, le défi qu'il pose au minorité francophone de l'Ouest, et certaines conclusions qui s'imposent.

La Loi sur les Langues Officielles (LLO) est en vigueur au fédéral depuis déjà 23 ans,[14] D'un côté, un certain nombre d'anglophones comme le Premier Ministre de l'Alberta Don Getty la trouvent "irritante". De l'autre, bon nombre de francophones qui cherchent de véritables changements dans les services fédéraux et provinciaux se plaignent de la faiblesse des "langues officieuses" at des "23 ans d'immobilisme" tant dans le dossier de certains institutions fédéraux que dans celui de l'éducation.[15] Dans maints bureaux de l'Ouest canadien, on a de la difficulté à se faire servir en français. En Alberta les taux d'assimilation sont de 75%,[16] situation qui n'est guère remedié par le 3% de postes fédéraux désignés bilingues, dont la plupart sont occupés par des anglophones. Il faut admettre que certains groupes sans statut "officiel", indigènes, allophones ou de couleur, de gens handicapés ou de syndicalistes, se croient encore plus démunis ou défavorisés.[17] Malgré quelques faiblesses, la LLO va plus loin que les remèdes de beaucoup d'autres lois anti-discriminatoires et d'équité. Alors, sans prétendre que la situation actuelle des minorités de langues officielles est idéale, l'effet de la loi, ainsi que le travail de l'ombudsman, le Commissaire aux Langues Officielles, permettent d'en tirer certaines conclusions.

Comme on voit dans les exemples suivants, la plupart les reclamations de la minorité sont bien modestes: Sécurité: Un bande de voyous rodent autour de votre maison. Vous appelez la Gendarmerie Royale pour expliqer vos craintes et obtenir de l'aide. Dans la plupart des petites villes, la réceptionniste est unilingue. Santé: Un détenu unilingue en prison fédéral, veut avoir certains services psychiatriques en français. Il croit que c'est son droit en tant que citoyen. Renseignements: Le gouvernement vous coupe votre remboursement d'impôt, votre assurance-chômage, ou votre pension. Vous voulez en connaître les raisons et en faire appel. Accès aux programmes: Une femme qui détient une 9e année d'éducation en français veut une formation de sécrétaire pour suppléer aux besoins de sa famille. Pourtant, le Centre d'Emploi lui refuse toute aide, malgré des demandes répétées, car elle a échoué un test de niveau de scolarité au Community College -- administré en anglais. Les règles d'Emploi lui impose ce test. Pourtant, le Centre n'y reconnaît pas de responsabilité car le Collège est provincial. Cette dame doit, lui dit-on, laver les planchers ou soigner des enfants. Elle n'est pas qualifiée pour d'autres emplois. On lui fournira ni cours de langue anglaise, ni formation sécrétariale, car elle n'a pas la scolarité de base. Comment l'administration de la LLO marche-t-elle dans de tels cas? Quels moyens peut employer une minorité pour la rendre plus efficace? On les examinera d'abord en principe, pour voir ensuite les réalisations et les limites de la loi, dans ces cas précis.

J'ouvre ici une parenthèse. En discutant des stratégies je ne parlerai que du droit administratif. Ce n'est aucunement nier l'importance de l'action politique. Jusqu'à présent, les droits linguistiques restent un enjeu important du débat constitutionnel.[18]

D'autres luttes contre la discrimination restent au niveau de l'action politique, du lobbying, de la recherche des faveurs. Une fois la législation obtenue, il est souvent question d'une date de proclamation, de personnel-clé, de budget et d'effectifs: à chacune de ces étapes l'impulsion politique risque de s'affaiblir. Si plusieurs bureaux fédéraux sont impliqués, il y sera question de mandats et des priorités -- et là commencent les tactiques de delai bureaucratique, de piétinement et de pataugeage, si bien décrites par Nicole Morgan (1988). Mais le mandat au bilinguisme s'est établi depuis belle lurette, prioritaire et développé. Ainsi, on peut en déduire certains principes générales d'action anti-discriminatoires.

Etant donné ce cadre législatif et administratif, la minorité (francophone de l'Ouest à la recherche de ses droits linguistiques fédéraux) dispose de cinq stratégies d'action: (1) demande et négociation individuelle, (2) demande et négociation collective, (3) plainte sous la LLO, (4) plainte fondée sur les droits de la personne (aux trois niveaux provincial, fédéral, international), et (5) demande d'accès àl'information personnelle.

L'astuce n'est pas seulement de connaître chaque stratégie, mais de savoir les combiner.

1. Demande et négociation individuelle: les services-clés et les communications doivent être disponibles dans les deux langues. Il suffit de les demander. Dans certains cas, on verra plus tard, un Ministère (dans l'analyse qui suit, il faut entendre toute institution fédérale) peut justifier une carence par manque de demande francophone. Plus souvent un certain delai s'impose: il faut attendre l'arrivée d'un préposé bilingue, ou attendre son rappel téléphonique. La négociation consiste à arranger cela à la satisfaction du demandeur, sans quoi il peut porter plainte -- àcondition qu'il ait refusé de se faire servir en anglais. Malheureusement, la plupart des francophones de l'Ouest étant bilingues, ils cèdent sur leurs droits pour avoir un service efficace. Pourtant, dans les négociations individuelles comme collectives, en plus des droits linguistiques définis, on peut invoquer le mandat de "Fonction publique 2000" par lequel tout gérant doit viser les besoins locaux dans son "service au public".

2. Demande et négociation collective: les associations francophones ont obtenu pas mal de succès avec certains Ministères tel le Ministère de l' Emploi. Voici quelques exemples: des préposés bilingues désignés, des bureaux désignés, consultations sur des programmes de développement, et encouragement de soumissions en français. Depuis quelques années, chaque gérant fédéral devient responsable de fixer les priorités de son bureau; transiger directement avec des porte-paroles de la communauté est donc un avantage mutuel. Dans la région Alberta-TNO, le Ministère de l'Emploi s'est doté de plusieurs comités consultatifs formés de ses propres employés ainsi que d'autres groupes minoritaires, pour discuter des priorités. Cela a bien servi certaines régionales de l'ACFA, par exemple. Plusieurs ministères se sont équipés de lignes téléphoniques, où un francophone

répond directement aux questions du public, de loin préférable à un simple message enrégistré. Dans tous ces cas le client peut porter plainte si ce service est inadéquat. Aussi, la régionale peut se fixer des cibles àatteindre, concerter les demandes et si nécessaire les plaintes. Une telle concertation a obtenu certains services des Postes, malgré la résistance d'une haute gestion qui se veut "entreprise privée". La loi s'applique aussi à tout tiers parti qui fournit des services gouvernementaux: donc la privatisation (en principe) n'est pas une échappatoire.

3. Plaintes sous la LLO: Les francophones de l'Ouest ont toujours droit à des services dans leur langue, faute de quoi ils peuvent porter plainte, et même aller en cour s'ils ne sont pas satisfaits. Ce faisant, ils peuvent obtenir l'appui de l'ombudsman fédéral (le commissaire) qui depuis 1988 peut lui-même intenter une poursuite devant les cours, ce qui peut allèger le fardeau du plaignant. Cela ne se fait que dans les cas bien importants, et certains disent qu'un tribunal semblable à ceux de la Commission des Droits de la Personne serait plus efficace.
(En dehors du cadre de la LLO: la principale faiblesse dans les droits linguistiques est que le gouvernement vient de couper le programme de contestation judiciaire, qui a été un atout fort important dans la reclamation des droits d'éducation sous la Charte.)
La poursuite judiciaire est un dernier recours. Rappelons que l'ombudsman entend et vérifie cette plainte au niveau local. Si les évidences démontrent une plainte fondée contre tel ministère, non seulement son gérant local doit-il satisfaire le au plaignant, mais c'est à lui d'expliquer quel système il mettra en vigueur pour combler cette faille à l'avenir. C'est ce que les fonctionnaires appellent "le mandat". La responsabilité en est claire et nette -- à tel point qu'une plainte qui ne trouve pas de solution en région peut être reférée au sous-ministre. Chaque fonctionnaire sait qu'il y joue de sa carrière. Cependant, ce n'est pas le commissaire qui impose une solution, c'est à chaque fonctionnaire responsable d'indiquer les modalités, de se fixer des buts précis, et de veiller au bon fonctionnement du système. La commission prétend que 75% des plaintes linguistiques fondées sont résolues à la satisfaction du plaignant! A prendre avec un gaine de sel. Quelques astuces: pour influencer un ministère réfractaire, les plaintes doivent bien indiquer les circonstances. et être assez nombreuses. Le demandeur ne

doit aucunement concéder ses droits, et doit notifier le commissaire par téléphone aussitôt que possible afin de lui passer tous les détails. Cela ne prend que quelques minutes; pouvoir identifier l'heure exacte, et rappeler le dialogue, est de toute importance. Avec multiples plaintes, la gestion doit faire face à sa responsabilité sans blâmer un employé individuel. Concerter les plaintes sur certains services-clés est un but tout à fait légitime d'une association régionale. Des groupes de jeunesse, ou d'âge d'or, pourraient bien aider une telle campagne. Dans certains cas, la discrimination linguistique (manque systémique de service) s'accompagne d'autres formes de discrimination, par exemple contre les femmes, contre les personnes âgées, etc. Dans ces cas, sans concéder la plainte linguistique on peut la dédoubler d'appels à d'autres lois et devant d'autres agences anti-discriminatoires.

4. Plainte fondée sur les droits de la personne: la commission fédérale a des agents courtois, et qui connaissent bien leur spécialité. Ils peuvent vite vous indiquer si votre cas est légitime. Un cas qui ira au tribunal peut durer un ou deux ans, mais force plaintes se résolveront par négociation. Avoir cette commission à ses côtés est un atout considérable. Les commissions provinciales ne sont pas à dédaigner non plus: celle de la Colombie-Britannique par exemple a soutenu la plainte d'un couple francophone, et a obtenu restitution de leur emploi avec dommages suite à une plainte linguistique. Faire appel aux engagements internationaux et aux agences de l'ONU n'est pas ànégliger non plus: les indigènes et les femmes ont utilisé cette stratégie. Car le gouvernement canadien n'aime pas être embarrassé devant les auditoires internationaux. Ces appels l'encouragent à trouver une solution au problème.

5. Accès à l'information et protection des renseignements personnels (AIPRP; ATIP en anglais): un contestataire peut renforcer sa plainte (3 ou 4) en demandant qu'un ministère fédérale lui livre une copie de son dossier. Dans au moins un cas, une personne femme lésée dans ces droits linguistiques, a vite obtenu gain de cause par la seule demande d'accès, suite à quoi le gérant local se verrait obligé d'expliquer certaines remarques inscrites dans son dossier. Parce qu'une demande d'accès va au bureau-chef de la région, le gérant local a donc intérêt à résoudre le problème àla satisfaction du client, évitant

ainsi à faire ses explications au chef de région ou à Ottawa. Au moins, le client se protège d'une épuration ou "nettoyage" de son dossier, et peut poursuivre sa plainte en pleine connaissance de son contenu.

La règlementation du Conseil du Trésor (voir Tableau 1) peut apporter des changements profonds àcette situation. La minorité risque de perdre la plupart des droits acquis, si elle ne fait pas preuve d'une demande suffisante. Je vous réfère au tableau des effets du règlement deposé en janvier 1992. Il faut ajouter que les minorités attendent depuis 23 ans que le gouvernement définisse la "demande important" et de la "vocation du bureau" dans la Loi de Langues Officielles. Ce règlement entra en vigueur dans les prochains deux ans et demi. Il semble promettre une amélioration des services bilingues (première colonne), mais si on examine de près les conditions par unité géographique, le minimum de population francophone, et le niveau de demande exigé, il y aura une possibilité de perte de services.

La condition de "niveau de demande de 5%" semble mettre en danger cette promesse apparamment généreuse des services-clés bilingues dans plusieurs régions de l'Ouest. Pour les associations francophones, les deux ans de mesure de demande seront une période dans laquelle le mot d'ordre sera: marche ou crève -- utiliser les services au maximum ou les perdre tous. Dans ce contexte, la question de stratégies devient capitale. Qu'arrivera-t-il dans les cas concrèts cités au-dessus? Un bref resumé:

Sécurité: Là où la minorité est en-dessous de 30% de la population, c'est fort possible que disparaisse les services bilingues de la Gendarmie Royale. C'était déjà en quelque sorte un service "sur papier", car dans les petites villes la réceptionniste est unilingue. Elle doit chercher à rejoindre un agent bilingue par radio avec les delais que cela impose. Santé: Le détenu en prison n'a pas de chance. Il est probable que les quelques services, accordés dans le passé, disparaissent.

Renseignements: Problèmes d'impôt, d'assurance-chômage, de pension: tous font partie de la sécurité du revenu, un des services-clés garantis même aux faibles minorités. La condition de niveau de demande s'impose. Dans une interprétation stricte du règlement, certains bureaux bilingues peuvent être abolis. Dans une interprétation généreuse, les services peuvent s'offrir par téléphone àlongue distance, ce que fait déjà Revenu Canada. Dans un avenir idéale, les télécommunications pourraient utilisé pareillement par beaucoup d'autres ministères. Accès aux programmes: La question des qualifications aux programmes d'Emploi se règle aussitôt que la personne aurait fait une demande d'accès à son dossier. Selon un avocat qu'elle a consulté, une plainte de discrimination sexuelle aurait été possible. Soudainement, le gérant local découvre un moyen de la re-catégoriser, lui offrant des cours de langue seconde, et de formation à l'emploi échelonné sur quatre années. C'est un cas où l'on voit assez clairement comment les droits individuels côtoient les droits collectifs.

Dans le principe de "participation équitable"[19] se trouve un intérêt commun, malgré leurs besoins et préoccupations différentes, à tous les minorités de l'ouest. Ils s'appuient mutuellement déjà dans certains débats constitutionnels. Il y a lieu a élargir cette alliance "arc-en-ciel" à d'autres solidarités. Comparer leurs stratégies, afin d'adopter les plus efficaces en serait une première étape.

On doit discuter aussi du rôle de l'état. Une bonne définition doit mieux coller aux réalités fédérales et provinciales, et distinguer les enjeux législatifs et administratifs. Il est douteux que la structure du pouvoir soit partout pareille et monolithique. Une bonne analyse dévoilerait et les dangers de reculs et les possibilités de rémèdes.

Une étude plus approfondie de toutes les stratégies anti-discriminatoires devrait nécessairement comprendre les stratégies politiques. Je me suis limité au droit administratif en milieu fédéral; pourtant, cette administration s'insère dans un contexte constitutionnel, donc de toutes les actions politiques qui concernent les minorités. L'étude du développement du droit linguistique permettrait certaines comparaisons avec d'autres revendications anti-discriminatoires: des indigènes, des minorités visibles, des handicapés, des femmes en recherche d'équité d'emploi, etc. Pour une bonne partie de leurs besoins, ces groupes n'ont pas dépasse l'étape du lobbying. Une histoire comparative du développement des systèmes d'assistance sociale, des droits humains, et de la législation sur l'équité, permettrait de mieux prédire où mènerait telle pression politique, ensuite telle action legislative ou administrative.

TABLEAU 1. EFFETS DU RÈGLEMENT (JAN. 1992) DU CONSEIL DU TRÉSOR [20] VISANT LA DEMANDE IMPORTANTE ET LA VOCATION DU BUREAU POUR LES SERVICES AUX FRANCOPHONES DE L'OUEST

Niveau de service bilingue	Unité géographique	Minimum de francophones	Condition
Un bureau de poste et tous autres bureaux fédéraux	Parcs nationaux (vocation du bureau)	– – – –	
Bureau régional (1) (e.g. SHLC, Banque Féd. de Développement, Diversification Régionale)	aire de service comprenant plus d'un SDR	500 ou 5000	niveau de demande de 5% (7) – – – –
	GRANDES VILLES		
1+ bureau par organisme (2) selon % francophone, et services au public voyageur	RMR: <u>Vancouver, Winnipeg, Calgary, Edmonton</u>	5000	
6 services-clés (3) + autres selon la demande	RMR: <u>Saskatoon, Regina, Victoria</u>	moins que 5000	autres services: niveau de demande de 5% (7)
6 services-clés + bureaux les plus utilisés	Cas spéciaux: <u>Whitehorse, Yellowknife</u> (4)		
	SDR: PETITES VILLES, OU RURALES		
"tous les bureaux" (5)	SDR: <u>Falher</u>	500 et 30%	
GRC, 6 services-clés, (3) + autres selon la demande	SDR: <u>McLennan, Donnelly, Girouxville, Rivière de la Paix, Cold Lake</u>	200-499 et 30%	autres services: niveau de demande de 5% (7)
GRC, un bureau avec les 6 services-clés	SDR: <u>Plamondon,</u> certains villages au Manitoba	0-200 et 30%	
1+ bureau, selon % francophone	SDR: <u>St Paul</u>	500 et 5%	niveau de demande de 5% (7)
GRC, 6 services-clés (3) selon % francophone	SDR: Chilliwack, Nanaimo, Kamloops, Prince George, <u>Comox</u> (6)	500, sous 5%	niveau de demande de 5% (7)

Avis: Un "bureau" bilingue comprend certains bilingues, pas tout le personnel.

Source: Adopted from synoptic table, Office of the Commissioner of Official Languages (1990), p. 87.

Notes: (1) C'est un gain de service: agents, correspondence et renseignements téléphoniques. (2) Une perte de service est possible dans la RMR d'Edmonton. Dans une région de 15000 km carrés, qui comprend Legal et Beaumont, plusieurs bureaux déjà bilingues peuvent être rayés: de Postes, d'Emploi, d'Immigration, de la GRC. A Vancouver aussi, les clients francophones parcouriront de longues distances. A Calgary, perte possible de bureaux, et des réceptionnistes bilingues de la GRC. Les services aux public voyageur ne s'appliquent qu'aux gares de chemin de fer, et aux aéroports de l'Ouest: toute message concernant la sécurité du public, renseignements, affiches et annonces. (3) Les six services-clés: Centre d'Emploi, Postes Canada, le Secrétariat d'Etat, Impôt, Sécurité du revenu (pensions, allocations familiales, sécurité de la vieillesse), la Commission de la Fonction Publique. (4) Gain de services possible à Whitehorse et Yellowknife. Pourtant, les capitales de la Saskatchewan et de la Colombie-Britannique peuvent perdre les services-clés. Voir (7). (5) Peu de gain: probablement aux Postes, à la Gendarmerie Royale, à l'Emploi. (6) Situation bizarre à Comox: les résidents du comté de Comox auront droit aux services bilingues, tandis que les habitants des villes de Comox, Courtenay et Cumberland n'y auront pas droit. Le règlement n'offre pas de solution aux besoins des familles francophones militaires aux bases de Comox, de Victoria et de Chilliwack. (7) Condition très onéreuse. La demande sera mesurée par chaque Ministère selon des critères objectives spécifiées. Mais il faut que presque tous les francophones du lieu réclament un service, et toute de suite, pour que la demande atteindra cinq pourcentage.

Enfin, s'impose la question de définition de la collectivité. C'est évident que la langue en est une composante de l'identité. Pourtant, la théorie anthropologique démêle difficilement identité et ethnie, ses manifestations majoritaires et minoritaires, exclusionnaires et inclusionnaires, et leurs causes profondes historiques, economiques, religieuses, sociales.[21] A mon avis, un identité n'est pas une structure statique, mais bien plutôt un processus de conscientisation qui se refait constamment (ainsi E.P. Thompson).[22] Les théories de polysystèmes et de l'altérité peuvent aussi nous aider.[23] Dire qu'une ethnie peut se promouvoir par des droits linguistiques n'interdit pas à l'individu de s'identifier en ajoutant sa langue à plusieurs autres centres de loyauté et d'affirmation.

REFERENCES

Action Canada Newsletter.

Anderson, P. 1991, March 9. "Nation-states and national identity (Review of Fernand Braudel." *The identity of France) London Review of Books*, 3-18.

Association of Canadian Studies. 1989. *Demolinguistic trends and the evolution of Canadian institutions* (Canadian Themes series), Ottawa.

Brym, R. "Review – Ethnic Inequality in a Class Society." *Canadian Ethnic Studies* 21: 127-128.

Canadian Labour Congress. 1992. *Action Plan*. Ottawa: Author.

Cardinal, L., and Lapointe, J. 1990. "La sociologie des Francophones hors Québec: Un partipris pour l'autonomie." *Canadian Ethnic Studies* 22: 47-66.

Chambers, R. 1992. No Montagues without Capulets: Some thoughts on cultural identity. Paper presented at conference, Explorations in Difference: Law, Politics and Culture, March 19-21, University of Alberta.

Francophone Jeunesse de l'Alberta. 1991. *Portrait de l'histoire francophone en Alberta* (pamphlet). Edmonton.

Frideres, J. S., ed. 1989. *Multicultural and intergroup relations*. Westport, CT: Greenwood.

Friesen, G. 1984. *The Canadian Prairies: A history*. Toronto: University of Toronto Press.

Godbout, L. 1991. L'identité exprimée et l'identité vécue du francoalbertain (Communication inédite au colloque ACFAS). Faculté Saint-Jean, University of Alberta, Edmonton.

Herberg, E. N. 1989. *Ethnic groups in Canada*. Scarborough, ON: Nelson.

House of Commons Special Committee on Participation of Visible Minorities. 1984. *Equality now!* Ottawa: Supply and Services.

Jain, H. C. 1985. *Anti-discrimination staffing policies*. Ottawa: Secretary of State.

Jain, H. C. 1988. *Employment discrimination against visible minorities and employment equity*. Ottawa: Multiculturalism and Citizenship.

Li, P. S. 1988. *Ethnic inequality in a class society*. Toronto: Wall and Thompson.

Lodge, D., ed. 1988. *Modern criticism and theory.* New York: Longman.

McDonough, J. 1984. *The protection of the rights of visible minorities.* Edmonton: Alberta Legislative Library for the Commonwealth Parliamentary Association.

MacMillan, M. 1990. "Explaining support for language rights." *Canadian Journal of Political Science* 23:530-47.

Malraux, A. 1935. *Le temps du mépris.* Paris: Gallimard.

Morgan, N. 1988. *The equality game.* Ottawa: Canadian Advisory Council on the Status of Women.

Morin, E. 1987. *Penser l'Europe.* Paris: Gallimard.

Morisette, B. 1991. "The linguistic minorities reconsider their strategy." *Language and Society* 36:8-10.

Munro, K. 1990. "Teaching in the French language in Alberta: An historical perspective." *Alberta* 2:14-18.

Nielsen, G.M., and Jackson, J.M. 1991. "Cultural studies, a sociological poetics: Institutions of the Canadian imaginary." *Canadian Review of Sociology and Anthropology* 28: 279-98.

Nowlan, A. 1969. "Apology." In *The mysterious naked man.* Toronto: Clark Irwin.

Office of the Commissioner of Official Languages. 1990a. *Our two official languages over time.* Ottawa: Supply and Services.

Office of the Commissioner of Official Languages. 1990b. *Annual report.* Ottawa: Supply and Services.

Palmer, H. 1991. "Ethnic relations and the paranoid style: Nativism, nationalism and populism in Alberta 1945-1950." *Canadian Ethnic Studies* 23: 7-31.

Pivato, J. Totosy, S., and Dimic, M., eds. 1991. *Literatures of lesser diffusion.* Edmonton: Research Institute for Comparative Literature, University of Alberta.

Razack, S. 1991. *Canadian feminism and the law.* Toronto: Second Story.

Rea, J.E. 1970. "The roots of Prairie society." In *Prairie perspectives*, ed. D. Gagan. Toronto: Holt Rinehart Winston.

Reaume, D., and Freen, L. 1990. Second class rights? Principles and compromise in the Charter. *Dalhousie Law Journal* 54: 564-93.

Seliger, M. 1969. *The liberal theories of John Locke.* New York: Praeger.

Smith, D.B., 1985. "A history of French-speaking Albertans." In *Peoples of Alberta,* ed. H. Palmer and T. Palmer. Saskatoon: Western Producer.

Sniderman, P., Fletcher, J.F., Russell, P.H., and Tetlock, P. 1989. "Political culture and the problem of double standards: Mass and elite attitudes towards languages rights in the Charter of Rights and Freedoms." *Canadian Journal of Political Science* 22: 258-84.

Sniderman, P., Fletcher, J.F., Russell, P.H., and Tetlock, P. 1990. "Reply." *Canadian Journal of Political Science* 23: 548-555.

Tetley, W. 1991. "Les droits linguistiques: Source de friction, source de protection." In *Droits, liberté, démocratie* (cahier no. 75), ed. J. Lamoureaux. Montreal: Association Canadienne francaise pour l'avancement des sciences.

Todorov, T. 1989. *Nous et les autres: La réflexion francaise sur la diversité humaine.* Paris: Seil.

Treasury Board. 1992. *Official language regulations on service to the public.* Ottawa: Office of the Commissioner of Official Languages.

Turi, J.G. 1989. "The official and the non-official use of language." *Language and Society* 26:37-38.

Verney, D.V. 1986. *Three civilizations, two cultures, one state.* Durham, NC: Duke University Press.

Wolf, D. 1990. "Multiculturalism: A principled approach." *Policy Options* 12:24-25.

FOOTNOTES

1   The Supreme Court's version of this doctrine is discussed by Reaume and Green (1990). Both French and English majorities are prepared to sacrifice minority rights whenever these appear to conflict with their own, according to Charter Project researchers: see Sniderman, Fletcher, Russell, and Tetlock (1989); see also the ensuring debate between MacMillan (1990) and Sniderman, Fletcher, Russell, and Tetlock (1990).

2   Bearing in mind that majority rule was in Locke's time a liberating doctrine, see Seliger (1969), chap.10.2; Verney (1986), chap.8; Rea (1970), pp. 46-155; and Friesen (1984), pp. 216, 241, 454. Palmer (1991) shows

the WASP majority's intolerance of bilingualism and multiculturalism long before "irritant" federal policies came into existence.

3   There is a detailed chronology from 1867 in Office of the Commissioner of Official Languages (199a, 1990b).

4   The distinction is clarified by Turi (1989). The present situation in the West is described in the annual reports of the Commissioner of Official Languages and the Association of Canadian Studies (1989). On the key issue of education, see Munro (1990) and the annual reports of the Office of the Commissioner of Official Languages. After nine years of stalling, and several Supreme Court Challenges, the Alberta Minister of Education has introduced legislation implementing Charter (see. 23) rights to Frendh schools (*Edmonton Journal*, June 22, 1992).

5   According to the Association Canadienne-Francaise de l'Alberta's interpretation of census data. For an in-depth analysis of factors in assimilation, see Godbout (1991). This is part of an ongoing research project by several professors at the Faculté. Cardinal and Lapointe (1990) review sociological theory and argue that fair treatment requires more than the skimpy reforms to date. Francophone Jeunesse de l'Alberta (1991) and Smith (1985) outline Franco-Albertan history to 1981.

6   See other essays in this collection and, more generally, Wolf (1990); Li (1988), critically reviewed by Brym (1989); and Frideres (1989), especially Jean Burnet's article on the origins of multiculturalism in the West. Employment equity is emphasized in the House of Commons Special Committee on Participation of Visible Minorities (1984), McDonough (1984), and Jain (1985, 1988). Razack (1991) analyzed use of the courts against gender discrimination -- an option now largely closed by Ottawa's curtailment of the Court Challenges programme.

7   Tetley (1991) ends in 1989. Post-Meech changes are described in Morissette (1991) and in the annual reports of the Office of the Commissioner of Official Languages.

8   Adapted from Treasury Board (1992), Synoptic Table.

9   See Office of the Commissioner of Official Languages (1990b), 124-130.

10   Fruitful approaches to this problem are suggested by Herberg (1989), chaps. 4-19; and Anderson (1991), 3-18. For the current debate in the EEC, see Todorov (1989) and Morin (1987). Chambers (1992) argues that valued differences are the basis of culture and community. Specific strategies are suggested by the *Action Canada Newsletter* and the Canadian Labour Congress (1992).

11   Polysystem theory in Pivato, Totosy, and Dimic (1991); for examples of the debate on postmodernism and alterity, see Lodge (1988); Nielsen and Jackson (1991) define Canadian identity as lived culture(s).

12   The Supreme Court's version of this doctrine is discussed by Reaume and Green (1990). Both French and English majorities are prepared to sacrifice minority rights whenever these appear to conflict with their own, according to Charter Project researchers: see Sniderman, Fletcher,

Russell and Tetlock (1989); see also the ensuing debate between MacMillan (2990) and Sniderman, Fletcher, Russell, and Tetlock (1990).

13 Bearing in mind that majority rule was in Locke's time a liberating doctrine, see Martin Seliger The LIberal Theories of John Locke (New York: Praeger, 1969) ch. 10.2 "The Majority's power and its use"; Douglas V. Verney Three Civilizations, Two Cultures, One State (Durham NC: Duke University Press, 1986) ch.8 "French Canada and the Triumph of Majority Rule"; J.E. Rea "The Roots of Prairie Society" pp.46-55 in D. Gagan (ed.) Prairie Perspectives (Toronto: Holt Rinehart Winston, 1970); Gerald Friesen the Canadian Prairies: a History (Toronto: U of T Press, 1984), pp.216, 241, 454. Howard Palmer "Ethnic relations and the paranoid style: nativism, nationalism and populism in Alberta 1945-1950" Canadian Ethnic Studies 23.3 (1991) 7-31 shows the WASP majority's intolerance of bilingualism and multiculturalism, long before "irritant" federal policies came into existence.

14 There is a detailed chronology from 1867 in (hereafter OCOL) Office of the Commissioner of Official Languages/Commissariat aux Langues Officielles, Our Official Languages over Time/Nos deux langues officielles au fil des ans (Ottawa, 1990); and OCOL Annual Report 1990 / Rapport Annuel 1990, "Preface".

15 The distinction is clarified by Joseph G. Turi, "The official and the non-official use of language / De l'usage officiel et non-officiel des langues," Language and Society/Langue et Société 26 (Spring 1989) 37-38. The present situation in the West is described in OCOL Annual Reports, "Province by province review/De province en province"; Association of Canadian Studies, Demonlinguistic Trends and the Evolution of Canadian Institutions/Tendances démolinguistiques et évolution des institutions canadiennes (ACS, Canadian Themes series, 1989). On the key issue of education, see Kenneth Munro, "Teaching in the French language in Alberta: an historical perspective," Alberta 2.2 (1990) * and ACOL Annual Reports. After nine years' stalling, and several Supreme Court challenges, the Alberta Minister of Education has introduced legislation implementing Charter (s23) rights to French schools: Edmonton Journal June 22, 1992.

16 According to the Association Canadienne-Francaise de l'Alberta's interpretation of census data. For in-depth analysis of factors in assimilation, see Laurent Godbout (Faculté Saint-Jean, University of Alberta), "L'identité exprimée et l'identité vécue du francoalbertain," communication inédite au colloque ACFAS, Edmonton, Oct. 1991. This is part of an ongoing research project by several professors at the Faculté. Linda Cardinal and Jean Lapointe review sociological theory, and argue that fair treatment requires more than the skimpy reforms to date, in "La sociologie des Francophones hors Québec: un parti-pris pour l'autonomie," Canadian Ethnic Studies 22.1 (1990) 47-66. Francophone Jeunesse de l'Alberta, Portrait de l'histoire francophone en Alberta (Edmonton: pamphlet, 1991) and Donald B. Smith, "A history of French-speaking Albertans," pp.84-108 in Howard and Tamara Palmer, (eds.)

Peoples of Alberta (Saskatoon: Western Producer, 1985) outline Franco-albertan history to 1981.

17 See other papers in this collection, and more generally, Dennis Wolf, "Multiculturalism: a principled approach" Policy Options (Oct 1990) 24-25; Peter S. Li, Ethnic Inequality in a Class Society (Toronto: Wall and Thompson, 1988), critically reviewed by Robert Brym, Canadian Ethnic Studies 21.3 (1989) 127-128; James S. Frideres (ed.) Multicultural and Intergroup Relations (Westport, CT: Greenwood, 1989), especially Jean Burnet's article on the origins of multiculturalism in the West. Employment equity is emphasized in the House of Commons Special Committee on Participation of Visible Minorities, Equality Now! (Ottawa: Queen's Printer, 1984); John McDonough, The Protection of the Rights of Visible Minorities (Edmonton: Alberta Legislative Library for the Commonwealth Parliamentary Association, 1984); Harish C. Jain, Anti-Discrimination Staffing Policies (Ottawa: Secretary of State, 1985) and Employment Discrimination against visible minorities and Employment Equity (Ottawa: Multiculturalism and Citizenship, 1988). Sherene Razack, Canadian Feminism and the Law (Toronto: Second Story, 1991) analyses use of the courts against gender discrimination - an option now largely closed by Ottawa's curtailment of the Court Challenges program.

18 William Tetley, "Les droits linguistiques: source de friction, source de protection" pp.249-261 in Jocelyne Lamoureaux (dir.) Droits, Liberté Démocratie (Montreal: Association Canadienne Francaise pour l'Avancement des Sciences, cahier no. 75, 1991) ends in 1989. Post-Meech changes are described in Brigitte Morissette, "The linguistic minorities reconsider their strategy - Les minoritiés linguistiques repensent leur stratégie," Language and Society - Langue et Sociét e (autumn 1991) 8-10; and in OCOL Annual Reports.

19 Adapted from the "Synoptic Table / Tableau synoptique" of Treasury Board / Conseil du Trésor du Canada, Official Language Regulations on Service to the Public / Règlement en matière de service au public dans les deux langues officielles (Ottawa: OCOL, 1992).

20 Adapted from the "Synoptic Table / Tableau synoptique" of Treasury Board / Conseil du Trésor du Canada, Official Language Regulations on Service to the Public / Règlement en matière de service au public dans les deux langues officielles (Ottawa: OCOL, 1992).

21 Fruitful approaches to this problem are suggested by Edward N. Herberg, Ethnic Groups in Canada (Scarborough: Nelson, 1989) ch.4-9; Perry Anderson, "Nation-states and national identity" [review of Fernand Braudel, The Identity of France], London Review of Books (9 March 1991) 3-8; for the current debate in the EEC see Tzvetan Todorov, Nous et les autres: la réflexion française sur la diversité humaine (Paris: Seil, 1989), and Edgar Morin, Penser l'Europe (Paris: Gallimard, 1987). Ross Chambers' (Romance Languages, University of Michigan) "No Montagues without Capulets: some thoughts on cultural identity,"

unpublished paper in Explorations in Difference: Law, Politics and Culture conference (Law School, University of Alberta, 19-21 March 1992) argues that valued differences are the basis of culture and community. Specific strategies are suggested by the Action Canada Newsletter and the Canadian Labour Congress Action Plan (Ottawa; CLC, 1992).

22   E.P.Thompson, The Making of the English Working Class (New York: Vintage, 1963), Preface.

23   Polysystem theory in Joseph Pivato, Stephan Totosy, and Milan Dimic (eds.) Literatures of Lesser Diffusion (Edmonton: University of Alberta, Research Institute for Comparative Literature, 1991); for examples of the debate on post-modernism and alterity, David Lodge (ed.) Modern Criticism and Theory (New York: Longman, 1988); Greg M. Nielsen and John M. Jackson "Cultural studies, a sociological poetics: institutions of the Canadian imaginary" Canadian review of Sociology and Anthropology 28.2 (1991) 279-298 define Canadian identity as lived culture(s).

Renée Delorme
Calgary

14

Minoritaire de Naissance ou L'alienation des Communautes Francophones Minoritaires du Canada

AVERITSSEMENT

Cet article est un témoignage basé sur mes expériences et mes observations en tant qu'intervenante activement impliquée au développement des communautés minoritaires de langues officielles au Canada. Il n'est pas le résultat d'une recherche mener selon les normes universitaires. Quoique certaines données (surtot celles statistiques) soient accompagnées de références, l'analyse comme telle du sujet est davantage intuitive que discursive. Ainsi se voulait d'ailleurs, la conférence <<Freedom Within the Margins>>.

INTRODUCTION

Même si certaines minorités francophones possèdent toutes les institutions qui leur permettent de s'épanouir et savent que leurs gouvernements sont sympathiques à leur cause, ces dernières vivent le même drame que les minorités les plus démunies. Ce drame est celui de devoir vivre en marge de la société afin d'éviter le génocide linguistique et culturel. Ainsi, les Acadiens et les Franco-Ontariens, tout comme les Franco-Colombiens et les Albertains vivent en constant état de vulnérabilité, d'insécurité et d'aliénation.

    Minoritaire de naissance (Franco-Ontarienne) et munie d'une formation en développement communautaire, j'ai été amenée à vivre et à oeuvrer pour diverses communautés francophones en situation minoritaire au Canada. A partir de mon expérience personnelle, je tenterai de démontrer que le niveau de développement d'une minorité n'allège pas son état premier. En fait, le niveau de développement d'une communauté réussit tout au plus à exorciser, pour un certain temps, cette profonde peur qui est de perdre tôt ou tard ses racines.

ÉTUDE COMPARATIVE DE QUATRE COMMUNAUTÉS FRANCOPHONES MINORITAIRES AU CANADA

Les deux tableaux ci-joints illustrent les acquis et le développement de quatres communautés francophones minoritaires au Canada. Les communautés du Nouveau-Brunswick et de l'Ontario sont celles qui ont le mieux réussit à se doter de solides assises politiques, économiques et culturelles. Ces deux communautés sont relativement importantes par rapport à la population de leur province et leur poids politique est suffisant pour influencer les décisions de leurs gouvernements. A l'opposé se trouvent les communautés francophones de l'Alberta et de la Colombie-Britannique. Afin de survivre, ces dernières doivent déployer toutes leurs énergies afin d'obtenir et de conserver le infrastructures de base de leur développement (ex. écoles francophones).

En comparant les 4 communautés francophones (voir les deux tableaux ci-joints) il est évident que les Acadiens et les Franco-Ontariens jouissent d'un niveau de développement très avancé par rapport aux deux communautés de l'Ouest. Ils possèdent tout ce dont une communauté a besoin pour non seulement survivre, mais aussi pour s'épanouir. En fait, ces deux communautés pourraient "s'assirent sur leurs lauriers" et jouir de leurs acquis. Curieusement ce n'est pas le cas. Au contraire, les deux communautés francophones minoritaires les plus développées du pays vivent les mêmes craintes que les deux communautés les plus démunies. Le spectre de l'assimilation et la peur de perdre les acquis sont vécus de façon tout aussi intense dans les quatre cas.

Afin d'illustrer ce fait, voici quelques extraits d'une série d'articles intitulés *Les enfants du divorce ... à venir?* préparée par l'Agence de presse francophone en octobre 1991. Ces articles ont été rédigés par des journalistes locaux. Ils illustrent les réactions des francophones minoritaires face à la crise constitutionnelle du Canada.

M. Jean L. Pedneault, journaliste au nord-ouest du Nouveau-Brunswick écrit:

> Au Madawaska, les gens (...) sont indépendants, voire même autosuffisants. (...) Ni Américains, ni Québécois, les Madawaskayens émettent des réserves sérieuses concernant le projet d'union des provinces maritimes. L'intérêt pour l'union économique qui semble séduire ailleurs s'estompe en ce milieu francophone (96 pour cent) lorsqu'il est question d'union politique. La crainte de voir la langue et la culture diluées dans l'économie inquiet. "La population du Madawaska veut un développement économique plus accéléré, mais elle ne veut pas une structure qui va menacer sa langue et sa culture," affirme M. J. Pius Bard, maire d'Edmundston et président de la légendaire République du Madawaska."

> (...) Les gens du Madawaska savent bien que l'époque de l'État-Providence est révolue. Ils ne veulent pas être traités en minoritaires. Ils se considèrent depuis longtemps comme des égaux par rapport au Québec, à l'Ontario et au reste du pays. Ils veulent une meilleure économie, ainsi que la protection de la culture et de la langue."

Au nord-est de cette même province, lejournaliste M. Bertin Couturier a rédigé ce qui suit:

> "Contrairement à d'autres régions du Canada, les Acadiens de la Péninsule n'ont pas à se préoccuper du problème de l'assimilation. Bien sûr, il faut toujours faire preuve de vigilance. Ce qui explique la ténacité dont font preuve les gens de la Péninsule" explique Percy Mallet de Shippagan, qui est agent touristique pour la province du Nouveau-Brunswick. (...) "Il m'arrive souvent, dit-il, d'entendre parler des francophones de Terre-Neuve, de Vancouver et même de l'Ontario. Ces gens-là connaissent notre histoire et la lutte que nous avons menée pour survivre en tant que peuple"."

> "(...) Si la province de Québec se sépare du reste du pays, ce sera extrêmement dramatique pour notre peuple sur tous les plans. Au niveau linguistique, comment voulez-vous que nos droits soient respectés dans un Canada anglais? Et sur le plan économique, nos institutions auront bien du

mal à recevoir leurs argents provenant du Secrétariat d'État."

"(...) On a toutes les misères au monde à se faire entendre dans notre province, bien que nous représentons le tiers de la population relève avec de justesse Martin Légère. "Imaginez alors la situation, si l'on doit vivre à l'intérieur des Maritimes. On va être totalement noyé dans une marée anglophone. Pour nous c'est un scénario inacceptable"."

En Ontario la situation ressemble à celle du Nouveau-Brunswick. Le journaliste, M. Robert Bousquet écrit:

"(...) Glengarry-Prescott-Russell (...) est la circonscription fédérale qui compte la plus forte concentration de francophones à l'ouest du Québec, soit deux habitants sur trois. (...) Le député fédéral Don Boudria se considère choyé quant à l'intérêt que ses concitoyens portent au débat constitutionnel, et à la question de la place des Canadiens français au sein du pays. "ils sont plus inquiets dans mon compté qu'ils ne le sont ailleurs. (...) En vérité, cette inquiétude concerne davantage les autres communautés francophones du Canada. M. Boudria convient que le nombre de citoyens d'expression françaises dans sa circonscription leur accorde "une certaine confiance de conserver leur langue plus qu'ailleurs, mais ils ne veulent pas tomber entre deux chaises. Ils veulent être des Canadiens et se sentir chez eux en français et en anglais"."

Au nord de l'Ontario la journaliste Florence Meney explique:

"En général, les francophones du Nord ont fait de grands progrès depuis trente ans dans leur lutte pour faire reconnaître leurs droits: "Nous disposons maintenant non seulement de paroisses et d'écoles d'expression française, mais aussi de tout un réseau de centres culturels, de journaux, de théâtres, d'entreprises de gens d'affaires, d'artistes, bref, d'une vie en français. (...) avec la loi 8 de 1986 sur les services en français, nous avons obtenu une place officielle dans la vie politique et institutionnelle de l'Ontario." (...) Si le Québec réclame le démantèlement des pouvoirs du fédéral au profit des provinces, cela risque à long terme de manacer les droits des francophones, droits acquis à force de batailles au cours des trente dernières années."

Selon le journaliste M. Denis-Martin Chabot, en Alberta:

"Même si les commissions scolaires acceptent plus facilement qu'auparavant de créer des écoles françaises, les 60,000 Franco-Albertains n'en ont toujours pas la gestion. Ils doivent, dans la plupart des cas, s'en remettre à des autorités scolaires anglophones et quémander chaque nouveau service. (...) Pire que l'assimilation, la nouvelle crainte des Franco-Albertains est de servir de monnaie d'échange dans le cadre des présentes négociations constitutionnelles. "On pourrait tout perdre," craint Mme. Levasseur-Ouimet. "Ce gouvernement (conservateur) ne s'est jamais montré très généreux envers les francophones. C'est pas demain qu'il le sera"."

TABLEAU 1. DONNÉES DÉMOGRAPHIQUES DES MINORITÉS D'EXPRESSION FRANCAISE*

Province	Pop. Total	Minorité Fr. L.M.F.	% Pop. Total	Pop. Bilingue
C.-B	2,883,375	45,830	1.59%	179,130
Alberta	2,365,830	56,040	2.37%	152,018
Ontario	9,101,690	482,440	5.3%	1,066,281
N.-B.	709,445	237,220	33.44%	206,733

*   Stat. Can. 1986

Notes: - Minorités francophones concentres à env. 80% en milieux urbains (Vancouver, Victoria, Edmonton, Calgary, Timmins, Sudbury, North Bay, Ottawa, Toronto, Windsor, Moncton), sauf pour le Nouveau-Brunswick dont la pop. est répartie le long de la côte du Nord-Est de la province dans des petits villages et des petites villes.
        - L'Ontario a la plus grosse minorité en chiffres absolus.
        - Le N.-B. a la plus grosse minorité/rapport à sa pop. totale assurant un certain pouvoir politique et économique.

Pendant ce temps en Colombie-Britannique, le journaliste M. Daniel Bélanger explique:

"Chinois, Japonais, Allemands, Coréens, Italiens, Français, Hindous, Portugais... A travers cette diversité ethnique, la communauté francophone de la Colombie-Britannique passe presque inaperçue. Elle est invisible. (...) Le multiculturalisme se vit et se voit autant dans les rues que dans les cours décoles. Sur l'échiquier des nombres, les Francophones forment à peine 2 pour cent (45,845) de toute la population Britanno-Colombienne. (...) Pour ce qui est de l'avenir du Canada, M. Painchaud est plus prudent. La francophonie à l'extérieur du Québec n'est pas la priorité du gouvernement. "Il faut d'abord régler globalement le problème autochtone. Cela va possiblement redéfinir la carte canadienne. Une fois ce dossier réglé, le prochain défi sera de vaincre l'intolérance et d'apprendre à accepter les autres comme les Noirs àMontréal et à Toronto, les Asiatiques en Colombie-Britannique, ou les minorités slaves dans les Prairies," explique le producteur.

(...) La Colombie-Britannique rejoint peu à peu les autres provinces en ce qui a trait à la prestation de service en français, mais le passé n'est pas garant de l'avenir."

CONCLUSION

Jusqu'à présent, la principale stratégie de développement qu'ont adopté les communautés francophones est celle de plus ou moins vivre en "vase clos." C'est à dire de vivre en marge de la société avec ses institutions, sa langue et sa culture. C'est aussi la stratégie qu'a adopté le Québec en tant que communauté minoritaire au Canada et la raison pour laquelle elle réclame un statut de société distincte. Cette stratégie est, à mon avis, à la base du problème de communication et d'incompréhension qui existe entre les "deux solitudes" canadiennes (les peuples anglophones et francophones). Si les communautés francophones veulent améliorer leur état en tant que communautés minoritaires un changement de stratégie s'impose. Il est urgent que les communautés francophones "rayonnent." On doit encourager le dialogue entre les deux communautés de langues officielles ainsi qu'entre toutes les autres communautés ethniques. Il est plus facile de respecter sinon de tolérer les différentes d'autrui lors/qu'on les connaît. Cette stratégie comporte évidemment beaucoup de risques pour les communautés minoritaires puisqu'/elle exige de ces dernières qu'elles s'exposent aux influences culturelles et linguistiques

TABLEAU 2. ACQUIS DES MINORITÉS FRANCOPHONES

	Colombie-Britannique	Alberta	Ontario	Nouveau-Brunswick
Éducation	• 3 écoles et programme cadre dans 25 districts • formation des maîtres dans 2 universités	• 21 écoles dont 6 homogènes • gestion scolaire • formation des maîtres dans 2 universités • Faculté St-Jean	• 302 écoles • 2 systèmes scolaires homogènes (catholique et séparé) • gestion scolaire parallèle • 2 collèges universitaires • 6 collèges communautaires • 2 universités bilingues	• 147 écoles • 3 centres scolaires communautaires • gestion scolaire parallèle • 1 université francophone avec 3 campus • 4 collèges communautaires
Économie	• plusieurs entrepreneurs et mouvements coopératifs s'impose nt de+en+	• plusieurs entrepreneurs	• mouvements des caisses pop et des coopératives imposant (1.7 milliard $ en 1988) • 18,176 entrepreneurs francophones	• 7,088 entrepreneurs • mouvement coopératif imposant (792 millions $)
Communication	• hebdo "le Soleil de la Colombie" • Radio Can local	• hebdo "le Franco" • Radio Can local	• quotidien "le Droit" • 13 hebdo • Radio Can local • TV Ontario • 7 radios privées • 2 radios communautaires	• quotidien "l'Acadie Nouvelle" • 3 hebdo • Radio Can local • 6 radios communautaires

TABLEAU 2. ACQUIS DES MINORITÉS FRANCOPHONES (...SUITE)

Culture			
• 5 centres culturels • quelques festivals (dont la Fête Colombienne" qui attirent 20,000 enfants) • 1 troupe de danse • 2 comp. de films et vidéo • 1 chorale • 175 artistes prof. • la Maison de la francophonie • 1 Comité culturel prov. **NOTE:** Francophones de transit. Essentiellement pas de racines et de culture locales.	• 10 ass. culturelles • 10 troupes de théâtre (dont 2 prof.) • 6 groupes de danse folklorique • 10 évenm. spéciaux culturels/année • 100 artistes prof. • 10 groupes d'artistes amateurs • regroupements sectoriels (femmes, aînés, jeunes etc.) **NOTE:** Certaines communautés francophones avec racines/culture typiquement de l'Ouest (Communauté du Nord) • Certaine culture locale.	• + de 20 centres culturels diffuseurs la culture. • innombrable clubs et comités culturels • troupes de théâtre: 6 prof., 1 pour les écoles, 20 amateurs (50 profes., 400 amateurs ... 600 représentations/année • festivals d'envergure (ex. Festival franco-ontarien et La nuit sur l'étang). • 4 maisons d'éditions • centre folklorique franco-ontarien • 1,339 artistes professionnels (dont plz de réputation mondial) • 8 ass. artistiques profes. **NOTE:** culture et racines essentiellement Franco-Ontariennes. Aucun lien québécois ... culture locale.	• + de 15 institutions diffuseurs de produits culturels (ex. muses, salles de spectacles, Village acadiens, etc.) • imp. infrastructure communautaire (3 csc, 13 soc. culturelles, 30 festivals, réseau de tournée scolaire, etc. • + de 15 entreprises artistiques (ex. théâtre, danse, etc.) • 250 artistes prof. (réputation national et intern.) • plz ass. prof. pour artistes et artisans • Centre acadien du tourisme • 2 maisons d'éditions **NOTE:** les Acadiens se définissent comme "peuple" (350 ans d'histoire). culture locale très forte.

NOTE: Les minorités de l'Ontario et du Nouveau-Brunswick ont des pouvoirs politiques et économiques réels.

TABLEAU 2. ACQUIS DES MINORITÉS FRANCOPHONES (...CONT'D)

Organisation Communautaire	• env. 6 org. prov.	• env. 8 org. prov.	• + de 39 org. prov.	• env. 20 org. prov.
Politique	• 1989, loi scolaire prov. révisée pour offrir droit à l'éd. en franç.	• loi 60 ... anglais seule langue officielle de l'Alberta • 1988, loi scolaire prov. révisée pour offrir droit à l'éd. en franç. • 1990, Cours Suprême donne droit à la gestion scolaire.	• 1970, française à statut officiel al'Assemblée législative • 1984, français à statut officiel devant les tribunaux et en éducation • 1986, loi 75 sur la gestion scolaire franç. • 1988, loi sur les services publics prov. en franç. (dans 22 régions)	• 1969, loi sur les l.o. (prov. devient bilingue) • 1973, ministère de l'éducation reconnaît la dualité linguistique • 2 réseaux scolaires parallèles et homogènes • 1981, loi reconnaît l'égalité des 2 communautés linguistiques au N.-B. • 1982, loi constitutionnelle enchâsse la reconnaissance des 2 l.o.

extérieures et par conséquent aux possibilitées d'un génocide culturel. C'est pourquoi une telle stratégie ne pourra être vraiment efficace que si ensemble les communautés canadiennes (minoritaires et majoritaires) l'adoptent.

BIBLIOGRAPHIE

Bélanger, Daniel; Bousquet, Robert; Chabot, Denis-Martin; Couturier, Bertin; Meney, Florence; Pedneault, Jean L., *Les enfants du divorce ... à venir ?*, serie d'articles commandités par l'Agence de la presse francophone, octobre 1991.

Secrétariat d'État du Canada, Ottawa, *Fiches sommaires des communautés minoritaires de langues officielles*, 1991.

Leclerc, Jean-Claude, 4 mai, 1992. *Quebec's not the only area in trouble*, article du Montreal Gazette.

PART VI

IMMIGRANT HISTORIES

Être Minoritaire au sein d'une Minorité: Mon Expérience Personnelle en Tant Que Libanaise au Sein de la Communauté Francophone de Calgary

Je suis d'origine libanaise et je vis au Canada depuis quatre ans. Dès mon arrivée à Calgary en novembre 1987, je me suis impliquée dans la communauté francophone. Pourquoi? Le français étant ma deuxième langue, certains pourraient dire que c'était par facilité. Et ce n'est pas tout à fait faux. Mais je parlais déjà anglais avant de venir ici, avec un accent, bien sûr, mais qui n'en a pas? J'aurais donc pu faire comme la plupart des émigrants qui arrivent en Alberta i.e. m'intégrer à la majorité anglophone même si cela signifiait oublier graduellement le français que j'avais appris à l'école. Cela aurait peut-être été dommage mais sûrement pas la fin du monde.

Si les choses se sont passées différemment, c'est surtout par hasard. Deux semaines à peine après mon arrivée à Calgary, alors que je ne savais même pas encore prendre le bus, je travaillais à l'A.C.F.A. régionale de Calgary. Là, j'ai appris beaucoup de choses sur le Canada, la politique canadienne et surtout les droits et revendications des Canadiens francophones. Je dois avouer qu'à l'époque j'entendais plutôt parler de Canadiens français, mais depuis j'ai compris bien des choses entre autres que j'avais des droits moi aussi. Quatre ans plus tard donc, je me permets le luxe de refuser l'emploi du mot "canadien français" pour adopter à la place un mot qui, à mon avis, correspond plus à la réalité canadienne, celui de "canadien francophone".

Mais en arriver là n'a pas été facile et ne s'est pas non plus fait du jour au lendemain. D'abord, il m'a fallu comprendre ce que le

terme canadien français signifie: une personne née au Canada,
dont les parents et les grands-parents sont eux aussi nés au Canada.
En deux mots, c'est un descendant des premiers colons français qui
sont venus s'installer en Amérique du Nord et donc un membre de
l'un des peuples fondateurs du Canada. Un Canadien français ou
une Canadienne française est, pour les mêmes raisons, une
personne nécessairement catholique.

Je n'ai pas grand chose en commun avec les Canadiens
français. Je ne suis pas catholique, pas même chrétienne. Je n'ai
pas de sang français dans les veines, du moins je ne le pense pas.
Aucun de mes ancêtres n'a, à ma connaissance, colonisé ne fut-ce
qu'un mètre carré de l'Amérique du Nord. Au fait, ils étaient bien
plus occupés à essayer de se débarrasser des colons qui avaient
envahi leur patrie. Aucun d'eux n'a donc contribué à la fondation
du Canada.

Non, je ne suis pas canadienne française. Mais depuis que le
Canada est devenu d'abord mon lieu de résidence et ensuite ma
patrie, je considère que j'y ai une place moi aussi. Et si cette place
se trouve au sein de la communauté francophone, c'est parce que ça
fait quatre ans déjà que je lutte avec les francophones afin de
promouvoir leurs droits et les miens. Ces derniers ne sont pas
toujours les mêmes. Les Canadiens français voient dans les écoles
par exemple un moyen de transmettre à leurs enfants leur langue
française, leur culture canadienne française ainsi que leur foi
catholique puisque, pour la plupart d'entre eux, les trois sont
inévitablement liés. Quant à moi, je ne vois dans les écoles que des
établissements purement scolaires. leur existence n'en est pas
moins essentielle à mon avis puisque cèst grâce à eux que le
français continuera àexister en Amérique du Nord. Nous luttons
donc ensemble, si l'on peut dire, même si nous ne le faisons pas
pour les mêmes raisons. En effet, nous voulons tous améliorer,
développer et augmenter le nombre des écoles francophones qui
existent déjà. Mais les Canadiens français veulent en même temps
conserver un système scolaire établi depuis longtemps, un système
scolaire quirépond uniquement aux besoins de l'élite canadienne
française. Moi, par contre, je voudrais voir toutes les écoles
francophones ouvertes à toute personne, indépendamment de sa
race, sa couleur, son origine, sa religion, à toute personne donc qui
désire quelle-même ou que ses enfants apprennent le français.

Pour les Canadiens français, les organismes culturels et
communautaires sont un autre moyen de promouvoir leur héritage
culturel et surtout de faire valoir leurs droits en tant que membres
de l'un des peuples fondateurs du Canada. Ayant une histoire et une
culture différentes ainsi que des racines ancrées dans un autre
pays, je ne peux faire partie de ces organismes que s'ils s'ouvrent à

tous les francophones sans exception et seulement s'ils revendiquent des droits linguistiques plutôt que culturels et historiques. Certains pourraient me dire que ces droits linguistiques sont basés sur l'histoire même du Canada. Cela, je ne le nie pas. Bien sûr qu'ils le sont, mais est-ce tellement important quand l'histoire même des Canadiens français montre que l'isolement ne représente pas le meilleur moyen de survie? L'histoire peut être apprise et respectée. Elle peut également servir d'exemple mais pas de prétexte pour vivre dans le passé. Les émigrants qui affluent au Canada depuis des générations ont donné à ce pays un visage nouveau dans lequel couleurs et races s'enchevêtrent. La plupart des Canadiens français de Calgary, pour ne parler que de ceux-là, voient un danger, une menace à leur propre survie dans cet afflux d'étrangers, tandis que moi personnellement j'y vois un avantage pour ces mêmes Canadiens français. Vous me direz que c'est normal puisque je fais moi-même partie de ces groupes d'émigrants. Je dois avouer qu'il est difficile d'avoir des préjugés contre soi-même. Mais si je dis avantage, c'est surtout parce que je vois beaucoup de francophones arriver au Canada. Ces derniers, s'ils sont acceptés dans la communauté francophone et s'ils s'y intègrent bien, vont nécessairement contribuer à la promotion du français.

Sans être la seule, je suis l'une des rares personnes d'origine ni française ni canadienne française à être impliquée dans la communauté francophone de Calgary. Pourquoi, vous me direz. Et c'est vrai, pourquoi? Pourquoi ne pas m'être plutôt impliquée dans la communauté anglophone de Calgary qui, parce qu'elle est plus grande, est inévitablement formée d'un plus grand nombre de gens originaires de différents pays? Pourquoi ne pas m'être plutôt jointe aux groupes d'émigrants qui pourtant ne manquent pas ici? Et pourquoi est-ce que les Canadiens français accepteraient parmi eux des gens comme moi qui, s'ils deviennent plus nombreux, pourraient au fil des années les rendre minoritaires au sein même de leur communauté? Est-ce parce que le mot multiculturalisme est à la mode et que le gouvernement fédéral sans lequel les groupes francophones ne peuvent exister semble en raffoler? Peut-être. Mais, au fond, la communauté francophone de Calgary ne m'a jamais tout à fait acceptée. Elle ne m'a jamais rejetée non plus, ça je dois bien l'avouer.

Il m'est difficile de vous expliquer une telle situation. Je vais quand même essaryer de le faire en reprenant l'exemple des écoles. J'en ai beaucoup parlé tout à l'heure parce que je considère que l'éducation est primordiale, qu'elle est à la base de tout. Je suis sûre que les Canadiens français de Calgary reconnaissent eux aussi l'importance des écoles. La preuve c'est qu'ils luttent depuis plusieurs années déjà pour essayer d'établir l'un de leurs plus grands projets: un centre scolaire communautaire. Mais, encore une fois, ce projet est parrainé par la commission scolaire catholique de Calgary, ce qui signifie que les élèves, les professeurs et les autres employés de cet établissement devront être catholiques pour y être acceptés.

Franchement, je ne comprends pas pourquoi les Canadiens français veulent priver le reste des francophones d'une éducation en français. L'un d'eux à qui j'avais un jour posé cette question, m'a répondu: "Mais le centre scolaire communautaire ne sera pas seulement une école. Une fois les classes terminées, tous les enfants, quelle que soit leur origine ou leur religion, pourront y aller pour participer aux activités culturelles et sportives qui s'y dérouleront." Comment est-ce que je pouvais réagir à une telle réponse? Je n'ai pas le droit de travailler dans ce centre, mes enfants... au fait, je n'en ai pas et maintenant que j'y pense, je suis bien contente de ne pas en avoir... mais si j'avais eu des enfants, ces derniers n'auraient pas pu étudier dans ce centre. Est-ce que cela signifie que je ne suis pas acceptée dans la communauté francophone de Calgary? Bien sûr que non puisqu'on me permettrait d'aller au centre les après-midi et les fins de semaine pour danser et jouer à la balle.

Il doit vous sembler bizarre de tant entendre parler de religion à une époque où il y a de moins en moins de pratiquants. Mais il ne faut pas oublier que la religion catholique fait partie de l'histoire et de la culture des Canadiens français. Il ne faut donc pas s'étonner qu'une grande partie de ces Canadiens français s'y accrochent encore afin de ne rien perdre de leurs traditions et donc de leurs droits. Ces geens-là semblent s'en servir comme d'une arme contre les gens qui, comme moi, viennent à peine d'arriver chez eux et demandent déjà des changements au sein même de leur communauté. Mais, je le répète, le Canada n'est plus ce qu'il était au début du siècle. Pour éviter de se faire écraser par la majorité anglophone, pour également préserver et promouvoir leurs droits, les Canadiens français devraient essayer de se faire des alliés de tous les francophones qui vivent au Canada. Après tout, l'union fait la force.

C. Hus and S. Deutschlander
Concordia College and German-Canadian
Association of Alberta
Edmonton

Immigrants of German Origin on the Prairies: Diverse Cultural and Ethnic Identities

The German immigrant experience on the Prairies is one of diverse culture and identity. Emigration to Canada after World War II has occurred mainly from Eastern Europe, which had for hundreds of years been the homeland for a large number of German settlers. As a result of outside pressures in conjunction with unifying forces from the inside, a simplified and superficial image of German culture has evolved. If the German cultural heritage is to be revived for succeeding generations, a new awareness of contemporary German culture must be sought. In this essay we examine the stereotyping of German groups by outsiders as opposed to the process of subjective identity formation. We will analyze the role of churches, schools, clubs, and businesses as sustainers of German culture and traditions.

IMMIGRANTS OF GERMAN ORIGIN.

Canadians of German ethnic origin form the second largest ethno cultural group on the Prairies. They show a particularly high concentration in the province of Alberta (Weissenborn 1978). During the early post-war period, immigrants of German origin formed the second largest group to enter Alberta. Most of these immigrants, however, did not come from within the German national boundaries.

The phrase "of German origin" describes a wide range of cultural and geographical characteristics. Throughout the period of German migration to Canada, national borders in Europe changed dramatically. In addition to the shifting political boundaries of the German state, the German population has migrated widely both within and beyond Europe. The vast majority of German-speaking immigrants in the three Prairie provinces originated from German-speaking enclaves in Eastern Europe or the United States. For example: as early as 1886, the province of Manitoba registered 11,086 German settlers, but only a fraction of these listed Germany as their place of birth. Most were born in Russia and Poland (McLaughlin 1985, 10). Consequently, people of German descent display many different linguistic and religious characteristics.

The concept of ethnicity is not easily defined. It encompasses not only nationality, citizenship, and birth place, but also includes language as well as religious, political, and economic traditions. A common ethnic identity may find expression in a particular way of perceiving the world and a common manner of interpreting events. It may stimulate a feeling of solidarity and give meaning to life in a special way. Germans on the Prairies constitute such a diversified group, with such different histories and varieties of experience that they lack a common identity. Indeed, they can be better understood as "an involuntary group of people who share the same culture or descendants of such people who identify themselves and/or are identified by others as belonging to the same involuntary group" (Isajiw 1974, 122). Their identification as an ethnic group develops to a large extent through the apperception of other ethnic groups. The Germans' sense of distinctiveness evolved mainly from stereotypes of their mentality and character as expressed by non Germans. Before World War I, German immigrants were considered of dominant race with untiring energy and great foresight (Palmer 1982, 27). They were generally regarded as sober, industrious and loyal subjects.

Use of the German language is perhaps the central criterion by which German ethnicity is defined, but even the concept of "mother tongue" is imprecise. It has been defined differently in different Canadian census periods, first as the "language of customary speech" (1921) and later as the "language first learned in childhood and still understood" (1941).

The definition of "ethnic origin" used by the Canadian census provides an even more confused account of German ethnicity. The 1981 census defines ethnic origin as the ethnic or cultural group to which the respondent's ancestors belonged when they first came to Canada. It takes into account both maternal and paternal ancestors, whereas the 1971 census considered ethnic ancestry only on the male side. Immigration Canada classifies a person as German according to citizenship, racial origin, or tongue (Keyserlingk 1984).

Muddled conceptualization by bureaucrats is not the only source of inconsistency. The stigma associated with German ancestry, which arose particularly during both world wars, lead many respondents to deny their German heritage. In 1912 the Prairie provinces showed a German population of 148,000, which by 1921 had decreased, according to the census, to 123,000.

THE IMPACT OF POLITICAL CHANGES IN THE OLD WORLD ON HETEREOGENEITY IN THE NEW..

Political and economic difficulties as well as religious conflicts, combined with a growing population, motivated Germans to migrate early in their history. In the seventeenth century Czar Peter the Great opened the Russian state up to German settlers, and during the eighteenth century the Empress Catherine the Great promised them religious freedom and exemption from military service. Germans founded farming settlements in Volhynia, Bessarabia, the Caucasus, and in areas around the Black Sea, and the Volga. Germans settled in Galicia, Transylvania, Bohemia, Moravia, and the Sudeten range.

In the nineteenth century the German empire emerged as a power in its own right and consequently posed a threat to Russian hegemony. All German colonists were now considered Russian citizens and became subject to duties and provisions as determined by the Crown. When military service became compulsory in 1874, many Germans felt forced to leave. These ethnic Germans had resisted assimilation into their host countries for many generations. Many of them turned to Canada: the vast Prairie provinces needed farm labour, and the Canadian government offered land and religious freedom. In Canada the German immigrants from Eastern Europe hoped to preserve their independent existence. With a strong sense of their cultural roots, particularly among the Mennonites and Hutterites, they sought to reconstruct "their old way of life in the New World" (Bassler 1978, 9).

Before World War I the mainstream of German immigrants settled in western Canada, particularly in the Prairie provinces. Most of them settled in clusters of religious and ethnic homogeneity. In Manitoba the Mennonites dominated, in Saskatchewan the Catholics, and in Alberta the Lutherans.

During the 1920s Germans again became "preferred immigrants" to Canada. Baltic Germans, who had lost their estates when the Bolshevics seized power in 1917, aquired homesteads on the Prairies. Many did not succeed in farming and moved to urban areas. When the Great Depression hit the Prairie provinces, immigration virtually ceased. One group of Sudeten Germans, who left Czechoslovakia when Hitler occupied their homeland, settled as farmers during this time.

After World War II about eighteen million Germans became displaced persons. The Soviet Union expelled nearly one million Germans. Former German territories such as Pomerania, Silesia, and West and East Prussia were restructured, and many Germans fled westward into the remaining German territory. German immigrants to Canada, who came via West Germany, originated from various East European countries and displayed a wide spectrum of political and social backgrounds. Most had experienced incredible hardship, and Canada seemed to offer a safe haven with ample opportunities.

Since 1960 only small numbers of Germans have immigrated due to the economic recovery in West Germany. Of these most recent immigrants only a fraction chose the Prairies.

This brief account illustrates that German settlers on the Prairies comprised a very heterogenous group with distinctive religious and occupational backgrounds.

ETHNIC IDENTITIES AMONG GERMAN CANADIANS

In this section we explore common perceptions about German Canadians held by outsiders and how these perceptions are partially reinforced by German Canadians themselves.

EXTERNAL IDENTIFICATION AND STEREOTYPING

In Canada, ethnic Germans are a group with a dual image that has a negative and a positive side to it. The negative side is strongly coloured by the two world wars, from which the Germans emerged as the losers. German Canadians are considered belligerent, and since World War II the term "Nazi" has been indiscriminately applied to individuals and the group. During and after the wars, this stereotype fuelled various forms of discrimination, including the detainment of civilians in camps and the beating of children in school. These experiences alienated many Germans from their native culture. Decades after World War II, the image of Germans as Nazis still holds great attraction and is thoroughly exploited. In movies like *Hogan's Heros* and *Raiders of the Lost Arc*, Germans are portrayed as authoritarian, with a fascistic love of uniforms. The German soldier is at best a blind follower of orders, at worst a cunning sadist. The newspapers rarely portray Germans in a favourable light for obvious sensationalist reasons.

In contrast to this view of Germans as warmongers, there is an alternative stereotype popular in Canada. Germans are hard working (epitomizing the Protestant work ethic), diligent, thorough, and competent. They live in tidy houses with white picket fences and speak with a strong German accent regardless of length of time spent in Canada. In economic terms, they are generally well-to-do and ambitious, many running their own businesses. They are not often found on welfare lists. In their leisure time, they go to German clubs (with Fachwerk 1 exterior, white-and-red chequered tableclothes on the tables, stained glass windows, and wood-veneered walls) where they eat sauerkraut and drink beer. On this view, they seem to have assimilated well into Canadian society. This impression is promoted by their non-visibility in terms of distinctive physical features.

SELF-IDENTIFICATION/SELF-IMAGE

For the purpose of discussing ethnic identity formation, we treat German Canadians as two groups, immigrants and succeeding generations. As was mentioned before, the majority of first-generation German Canadians are post-war immigrants who arrived during the first two decades after World War II.

SELF-IDENTIFICATION AND SELF-PERCEPTION OF IMMIGRANTS

To look at German Canadians as a single "German-speaking group" is indeed a falsifying oversimplification. Within the immigrant population, group loyalty is based primarily on cultural-religious criteria, which are often determined by the particular geographical area from which the group originated. Existing German Canadian organizations and churches in Canada reveal the importance of the geographical element; there are the Baltic Immigrant Aid Society, American Historical Society of Germans from Russia, Sudeten German Club, Swiss Society, Club Austria, Friends of Berlin and Danube Swabians, to name only a few. Some German churches in Edmonton have a predominance of German immigrants from one of these regions. Each of these groups has emerged from a centuries-long tradition in

Eastern Europe, during which their dialects and rich cultural traditions evolved. After immigrating to Canada, such groups formed their own organizations to preserve the link with their homelands.

With these factors compounded by experiences such as discrimination or even persecution, the members of the groups have developed strong common bonds with each other. On the basis of this commonality, new congregations sprung up that offered church services in German and the liturgical traditions from their countries of origin. Later, after having established themselves and overcome the first few years of hardship, they founded their clubs as a refuge from the surrounding society. According to various personal accounts, arrival in Canada after the last world war and (and also after World War I, for that matter) was a traumatic experience. They felt unwelcome even after the category of "enemy alien" was removed from them by the Canadian government as a group, since they still encountered a hostile social environment. They were not made to feel welcome in West Germany after their exodus from Eastern Europe, which uprooted them completely from a stable life. This treatment may have not been perfect either but had, at least, given them an identity and stability.

Immigrants who arrived during the late 1970s and 1980s did not have to carry this emotional baggage with them. These individuals left Europe of their own free will, motivated by the spirit of adventure or in pursuit of business opportunities that the increasingly prosperous but overpopulated West Germany could not offer. Furthermore, they did not immigrate in large numbers or as collectives, but trickled in individually. These individuals did not feel the strong need to join ethnic clubs or seek fellowship with people of their own kind, and they therefore mingled more readily with Canadians at large. Most ethnic Germans of this period settled in cities.

SELF-IDENTIFICATION AMONG THE SECOND GENERATION

The second generation of German Canadians, either Canadian born or immigrating in early childhood, has a different self-image than the parent generation. Those who experienced the early postwar years share some of the traumas of being perceived as members of an enemy nation. Some learned German from their parents, who continued speaking German in the home, but for various reasons this practice usually declined in later years. Most second-generation German Canadians experienced their parents' idiosyncracies and habits in everyday life, recognized them as different from Canadian society in general, and did not emulate them. But for this generation one important psychological element was missing: the memories of a different life in the old country. They never lived through the war, they never experienced the loss of their livelihood. They grew up to become Canadians, albeit German Canadians. Few of this group joined the clubs their immigrant parents had founded. Second-generation German Canadians have to a far greater extent than their parents become truly assimilated.

GERMAN CULTURAL ACTIVITIES

The cultural stereotype of the sauerkraut-eating, beer-drinking and dirndl-or-lederhosen-wearing German is strongly reinforced by German Canadians themselves on occasions such as Heritage Days, Octoberfest, and the Schuhplattler Dances. The construction of clubhouses in one particular architectural style further perpetuates the stereotype. One extreme example is found in Kimberly, British Columbia, where the tourist finds himself or herself in the surroundings typical of a small town in Bavaria. These cultural showcases reduce the true complexity of the German ethnic group to a one-dimensional image, easily recognized by outsiders. Furthermore, this image is not necesssarily shared by all German Canadians, since the membership of German Canadian clubs constitutes only a very small percentage of the total German Canadian population. Furthermore, the existing groups are somewhat self-contained and rarely noticed by the public. Many groups do not have their own clubhouses and show little interest in projecting their particular features of German culture onto the outside world. They do not have a great public impact on the overall stereotypical portrayal of German culture in Canada because their numbers are quite small. As a result, schisms have developed within the German-speaking community itself. Various groups emphasize different features and do not necessarily identify with those of others. This divergence is particularly pronounced between the immigrant population and succeeding generations. Therefore, post-war immigrants who, since the beginning of settlement in Canada, have tried to re-establish their traditional life-styles are economically integrated into Canadian society but have psychologically remained tied to their countries of origin.

ENHANCED SUPPORT FOR CONTEMPORARY GERMAN CULTURE

The traditional carriers of German culture on the Prairies, such as churches and clubs, are losing members and influence. The German immigrants who founded and sustained these organizations are becoming too old to continue to do so or have died. Their children are well adapted into mainstream Canadian society and often lack the sentimental feelings and bonds to "German-ness". They may be interested in their roots and heritage, but in a different way than were their parents.

The newer generation of German immigrants experienced the immense social and political changes on both sides of the Iron Curtain during the post-war period. Their understanding of German culture differs widely from that of the pre-war generation. They are not attracted by the outdated and often oversimplified image of German culture that the clubs and churches present.

But there is new energy and interest on the horizon. Recent years show an increased acknowledgement and valuation of the diversity of cultural values in the Canadian mosaic. The search for personal identity often leads to the quest for family roots and cultural heritage. A first step is to recognize the diversity of German cultural heritage and to create an awareness of the different traditions. A greater degree of acceptance as promoted through the multicultural concept may sharpen this awareness.

Another aid to sustaining German culture is a newly observed interest in the German language from within the non-German segment of the Canadian population. Diversified educational curricula with local options and programs, both within and outside the public school system, are catering to this interest. Owing to block patterns of settlement, German ethnic populations on the Prairies have always shown better German-language retention than those in other parts of Canada. This retention has lead to the establishment of more German-language teaching facilities. In recent years, German teachers have seen their classes transformed from mother-tongue to second-language classes.

Germany, as a strong trading partner, has attracted Canadian business activity. This economic strength has also enabled German tourists to visit Canada in increasing numbers. Knowledge of the German language is becoming a valued skill in business transactions. Trade relations also stimulate cultural exchange and therefore enhance interest in the social customs and values of contemporary German culture. Language confers access to cultural tools such as books, films, and theatre, as well as personal records and letters.

Finally, the idea of cultural rights also helps to promote access to the rich German cultural heritage. Cultural rights are a relatively new concept. Political rights and freedoms originally encompassed cultural rights which were taken for granted. Accelerating awareness of the suppression of Native culture has created a new Recognition of the importance of cultural rights and the need to protect them. Cultural rights mean the freedom to participate in ethnic group activity and to have access to cultural goods such as literature, music, and the different forms of visual arts. The diversity of the German immigrant experience calls for new ways to access this rich, cultural heritage.

As the stereotypes of German culture are broken down, Canadians generally begin to perceive the German experience as integral to an emerging multicultural national identity.

REFERENCES

Bassler, G.P. 1978. "Die Anfaenge der deutschen Massenwanderung nach British Nordamerika im 19. Yahrhundert." In *Annalen*. Deutschkanadische Studien. 2; 4 - 18.

Canada. Statistics Canada: 1921, 1941, 1971, 1981 Census. Otawa

Isajiw, W.W. 1974. "Definitions of Ethnicity." In *Ethnicity*. 1, 11-24.

Keyserlingk, R.H. 1984. "The Canadian Government's Attitude Toward Germans and German Canadians in World War II." In *Canadian Ethnic Studies*, Vol.XVI, No.1, 16 - 28.

McLaughlin, K.M. 1985. *The Germans in Canada*. Ottawa: Canadian Historical Assocation, Multiculturalism Program.

Palmer, H. 1982. *Patterns of Prejudice: A History of Nativism in Alberta*. Toronto: McClelland and Stewart.

Weissenbarn, G. 1978. "The Germans in Canada: A Chronological Survey of Canada's Third Oldest European Ethnic Group from 1664 to 1977." In *German-Canadian Yearbook, Vol.III,* Froeschle, H. ed. Toronto. 22 - 56.

John W. Friesen
Department of Educational Policy Administrative
Studies
The University of Calgary

17

"Welcome to Our World": The Sad Saga of Doukhobor Immigration and Settlement in Canada

> *There are two simple theories of ... Canadian*
> *immigration policy and practise. One sees racism as*
> *having disappeared while the other sees racism persisting*
> *in changed form. (Taylor 1991, 3)*

It is now possible to trace nearly a century of Doukhobor history in Canada, dating from the spring of 1898 when Canadian officials were first contacted about possible Doukhobor immigration. The Doukhobers' attraction to Canada was motivated by government policies formulated mainly by Clifford Sifton, minister of the interior from 1896 to 1905. Sifton viewed immigration as a business proposition and a long-term investment for Canada. He believed that settlers from almost any country should be encouraged to immigrate, and preferably settle on the Prairies and thus ensure maximum national productivity. His goal was to get the job done as quickly as possible with as many people as possible, and so he simplified legislation to promote home-steading, freed many of the encumbered lands, and conducted large-scale promotion of immigration in the United States and overseas (Hall 1977). Sifton expected immigrants to fend for themselves once they were settled, and the conditions of immigration for that purpose were exceedingly simple. In the case of the Doukhobors, he required that they occupy and till the lands and promise to incite no insurrection against the government. Naturally, the Doukhobors readily agreed to these terms

From the time of their entry into Canada, it is possible to identify a *consistently racist attitude* towards the Doukhobors, on the part of both government and citizenry. This is not to suggest that Doukhobor reaction to such treatment was always entirely laudable, but one should also point out that their disruptive reactions have always emanated from the radical sector of the community best known as the Sons of Freedom. In addition, the best-known writings about Doukhobors have been very negative towards them (Callwood 1984; Holt 1964; O'Neal 1962).

In August 1898 James Mavor, a political economist at the University of Toronto, received a letter from Prince Peter Kropotkin, a Russian anarchist, in which the latter drew attention to Count Leo Tolstoy's efforts to help the pacifist Doukhobors to leave Russia. In 1895, already ostracized by their compatriots for their unorthodox views, which included pacifism, communalism, and a disdain for human institutions of any kind, the Doukhobors staged public demonstrations in many southern Russian communities to show their disapproval of increasing militarism. As a result, many of them were flogged, imprisoned, and exiled. Three years later the Russian government gave permission for the group to migrate, and Canada was on their list of possible destinations. After acceptance of their own precisely worded "demands":–that they be exempt from military services, and that they be permitted to settle in solid blocks or reserves and thereby carry on their traditional village or communal lifestyle–the Doukhobors set sail for Canada. On January 20, 1899, the first boatload of twenty-one hundred Doukhobors landed in Halifax, and their numbers swelled to seventy-five hundred that year, the largest group of immigrants to arrive in North America at one time (Tarasoff 1982, 259). Although many Doukhobors have since assimilated by denying their ethnic roots, sometimes even to the extent of changing their surnames, estimates are that there are from twenty-five to thirty thousand Doukhobors in Canada today (Friesen and Verigin 1988; Tarasoff 1982).

It is generally the case that intolerant, racist, or antagonistic attitudes do not arise from a single base. Ethnic racism in Canada is often traced to the Loyalist origins of English Canadian society, which have been a strong component of prevailing conservative thought in the country. However, the situation is much more complex than that. Anglo-Saxon nativism, for example, was merely a subcategory of a broader notion of "white" racial superiority, which was shared by many people of northern European background who were not anglophones, but who had a belief in the superiority of northern Europeans over "non-preferred" continental Europeans, Asians, and blacks. In addition, hostility towards minorities arose from class prejudice, economic self-interest, and a fear that some ethnic groups could not be assimilated (Palmer 1982, 169; Taylor 1991, 4). The latter objection was based on the assumption that cultural diversity was a potentially divisive force in Canada and people who could not be assimilated were simply undesirable citizens. Any group that failed to assimilate was disloyal to Canada. Clearly this has been the strongest negative strain of intolerance with which the Doukhobors have had to contend.

THE SASKATCHEWAN EXPERIENCE

Beginning in June 1899 the Doukhobors mapped out a total of sixty-one villages in the east and central Saskatchewan districts of Kamsack, Blaine Lake-Langham, Swan River Pelly, and BuchananCanora. Fifty-seven of these villageds prevailed. The intent was to operate the villages with an overall communal plan, and although this was not exactly the result, the Doukhobors' concept of community was effectively maintained by isolating themselves from social interaction with their neighbours and by promoting strong ethnocentric loyalties. One *could* argue that Doukhobor "togetherness" worked against them in some way, but it was also partly strengthened by the external forces of suspicion and intolerance.

On the positive side, it is interesting to note that one of the first encounters the Doukhobors had with outsiders had to do with schooling. There was a positive glimmer in the encounter, thanks to the efforts of the Society of Friends (Quakers), who began schools among the Doukhobors in 1900. At that time, two women, Eliza H. Varney of Bloomfield, Ontario, and Nellie Baker of Kingston, Ontario, worked out of three pitched tents; one provided living quarters, another served as a dispensary, and the third functioned as a school. The two women reported encouraging results. Miss Baker indicated that after barely two months of instruction, some of the children were able to correspond "in fairly understandable English" (Tarasoff 1969, 100). Although the Quakers continued their educational efforts among the Doukhobors, reports were that many of the pupils drifted away from school because of the indifferent attitude towards schooling of Peter Verigin, the beloved Doukhober leader (also called Peter the Lordly) (Woodcock and Avakumovic 1977, 212 - 14). This contradicts an earlier report suggesting that Verigin *encouraged* co-operation with the various school districts, but it is also possible that Verigin might have changed his mind after discovering that the Quakers had more than the three R's in mind when teaching Doukhobor children. Like other denominational groups, they included religious conversion in their list of educational objectives, which did not include a full appreciation of all of the tenets of the Doukhobor faith. At the very least, this situation indicates that the Doukhobors were not *adamantly* opposed to schooling. In fact, their perceptions appear to have been honed by a multiplicity of positive factors, in particular, the attitudes of their teachers. The activities of the Quakers appear to have been somewhat sensitive to the Doukhobor life-style (particularly their peace stance), and this suggests that if the Doukhobors had also been afforded even a minimum of understanding by public authorities, their attitudes towards other forms of schooling might have become more aligned with those of the rest of the Canadian populace.

The first clash with the Doukhobors over schooling occurred in Yorkton, Saskatchewan, in January 1900, when some Doukhobors refused to send their children to school (after all, this requirement was not included in their list of immigration obligations), and they also refused to pay a school tax of eight dollars. Their position was that since their children did not attend school, there was no need to pay the tax. The school district seized a horse from a Doukhobor village to compensate as a fine *even though school officials made it clear that they were not too anxious to have Doukhobor children attend their schools.* The Doukhobors later complained to the Council of Public Instruction that not only did they not have access to public schooling, they were charged inordinately high taxes. The school district board members defended themselves by insisting that no Doukhobors had ever made application to the district office for their children to attend school. Further, officials argued that they had no plans to build additional schools for the Doukhobors, since the latter had not registered for their lands and would probably not remain long in the district. The provincial attorney-general pointed out that taxation implied privilege, and thus Doukhobor children should be accommodated in local schools. By 1906, it was reported that Doukhobor children in one district were attending school, but there were many districts where this was not the case (Lyons 1973, 62).

It soon became evident that farming neighbours of the Doukhobors did not approve of the life-style of the communalists and grew jealous of Doukhobor successes. In a very short time, the Doukhobor farming community included in its assets 600 horses, 400 oxen, and 865 cows. In addition, they built bridges and ferries over rivers, which they operated free of charge to all travellers, and established a flourishing co-op in Yorkton. Neighbouring farmers bitterly attacked Doukhobor marriage customs and exploited

Doukhobor men who found it necessary to work for their neighbours in order to remain active and to subsidize communal income. The farmers underpaid their Doukhobor help and insisted that because they were not British, the Doukhobors were not fit to become Canadian citizens. In some instances, neighbouring stockmen also deliberately drove their cattle into Doukhobor crops to destroy them.

Protests against the Doukhobor privilege of living communally eventually precipitated a letter from Clifford Sifton's office on February 15, 1902, demanding that the Doukhobors register their lands with the government on an individual basis. The letter caused considerable consternation in the community because the Doukhobors felt its demands were contrary to the conditions of their original acceptance as future citizens. Doukhobor emissaries had originally envisaged that their Canadian sojourn would be patterned after the Mennonite experience of 1874 - 78 in Manitoba, where Mennonites lived with "partial communism and passive resistance to the state" (Tarasoff 1982, 259). Although the Doukhobors were not aware of it at the time, the Mennonites had managed to bypass the state requirement of swearing allegiance to the Crown when laying claim to settlement lands, simply "solemnly affirming" their loyalty (Smith 1927).

When Peter Verigin the beloved Doukhobor leader, arrived in Saskatchewan in December, 1902, he tried to negotiate with government officials over the requirement of swearing allegiance, but to no avail. The opposition Conservatives tried to use Doukhobor resistance to embarrass the government and thus Sifton and his colleagues remained firm in their resolve to force Doukhobor compliance with the law. Some time passed before the government was able to enforce their order; in the meantime Clifford Sifton was replaced in office by Frank Oliver, who set about finishing that particular assignment. He sent homestead inspectors to the Doukhobor villages to determine whether or not the Doukhobors had met the government requirement of cultivating an acceptable portion of occupied lands. In 1906 he appointed Methodist missionary John McDougall to report in detail on Doukhobor organization and activities. McDougall recommended that the Doukhobor commune be dismantled and the requirement of individual registration of land be enforced. When the Doukhobors protested, again claiming that their original terms of acceptance had been violated, Oliver remained firm. Eventually, 236 Doukhobors agreed to the government terms and established themselves as independents. The rest of the community dwellers were forced to occupy special reserve lands, on the basis of fifteen acres per homestead. Obviously, this was insufficient land to meet

Doukhobor needs, and they were thus forced to devise an alternative plan to make a living.

In the meantime, much of the previously occupied Doukhobor land was made available to incoming settlers for free registration. On June 1, 1907, a long line-up of would-be settlers formed outside the land registration office in Yorkton, Saskatchewan, and waited up to forty-five hours in downpouring rain. The actual registration process was the scene of disturbances and confrontations and five police officers were called on to maintain order. The Doukhobor holdings were very attractive to outsiders; after all, it was a very special privilege to be able to apply for land that was already cultivated. At the time of their relocation the Doukhobors had 49,429 acres of cultivated land, or 5.6 acres per person (Berton 1984; Thorsteinson 1917).

Public sympathy for Doukhobor losses was minimal, and the community was left on its own to devise a new direction for its future. When the Doukhobors applied for a limited remuneration for their lands, the government flatly turned them down. With their hearts full of memories of governmental attitudes in their former homeland of Russia, the Doukhobors were perplexed as to their future. Soon, however, Peter Verigin came up with a plan. It consisted of buying previously owned land in the interior of British Columbia and relocating the community. During the years 1908-13, Verigin moved his people to the areas of Nelson, Trail, Slocan City, Castlegar, and Grand Forks, B.C., and engineered a new model of utopian society. Within a few years the community operated fruit farms, worked for their neighbours and developed eight sawmills and two jam factories at Nelson and Brilliant (near Castlegar). They manufactured the "K-C" brand of jam, which featured only the best of the fruit crop and generous portions of primary ingredients such as sugar (Friesen and Verigin 1988). Some community members remained in Saskatchewan to till the reserve lands allotted to them by government. Thus, despite their betrayal at the hands of another government, the Doukhobors regained their breath and gave the new nation another chance.

THE BRITISH COLUMBIA EXPERIENCE

Doukhobor spirits were high when they migrated to the B.C. interior. Here they felt they were free from governmental restrictions and encumbrances and their land base was safe. Initially, Peter the Lordly purchased lands in his own name "to protect the community," he said, and within a few years formed the Christian Community of Universal Brotherhood (CCUB). Then, true to his word, he turned all of the accumulated assets over to the organization. After that the CCUB operated with a board of directors, although Verigin's influence was always very strong. He also oversaw the development of ninety villages that were specially designed for the new kind of more cloistered life-style. Each village consisted of one or two large houses that accommodated 30 - 50 people and a series of outbuildings used to house machinery and for storage. By 1912 some 5,550 Doukhobor souls made up the community, and life was good (Mealing 1984).

In 1915 the CCUB created a "branch office" in southern Alberta where Verigin purchased 11,260 acres near Lundbreck and Cowley and sent 300 Doukhobors to establish new colonies. His plan was that these occupants would raise grain and grind it in their own flour mill and then exchange the flour with his British Columbia followers for the goods they produced, such as lumber and fruit. Again he purchased already occupied farms in order to avoid taking the oath of allegiance to the Crown.

Peter Verigin was killed on October 24, 1924, when the train on which he was a passenger enroute from Brilliant to Grand Forks was rocked by an explosion. After his funeral, his companion of many years, Anastasia Golubova, declared herself rightful heir to his position, his followers felt otherwise and issued a call to his son in Russia, Peter Petrovich Verigin, to be their new leader. Peter Petrovich arrived in 1927 and took control of the community. In the meantime, in 1926, somewhat disillusioned by her rejection, Anastasia attracted 165 followers to Shouldice, Alberta, where she purchased lands and founded the Lordly Christian Community of Universal Brotherhood. The experiment lasted until 1945, when only Anastasia and a female companion, Fedosia Verigin (a niece of Peter the Lordly), remained as the occupants. For historical interest, it must be mentioned that ruins of the village remain today and are located about twelve kilometres east and two kilometres south of Arrowood, Alberta (Verigin 1977).

Peter Petrovich was never the leader his father had been because he lacked the dignity and finesse his father had in dealing with people. He was a demanding and boisterous man often involved in fist-fights brought on by excessive drinking. On arrival in Canada he took the name *Chistiakov* (the cleanser) for himself and announced that he would clear the deadwood from community ranks. His eleven-year reign was marked by an admixture of effective reorganization and explosive confrontations. On a more positive note, he began cultural clubs for Doukhobor youth and organized youth choirs that have a strong legacy today. His work fostered a series of long-lasting cultural forms, which later assisted his followers in remaining true to their faith. At the same time, he advocated participation in public schooling. However, despite his vision, he was unable to ward off the growing public resentment against the Doukhobors, which ultimately resulted in the permanent destruction of their commune.

THE LAST SPIKE

In 1938 the writing was on the wall for the CCUB Although their assets at this time amounted to about six million dollars, spread across the three most westerly provinces, they also carried demand notes for $319,276, which made up about 4 per cent of their worth. Suddenly, without any warning, and with the approval of the Government of British Columbia, the holders of said notes, the Sun Life Assurance Company and National Trust Company, demanded immediate payment. When the Doukhobors were unable instantly to liquidate enough assets to pay off the loans, foreclosure was declared on the CCUB and eviction notice was given to the occupants. An appeal to the B. C. Supreme Court failed when the court moved that the farmer's Land Protection Act did not apply to corporations. In 1940 the Government of British Columbia passed the Doukhobor Lands Acquisition Act and took control of said lands. The government paid a total of $296,500 for the lands and administered them for sale to the former occupants through their Land Settlement Board. Remaining assets were liquidated without the benefit of public auction, with goods often sold for less than the wholesale price, as the trustees put it, "simply to pay off the debt" (Tarasoff 1982). The government also refused to reimburse the community for $202,206 that it had spent on public works, which works had been available for public use since the early days of Doukhobor emigration.

The burden of foreclosure fell heavily on Peter Petrovich's shoulders, and he died on February 11, 1939. True to form, he cursed his doctors and his well-wishers to his last breath. Sensing his imminent demise, on November 11, 1938, he called a national convention of Doukhobors at Castlegar and announced the formation of a new Doukhobor organization, to be named the Union of Spiritual Communities in Christ, to replace the CCUB. The new organization would carry on the vision of communal living in spirit, although its physical reality might not be possible for some time. Today, many older Doukhobors dream of the rebirth of the commune and refer with hope to the experience of their one-time neighbours in Russia, the Hutterites, who at least twice in their 450-year history of communal living have operated without that structure in several locations. This would include the years 1690 -

1762 in Transylvania and 1819 - 59 in Radichev (Hostetler 1974, 312 - 13).

After Peter Petrovich's death, his followers again turned their gaze towards Russia in search of Petrovich's son, Peter, who, on investigation, was reported missing in a concentration camp by the Red Cross. Subsequently, in 1940, John J. Verigin, Peter the Lordly's seventeen-year old grandson, was named secretary of the society, and he became honorary chairman in 1961, which position he still holds.

Few Canadian groups other than the Doukhobors can claim the honor of being the target of four separate governmental commissions. The first of these was the McDougall Commission, which in 1906 was to enquire into the desirability of the communal life-style; McDougall urged its abandonment. William Blakemore was appointed a commission of one in 1912 to inquire about Doukhobor resistance to public schooling; he was mild in his recommendation that Doukhobor leaders be talked into acceptance, but government leaders were in a hurry and thus forced mandatory attendance without consultation. In 1947 Judge Harry Sullivan headed up a commission to study disturbances in the Doukhobor community, but he gave up his assignment in exasperation. Subsequently, in 1950, a group of scientists under the leadership of University of British Columbia anthropologist Harry Hawthorn took up where Sullivan left off, and two years later recommended that Doukhobor marriages be recognized, that Doukhobors be given the right to vote, there be a lower penalty for nudity, remaining Doukhobor lands be disposed of, educational efforts among the Doukhobors be intensified and the zealot faction should be relocated, by force if necessary. In addition, the commission recommended that still another commission on Doukhobor Affairs be set up (Tarasoff 1982).

THE SCHOOL AS WEAPON

Perhaps the most heinous of atrocities committed by Canadians against the Doukhobors has to do with schooling. The background to this story originates in the fact that formal schooling was not high on the list of priorities for the Doukhobors who followed their leader, Peter the Lordly, to British Columbia. Their intentions were, once again, to perpetuate their traditional life-style via established internal structures and procedures. This included the socialization of their children along traditional lines. The Doukhobors were unaware of the implications of moving to an established province with a dominant cultural (British) influence. Neither the citizens of British Columbia nor their government were prepared to dispense a great deal of patience to any newcomer groups who might find their laws unsuitable. This was particularly true with regard to schooling, which meticulously reflected the values of the dominant culture of the most westerly province and functioned in accordance with established laws and regulations (Lyons 1973, 114).

Although the fact not immediately apparent to outsiders, the Doukhobors traditionally educated their children with more exactitude than was evident from the recitation of prayers and the singing of songs. A good indicator of specifics inherent in the Doukhobor concept of community socialization is a list of rules formulated around 1912 to govern the behaviour of the children in Doukhobor villages. The following are representative of the ten dictates on the list:

1. In the morning it is obligatory for all children to wash and pray to God, then to read the Lord's Prayer and other psalms; ...
5. All children must be brought up in the spirit of Christian peaceful life; and with the growth of the body one must try and develop a reasonable soul in tune with God which brought us Christ and his sacred teachings; ...
7. The denial of greed and envy in children is to be looked upon as a high and necessary virtue; ...
10. All children, without exception, must come every day to the *sobranye* to sing prayers and hymns and to read psalms. (Tarasoff 1963)

When Commissioner William Blakemore completed his work in 1912, he noted that Doukhobor resistance to schooling targeted the *content* and *format* of schooling, not the institution or process of schooling per se. The Doukhobors contended that the schools operated according to undesirable and immoral dictates and promoted the worldly values of easy profit, thievery, cheating, and exploitation. This was a cultural protest, not an anti-school movement. In addition, the Doukhobors spurned the school's advocacy of military training, which for them represented a validation of the useless shedding of innocent people's blood. One Doukhobor woman even objected to a lady teacher who curled her hair and wore ribbons–clearly activities of the vain (Ashworth 1979, 139).

The Doukhobors were not prepared for the results of Blakemore's report, which recommended compulsory schooling for Doukhobor children. He *did* concede that the schools neglected to take cognizance of Doukhobor values and urged that the educational process be amended towards that end. He also suggested that

Russian-speaking teachers be hired and the curriculum be modified to incorporate only "elementary subjects," which would essentially only promote literacy. The hardest blow came from Blakemore's recommendation that the Doukhobor exemption from military service be cancelled.

In 1914 the pressures towards Doukhobor conformity continued with the passing of the provincial Community Regulation Act, which obliged the Doukhobors to provide vital statistics of births, deaths, and marriage; it also stipulated compulsory education for Doukhobor children. Failure to comply would result in fines, and failure to pay would justify the seizure of community goods. Two years later, when all efforts to produce some kind of compromise had failed, a school was built at Brilliant (now part of Castlegar), and by 1922 eleven schools were in operation, two built by the government and the rest by Doukhobors (Ashworth 1979, 142).

This section of the account should not be interpreted as leading towards a happy ending, for it was quite to the contrary. Almost as soon as school construction was complete, fines were levied on parents for failure to send their children to school. The following year the burning of schools began, but when these activities reached high proportions the government raised the amount of the fines and school attendance resumed. The truce was short lived, however, and within a few years the zealous faction of the Doukhobors again began burning schools and staging various forms of protest. When Peter Petrovich arrived in Canada he tried to eliminate the fanatical element from Doukhobor ranks, and many of them moved to Krestova, a few miles from Castlegar. From there, out of both frustration and zeal, they continued their protesting antics and, thanks to the press, generally conveyed a negative image of the entire Doukhobor community that has prevailed in Canada to this day (Friesen 1988, 85 - 90). In the meantime, Peter Petrovich urged his orthodox followers to try to adapt to public schooling, which might in the final analysis serve to enrich the Doukhobor way of life through the benefits available in Canada (Stoochnoff 1961, 21).

The most severe action in the story of the Doukhobor schools occurred in 1953 in British Columbia, when it was reported that many Sons of Freedom children were not attending school. These children were taken from their parents in groups, and 170 of them were forcibly detained for six years at New Denver, BC. Although parents had instructed the children to resist the authorities, the government successfully initiated the plan and subsided in 1959 only when the parents promised to comply with provincial laws. As one Doukhobor observer, Peter Maloff, a lawyer, observed:

"Taking the children with the alleged purpose of educating them only deepened the crisis, and for the children the memory of the separation might instill a life-long feeling of hatred towards the authorities which no amount of education could eradicate. (Ashworth 1979, 163)

Using the school as a weapon for assimilative purposes is not a new tactic and in the Doukhobor case, at least, has been stimulated by parallel teacher attitudes (Friesen 1983; Snow, 1977). For example, for the last several decades a very negative concept of the Doukhobor attitude towards schooling has been fostered by a popular, albeit unfortunate and biased, book entitled *Doukhobor Daze* (O'Neail 1974). Written by a teacher who worked in a Doukhobor village school from 1937 to 1938, the book offers an insensitive description of the Doukhobor life-style which the author apparently found quite pathetic and very amusing. The book comprises a personal diary of the teacher's daily experiences in the village community and offers only minimal information about how the Doukhobor schools actually functioned. Today, because of the emphasis on multicultural education in teacher training, we reel with disbelief at the antics of a teacher who clearly lacked both an understanding of and any sympathy for the Doukhobor way of life. However, teachers-in-training are cautioned about developing a student-centred approach to curriculum content and method of instruction. They are urged to display a positive feeling of self-esteem and be aware of the underlying value orientation of their own culture. This attitude must be extended to the pupils, whose culture should be afforded a place of respect within the school context. Teachers are to discuss stereotyped thinking and show how it leads to prejudice. They are to be aware of the damage that prejudice, racism, and discrimination can cause for the learner. Pupils are to be encouraged to explore their own cultural heritage and to value it. A classroom atmosphere is to be fostered that will allow each pupil to feel a part of the group while maintaining his or her own unique cultural identity–and feeling good about it (Friesen 1985; Tiedt and Tiedt 1990).

Against this multicultural education mandate, it is disturbing to read O'Neail's diary about her teaching experiences. After a brief description of the Doukhobor villages, she outlines her first day's experiences by examining the roster. Evidently unaware of the Russian origins of the Doukhobors, she expresses shock that the children's surnames all end in "off," and writes, "Abrissimoff, Babakaoff, Chernenkoff, Davidoff ... Zoobkoff–I'm bewilderedoff!"

And that's not all. There are three Petes, three Johns, three Mikes, three Fannies, two Tenas, three Marys, three Nicks, two Pollys, three Annies, four Bills. This could become very confusing, so–I shall change their names thus: Pete, Peter, and Pat; John, Johnny, and Jack; Mike, Michael, and Mickey ... So be it. (O'Neail 1974: (3).

When the first class is finally underway, the children are asked to recite the Lord's Prayer. Imagine Ms. O'Neail's chagrin when she hears these words repeated:

Our father bedart in heaven hello bedie name. Die king come die willie done in earth as it is in heaven. Give us this day our delly bread in forgive us our trespers as we forgive those who tresper against us. And lid us not into temtion but deliver us from eevil for dine is the king come the power and the glory forever and ever all man [sic] (5).

Evidently having enjoyed this rendition to the hilt, Ms. O'Neail reveals her obvious cultural superiority when she quotes one student's reaction to her announcement that the Lord's prayer is important. "And Mees Hulls, we didn't know it *means* sawmetheeng!" (5).

Thus the dairy continues with amusing notations on various aspects of Doukhobor life–as seen by an unappreciative outsider. Note the following entries apparently outlining glaring inconsistences in the Doukhobor life-style:

We have stopped tossing our meat under beds and cushions when we hear a knock at our door. The Doukhobors disapprove of meat-eating (they say) but we are not Doukhobors -- yet. And anyway, they do a number of things of which *we* disapprove! Besides, we've seen countless Doukhobors in restaurants in town, gorging on rare steaks, and gulping sausages. (95)

At recess Gertie and I heard a commotion outside and upon investigation found a terrific fist-fight in progress between John Ozeroff and Billy Reibin. The Doukhobors are "agin" militarism, fighting, war, army and navy, airforce, and anything else that has to do with aught but pacifism; except, that is, when it comes to good neighborly knock-'em down quarrels, and that is a horse of a different color. (102)

After an absence of more than twenty years, O'Neail returned to the village school where she taught, and expressed her delight at the changes—now there were Anglo names, such as "Elaine, Margaret, Linda and June" for the girls and "Robert, Leonard, Wayne and Ronnie" for the boys; modern furniture; "English dresses" for the girls; and "the first graders already speak English *before* they enter school!" O'Neail concludes "And I am happy for them and for their neighbors whose lives have been lifted from the gloomy and depressing surroundings in which they once lived (140).

It would be unfair to generalize that all teachers in Doukhobor schools held racist attitudes towards the Doukhobor life-style and were thus amused by obvious cultural differences. On the other hand, the fears of Doukhobor elders that schools could be contaminating influences on their young were not without foundation. Observers noted that by the 1930s community Doukhobor began to attend movies, and baseball, a sport learned at school, became a favourite activities. Automobiles became common means of conveyance, so that people could go to town on a Saturday night and meet with non-Doukhobor friends. Purchases made by Doukhobors at local stores indicated a strong measure of assimilation—hand lotions, hot-water bottles, bobby pins, perfumed soaps, toothbrushes, and powders and pills (Zubek and Soberg 1952, 194). With the breakup of the CCUB and the enhanced use of the automobile, it became possible to travel further afield and engage in behaviours that might not be possible under the disapproving eyes of the elders. Because of these various influences, by the 1950s large numbers of Doukhobor children attended high schools and institutions of post-secondary education, and, by Canadian standards, did well in their studies.

CONCLUSION: A CONTINUING HARASSMENT

Clearly, the Doukhobor experience in Canada demonstrates cultural discrimination of the worst kind. As the most obvious of detested Doukhobor practices abate, including objections to schooling and communal living, negative public sentiment is likely also to wane. In the meantime, some members of the Doukhobor community struggle to maintain their ethnic identity in a society that, while it is not too informed about Doukhobor philosophy and cultural mystique, is quite ready to deny its value.

Against this context, it would seem that Canadian multiculturalism, allegedly the great hope for the eradication of racism in this country, still has a long way to go.

REFERENCES

Ashworth, M. 1979. *The forces which shaped them: A history of minority group children in British Columbia.* Vancouver: New Star Books.

Berton, P. 1984. *The promised land.* Toronto: McClelland and Stewart.

Callwood, J. 1984. *Emma: The true story of Canada's unlikely spy.* Toronto: General Paperbacks.

Friesen, J.W. 1983. *Schools with a purpose.* Calgary: Detselig.

Friesen, J.W. 1985. *When cultures clash: Case studies in multiculturalism.* Calgary: Detselig.

Friesen, J.W. 1988. "The Doukhobors." In *The evolution of multiculturalism.* ed. C. Bagley. Calgary: Calgary Institute for the Humanities.

Friesen, J.W. and M.M. Verigin. 1989. *The community Doukhobors: A people in transition.* Ottawa: Borealis.

Hall, D.J. 1977. "Clifford Sifton: Immigration and settlement." In *The settlement of the west,"* ed. Howard Palmer. Calgary: Comprint.

Holt, S. 1964. *Terror in the name of God: The story of the Sons of Freedom Doukhobors.* Toronto: McClelland and Stewart.

Hostetler, J.A. 1974. *Hutterite society.* Baltimore: Johns Hopkins Press.

Lyons, J.E. 1973. A history of Doukhobor schooling in Saskatchewan and British Columbia. Master's thesis, University of Calgary.

Mealing, F.M. 1975. *Doukhobor life: a survey of Doukhobor religion, history and folklore.* Castlegar, BC: Cotinneh Books.

Mealing, F.M. 1984. "Doukhobor architecture: An introduction." *Canadian Ethnic Studies,* 16:73 - 88.

McDonald, N.G. 1974. "David J. Goggin, promoter of national schools." In *Profiles of Canadian educators.* ed. R.S. Patterson, J.W. Chalmers, and J.W. Friesen. Toronto: D.C. Heath.

O'Neail, H. 1974. *Doukhobor daze.* Sidney, B.C: Gray's Publishing.

Palmer, H. 1982. *Patterns of prejudice: A history of nativism in Alberta.* Toronto: McClelland and Stewart.

Smith, C.H. 1927. *The coming of the Russian Mennonites: An episode in the settling of the last frontier, 1874 - 1884.* Berne, IN: Mennonite Book Concern.

Snow, Chief John. 1977. *These mountains are our sacred places: The story of the Stoney Indians.* Toronto: Samuel Stevens.

Stoochnoff, J.P. *Doukhobors as they are.* Printed privately. Toronto: Ryerson Press.

Tarasoff, K. 1963. *In search of brotherhood.* Vancouver: Manuscript.

Tarasoff, K.J. 1969. *A pictorial history of the Doukhobors.* Saskatoon: Western Producer.

Tarasoff, K.J. 1982. *Plakun Trava: the Doukhobors.* Grand Forks, BC: Mir Publication Society.

Taylor, K.W. 1991. "Racism in Canadian Immigration Policy." *Canadian Ethnic Studies,* 23:1, 1 - 20.

Thorsteinson, E.J. 1917. "The Doukhobors in Canada." *Mississippi Historical Review,* 4:1, 23 - 48.

Tiedt, P.L., and Tiedt, I.M. 1990. *Multicultural teaching: A handbook of activities, information and resources.* (3ded.) Boston: Allyn and Bacon.

Verigin, L. 1977. "Spirit Wrestlers: Alberta's Doukhobors." In *Alberta: The pioneer years. ed.* H. Fryer. Langley, BC: Stagecoach Publishing.

Woodcock, G., and Avakumovic, I. 1977. *The Doukhobors.* Toronto: McClelland and Stewart.

Zubek, J.P., and Soberg, P.A. 1952. *Doukhobors at war.* Toronto: Ryerson Press.

PART VII

MULTICULTURALISM AND THE STATE

Nayyar S. Javed
Mental Health Clinic
Saskatoon

18

State-Imposed Multiculturalism: Social Change or Illusion of Change?

In recent years, public policy pertaining to multiculturalism has gained a significant degree of visibility in the media and everyday discourse. Multiculturalism is seen as a potent agent of social change that is desirable but simultaneously threatening to the "Canadian" (English/British) cultural tradition as well as Canadian nationalism. The groups that have attained power through their affiliation with the English/British cultural traditions seem to perceive multiculturalism as a threat to their position in society.

I argue that state-imposed multiculturalism has remained more of a rhetoric than a real commitment to eliminate inequalities, founded on the notion of separating "mainstream Canadians" from the so-called multicultural groups. Many other social definitions are used in defining these groups, all of which contain a hidden bias and emphasize their "otherness." The creation of their otherness in the Canadian consciousness has served to legitimize their exclusion.

In what follows, a distinguish between multiculturalism as a world-view based on the principle of equality and the state-imposed multiculturalism practised within Canadian public policy. This distinction is useful in examining the flaws in Canadian multicultural policies. I elaborate the role of "multicultural rhetoric" in creating the illusion of change through this policy in order to achieve clarity in assessing the outcome of the policy. I present the psychological implications of the multicultural rhetoric to raise questions regarding their impact on the treatment of the groups defined as "multicultural." I briefly consider funding stipulations as a regulatory strategy, to examine how the state has restricted the struggles of groups seeking equality. I conclude with recommendations for a systematic study of how multicultural policy has affected the Canadian consciousness, and ask why race and gender issues were excluded at the initial stages of formulation of that policy, as well as asking what forces compelled the state to include these issues in the 1980s.

MULTICULTURALISM AS WORLD-VIEW FOR LIBERATION VERSUS STATE-IMPOSED MULTICULTURALISM

Ideally, multiculturalism is a world-view based on values and practices directed at liberating human consciousness from parochial thinking and egocentric notions. It ought to lead members of a society to view their well-being as interconnected and thus treat one another as equal partners in all social and economic relations. This world-view encourages the elimination of social structures that support domination by the privileged few. In my opinion, however, multiculturalism as constructed and imposed by policy-makers in Canada does not have this character; it violates the world-view it professes to be.

Examining the political context of Canadian multicultural policy formulation, one might grow suspicious of Pierre Trudeau's motive in constructing that policy. His keenness to make Canada bilingual seemed to be the real goal. He needed to appease the ethnic groups that, at that stage of Canadian history, had become politically powerful. Mr. Trudeau could not totally ignore their concerns yet at the same time he was not committed to treating their concerns, in the same way as those of the French and English communities. A multiculturalism specially designed to convince these groups of equal treatment while treating them unequally served effectively to appease them. (Lewyicky 1992)

Because a commitment to equality was lacking in the formulation of the policy, the paradigm incorporated into the policy implementations was not based on the reality of those who were experiencing inequalities. The paradigms were borrowed from the experience of Western anthropologists and development workers in the so-called Third World. Therefore policy implementation focussed on cross-cultural understanding and communications without an analysis of racism and other forces of oppression. Consequently, multiculturalism had little effect on popular thinking, in which Canadians of non-European origin and of aboriginal ancestry continued to be viewed as not belonging to

Canada. The identification of the former group as "immigrants" even when they are bona fide Canadian citizens illustrates this view (Javed, in print, Milis 1992).

Recent polls indicating Preston Manning's popularity reflect Canadians' resistance to change. Romantic attachment to what the English settlers brought to Canada seems to be deeply entrenched in the collective consciousness of those who perceive themselves as "the real Canadians." Despite the economic and political crisis Canada faces, the obvious need for a major transformation in the management of national affairs, we Canadians are blindly adhering to the past. We know–I hope that we know–that what worked in the past is not going to work in the future, and that we need to face this reality, yet we are reluctant to accept the challenge. There seems to be an emotional block preventing us from facing our reality.

Our impulse to seek comfort by idealizing how things used to be has serious consequences for leaving us vulnerable to individuals like Mr. Manning who can delude us into thinking that what worked in the past can work in the future. Mr. Manning's solution for managing diversity in Canada is to perpetuate the inequality of the racialized groups. This may appeal to those who, whether privileged or not, are committed to the status quo, but inequalities can threaten national unity and thus weaken the state.

Historically, groups have been perceived as different from "real Canadians" on the basis of cultural and biological characteristics portrayed as "incompatible with the Canadian life-style." Inherent in this view is a racist bias that implies the inferiority of these groups which has served as a tool for legitimizing their exploitation in the labour market (Li and Bolaria, 1979). This exploitation, though morally reprehensible, has furthered the growth of the Canadian economy. It has also deprived Canada of the brain power of those within these groups who can contribute in developing a vision Canada needs to compete in the international arena. The perspectives of such individuals are a valuable resources that ought not be wasted for the following reasons.

The world has changed significantly. It is becoming abundantly clear that the relationship of domination and subordination has ceased to work. Droughts in Africa, political unrest all over the world, dismantling of the Soviet Union and of apartheid in South Africa are phenomena that clearly suggest a need for a major shift in the paradigms of human relations and state management. Canada, like the rest of the world, needs such a shift in its relationship with the international community and its management of internal affairs. Those who have dominated

Canadian international and other public policies do not seem to have answers to many perplexing questions. It is time that all Canadians participate in a collective search for their answers. The need for answers is urgent, and if we fail to respond to it Canada will face social turmoil and fall behind in the economic competition going on all across the globe.

The systematic inequalities, exclusion, and devaluation faced by the "multicultural groups" are depriving Canada of the potential that the individuals of these groups can offer. Millions of dollars spent on preparing "mainstream Canadians" for international business ventures can be saved by recognizing these individuals as valuable resources and utilizing their linguistic abilities and cultural knowledge for effective work in other countries.

Moreover, racial tension and unequal treatment of certain people is costly. Inequality needs to be eliminated because a fractured Canadian society cannot meet the demand far an economic evolution. Racial tension is an illness and has costly health implications for those who are systematically abused within social relations and in the job market. Stress-related health problems experienced by the racialized are not only immoral but also *expensive for Canada* (Canadian Task Force 1988).

Other ethnic cultures face many blocks in achieving equality with the dominant culture, which is also ethnic because it was implanted within Canada, but is nonetheless seen as the norm. At this stage in Canadian history, there seems to be a cultural hierarchy: the English culture occupies the top position and the other cultures are neatly arranged in a pyramid. Those seen as similar to English culture are deemed more "compatible" than those that are believed to be "different" and are labelled as incompatible. The cultures seen as compatible with the English culture, though considered desirable, are far from being its equal. Their value is restricted to a narrow sphere of the ethnic enclave. Beyond "ethnic events," they receive little attention from the "mainstream Canadian," so the cross-cultural understanding emphasized by the official multicultural policies remains superficial. At this stage, these cultures are not assimilated by the culture prevailing in Canadian institutions. In fact, the institutions' culture is resistant to change, and any attempt to accommodate other cultures is viewed as a threat to "the Canadian cultural tradition."

Recent statistics indicate that the lived reality of the ethnic groups that are racialized and are therefore identified as "visible minorities" has not changed much despite the official policy of multiculturalism. These people face systemic racism in the labour market and in other social relations, as shown by their virtual absence in management, in electoral positions, in trade union movements, in civic, provincial, and federal positions, and on all of the important decision-making bodies, including boards and commissions.

Official multiculturalism, by ignoring racism at its initial stage, has done little to eradicate the barriers preventing visible minorities (racialized groups) from participating in Canadian life in a meaningful way. Nor has employment equity legislation enacted in 1986 changed the situation much. It did not include measures for accountability, and any public policy or legislation without accountability ends up being an empty slogan. The reality of the visible minorities has not been changed by state-imposed multiculturalism, but an illusion of change has been created by a rhetoric that can be referred to as "the multicultural rhetoric."

MULTICULTURAL RHETORIC: AN ILLUSION OF CHANGE

"Multicultural rhetoric" consists of many deluding words and phrases, and social constructions of ethnic male, female, cultural, linguistic, and other characterizing features are obscured by the labels defining ethnicity. These labels conjure up many images, including the image of "the other" (Miles 1989).

Individuation is a fundamental value of all Western societies, including Canada. An individual's freedom and sense of entitlement are emphasized in assessing his or her mental health. In this context, representation of a group as "the other" can invoke primordial responses of fear and apprehension, because the "otherness" is portrayed as a threat to those who see themselves as the "Canadians" and, therefore, entitled to "earned" privilege.

Moreover, phrases and words like the "cultural mosaic," "visible minorities," "ethnicity," "cultural difference," "unity within diversity," and other pieces of this rhetoric create an image of a profound social change that, though badly needed, has not yet taken place. Thus, these images contribute to a false consciousness that functions as a tool for dissociating people from their reality. A pathological approach has been engendered by this dissociation from reality. "Mainstream Canadians"–another phrase in the multicultural rhetoric–seem to be experiencing a wave of panic because they have been deluded into believing that the visible minority or the multicultural groups are taking over. This fear further prevents them from seeing inequalities generated by systemic racism. They are trapped by their denial, so they fail to see many vicious faces of racism and tend to equate racism with racial riots and racially motivated physical assaults. They do not realize that exclusion of the perceived racial minorities is also an assault on identity and rights (Bhabha 1990).

The false consciousness affects those experiencing racism in many ways. Besides being victimized in all interactions with the privileged, they get confused and start to doubt themselves. The contradiction between their lived reality and the images presented by the multicultural rhetoric is a "crazy-making" dynamic and tends to create difficulty in grasping the reality. Individuals identified as visible minority start to deny their own reality and accept the one imposed on them by the dominant group. They become vulnerable to divisions and tokenism. Tokenism has served as a tool for division within the "multicultural" community and for slowing down the movement for change by maintaining an image of change. Those who are able to get in touch with their own reality experience stress because of a consistent devaluation of who they are. They are treated as "other" and thus as not entitled to belong to Canada.

MULTICULTURAL POLICIES AND GENDER ISSUES

In examining how the multicultural public policy has affected "visible minority women" it is useful to point out that gender issues, like racism were not considered in the formulation of that policy. Until 1981, when the first forum was held to initiate a dialogue between "immigrant and visible minority women" and the federal government, gender issues were ignored. This dialogue is still going on, and there is some awareness of the painfully unique experiences of this group of Canadian women. They are caught in a web of oppression created by an interaction of racism and sexism. They are a target of discrimination in the women's community because of their "race," and in society at large because of their race and sex, and within their homes and ethnic communities because of their sex. Experiencing devaluation in all settings and having nowhere to turn, these women are vulnerable to all sorts of abuse, mistreatment, and oppression. Ignoring their own pain, they are always there to provide emotional support to their racialized family and community. They are the ones who struggle to preserve their culture, organizing "multicultural" events and carrying on many of the multicultural projects. Most of their work is voluntary, although sometimes they may be paid a nominal sum. Teaching of the heritage languages illustrates how their labour is exploited by the state. Recently, the multicultural policy provided these women with forums to voice their concerns. Even though the issuers of male violence against women and women's social role limitations have not received much attention in public policy, these socialized women have grabbed the opportunity to network with one another and to obtain validation for their own reality, which they experience in the isolated space of being a woman and belonging to racialized groups. However, their responsibility to preserve and transmit heritage cultures has impeded their acculturation and added to their isolation and vulnerability to victimization. Moreover, cultural diversity and sensitivity is sometimes invoked by their male partners in order to excuse oppressive practices and has been used to manipulate the justice system in situations that needed judicial intervention. For instance, in court cases involving male violence, cultural differences and practices are often invoked to persuade the judicial system to go with men's interpretation of cultures.

FUNDING STIPULATIONS: THEIR EFFECT ON IMPLEMENTATION OF THE POLICY:

In the absence of a systematic assessment of how the funds allocated to multiculturalism affect its implementation, it is problematic to draw any definitive conclusions. However, as an advocate in this area, I have worked with various recipients of funds. Those of us working to bring about change have often felt that funding stipulations restrict us in many ways. We have observed with dismay that a significant amount of money gets spent on conferences and other public forums that enhance the visibility of elected politicians or on expanding the profits of businesses producing posters, buttons, or ribbons. Recently, "multicultural" work has become a lucrative industry for "white" male academics and consultants. Saskatoon Multicultural Council, fifty thousand dollars was given to a consultant company run by an all-"white" male academics for providing training to a few individuals on creating awareness on racism. Similar incidents are happening all across Canada. Out of the twenty-nine million dollars per year allocated to multiculturalism, very little is spent on ongoing programs; most of this money is spent on organizing conferences or carrying out short-term projects. It would be interesting to conduct a study on who occupies management positions in the multicultural organizations.

RECOMMENDATIONS

This essay is based on my personal experiences and my work with the "visible minority" individuals who either seek therapy or are engaged in advocacy work. It would be useful to explore some of the questions arising from the observations I have made in a more systematic way. We have had public multicultural policy for more than two decades, and public funds are spent on implementing this policy. It is time that we evaluate multiculturalism's performance, in order to correct its flaws and build on its strengths for a positive impact on real people's real lives.

REFERENCES

Appiah, K.A. 1990. "Racisms." In *Anatomy of Racism*, ed. D.T. Goldberg. Minneapolis: University of Minnesota Press.

Bhabha, H. 1990. "Interrogating Identity: The Posclonial Prerogative." In *Anatomy of Racism*, ed. D.T. Goldberg. Minneapolis: University of Minnesota Press.

Chomsky, Noam. 1990. *Pirates and Emperors.* Vermont: Amana Books.

Fanon, F. 1990. "The Fact of Blackness." In *Anatomy of Racism*, ed. D.T. Goldberg. Minneapolis: University of Minnesota Press.

Goldberg, D.T. 1990. "The Social Formation of Disurse." In *Anatomy of Racism*, ed. D.T. Goldberg. Minneapolis: University of Minnesota Press.

Javel, N. (1993). "Saliance of Loss and Marginality: Life Themes of "Immigrant Women of Color" in Canada." *In Racism in the Lives of Women: Testimony, Theory and Guides to Antiracist Practice*, ed. Adleman, J. and G. Enguidance.

Lewycky, L. 1992. "Multiculturalism in the 1990s and into the 21st Century: Beyond Ideology and Utopia." In *Deconstructing A Nation: Immigration, Multiculturalism and Racism in 90s,* ed. V. Satzewich. Halifax: Fernwood Publishing.

Li, P.S. and Bolaria, B.S. 1979. "Canadian Immigration Policy and Assimilation Theories." In *Economy, Class and Social Reality*, ed. J.A. Fry. Toronto: Butterworths.

Li, P.S. and Bolaria, B.S. 1983. *Racial Minorities in Multicultural Canada.* Toronto: Garamond Press.

Patel, D. 1980. *Dealing with Interracial Conflict: Policy Alternatives.* Institute for Research on Public Policy, Montreal.

Peter, K. 1981. "The Myth of Multiculturalism and Other Political Fables." In *Ethnicity, Power and Politics in Canada,* ed. J. Dahlie and T. Ferjando. Toronto: Methuan.

Said, E.W. 1979. *Orientalism.* New York: Vintage Books.

Krish Champakesa
Calgary Multicultural Centre
Calgary

Perceptions of a Culturally Diverse Society

The theme of the conference related to the politics of exclusion–to recognize voices from the margins, celebrate forgotten ways of knowing, learn new ways to listen to different voices, create common spaces for us, discover commanalities and appreciate differences and create a collective future with individual freedom. What an apt epithet for the culturally diverse, pluralistic society of Canada today, which in the last few years has been frantically searching for an elusive CANADIAN IDENTITY, community base with a COMMON VISION, in which the differences are not only accepted but seen as contributing to Canadian riches and prosperity for all twenty-seven million of us.

At a recent conference on Canada's future, organized by the Multicultural Communications Foundation at Edmonton, the valedictory address was given by a prominent native leader, KONRAD SIOUI of the Assembly of First Nations. In his address, Konrad spelled out a configuration for such a perception. He suggested a circle instead of a straight line, or a pair of lines. He reasoned that in the latter, two or more can move TOWARDS or AWAY from each other. If all participants sit in a circle, it helps them to focus on a COMMON CENTRAL VISION, and all can look OUTWARDS for more input. I cannot think of a better illustration.

OUTLINE OF A VISION - UNITY IN DIVERSITY

With commendable foresight on the evolving pattern of Canadian society and careful study of the problems with the MELTING POT south of our borders, the Government of Canada endorsed a MULTICULTURAL pattern of society as the most suitable model for Canada. MULTICULTURALISM fosters a society and a Canadian identity, IN WHICH PEOPLES AND GROUPS OF ALL CULTURES ARE ACCEPTED. MULTICULTURALISM PROMOTES HUMAN AND GROUP RELATIONS IN WHICH

ETHNIC, RACIAL, RELIGIOUS, AND LINGUISTIC
SIMILARITIES AND DIFFERENCES ARE EQUALLY VALUED
AND RESPECTED. THIS FOSTERS UNDERSTANDING AND
SHARING OF OUR DIVERSITY AND PROMOTES EQUAL
OPPORTUNITIES FOR ALL CANADIANS TO PARTICIPATE
FULLY IN THE ECONOMIC, SOCIAL, CULTURAL, AND
POLITICAL LIFE OF CANADA.

This model was declared as policy, enshrined in the Charter of
Rights and federal legislative enactments. The Hon. Gerry
Weiner, Minister for Multiculturalism and Citizenship, has
eloquently advocated this model at many forums with the crisp
message, MULTICULTURALISM IS CANADIANISM and belongs
to all Canadians.

Alberta has been a forerunner in the leadership role in
espousing this policy. It has a full-fledged Ministry of Culture and
Multiculturalism and the Alberta Multiculturalism Commission.
Alberta has also legislated the policy in enactments, and in 1988 the
Commission carried out an exhaustive survey INTERCHANGE
'88, across Alberta. This resulted in a visionary document, FOCUS
'90, outlining the concept of multiculturalism. After further
consultations, the Commission produced the MULTICULTURAL
ACTION PLAN, setting out the priorities and clear lines of action.
They formed a MULTICULTURAL ADVISORY COMMITTEE with
cross-professional and cross-cultural representation. They have
recently put out an EDUCATION KIT for adoption in the school
curriculum. STEVE ZARUSKY, Chairman and the talented
members of the Commission have vigorously advocated
multiculturalism at several forums. Many community
organizations, service providers, and their leadership across
Canada have responded positively and work actively for its
implementation.

But, even today multiculturalism is still perceived by many
segments of our society, some of them very vocal, as applicable
mainly to recent immigrants, albeit visible minorities. All our
efforts so far have not succeeded in REORIENTING this perception.
IN MANY FORUMS, A PERSISTENT VIEW IS HEARD OF "WE"
AND "THEY." The latter are referred to in the plural, as
multicultural communities, meaning all Canadians other than
those of English or French origin, and excluding the First Nations.
IF MULTICULTURALISM is synonimous with CANADIANISM
then, EVERYONE OF THE TWENTY-SEVEN MILLION OF US
COMPRISE ONE MULTICULTURAL CANADIAN SOCIETY.
Then what is the need for the use of the plural, except to drive a
WEDGE between "WE" and "THEY"?

In view of this dilemma, please permit me to use the words, "PLURI-ETHNICITY" or "TRANS-CULTURALISM", instead of the now commonly misunderstood term "MULTICULTURALISM".

A LOOK AT THE ORIGINS

Permit me to go back into the growth pattern of our society for an insight into Canadian ethnic composition as it has developed over the last few centuries.

The First Nations HAVE BEEN the inheritors of this land. They have been here for twenty-five to thirty thousand years. They taught immigrant arrivals how to survive, how to utilize the natural resources and live in harmony with the immutable laws of nature and the environment. Les Canadiens chose to come, stay, and settle down here in the 1750s. Loyalists, losers of the American Revolution, chose to make this country their home. thus was British Canada born in bitterness.

Patrick Watson, Chairman of CBC, a Canadian of Irish origins, has produced a short film on Quebec in the mid 1800s. During this period, many Irish orphans arrived in Canada; their parents had died in the crossing, due to a debilitating famine. They were adopted by Quebec families and became French-speaking Quebekers, still retaining their Irish names. The Irish, who came so tragically, were mostly bound for the USA, and those that couldn't make it, stayed.

Between 1867 and 1976 ten million people immigrated to Canada but six million left to settle in the United States.

In the early 1900s the immigrants were mainly from Europe. They had rural moorings. Their traditions were bound to Land–Agriculture, Farming, and Animal Husbandry. They were familiar with the Canadian climate and adapted to and settled down in the vastness of Canada, both as individuals and as close-knit communities. Examples are the Scots, Mennonites, Russians, Icelanders, and Ukrainians. At about the same time came other immigrants from the East, who helped to build the Trans-Canadian railway system and open up the West.

In the two decades just after the Second World War, the immigrants came from war-ravaged Europe. They were skilled and urban, and many of them came as refugees seeking a safe peaceful haven.

Since the 1970s, there has been a significant change in the composition of our immigrant arrivals. A very large number have origins in the Asian subcontinent, Far East, Middle East, Africa, and South America. In other words, they do not have English or French origins or other European backgrounds.

We now have Canadians from almost EVERY COUNTRY AND REGION OF THE WORLD. Most of them are classified as VISIBLE MINORITIES, commonly understood as NONWHITE. Today, ONE IN SIXTEEN of the Canadian population falls into this category. In large cities like Toronto, Calgary, Vancouver and Edmonton, they total ONE IN SIX. By the twenty-first century, this ratio is expected to rise to ONE IN FIVE.

CHARACTERISTICS OF RECENT IMMIGRANTS - MISPERCEPTIONS

Many misperceptions still exist, across segments of our society on the likely effects of this growing diversity of recent immigrants on our prosperity and way of life in Canada. Many apprehend a decline in affluence, working and living standards, health and social welfare, and ways of life modelled on an European pattern. Such an attitude turns a Nelson's eye to the real needs of Canada and what immigrants have brought to Canada.

Let us consider our needs. The demographics of birth rates, and age groups, and existing and projected demands for an increasingly skilled workforce maintain our international competitiveness and future prosperity DEMAND an increasing influx of a variety of skilled persons. They call for higher and higher educational and professional expertise. The projections also indicate that these people have to come from THIRD WORLD countries. In the foreseeable future, THERE SEEMS TO BE LITTLE CHOICE.

Why do immigrants choose to come to Canada in preference to any other country ? Canada is a

...Land of vast resources,
...Immense opportunities to work and have a good life, a
...high standard of living and prosperity,
...unique health and social services, and
...hardworking, peaceful, understanding, compassionate
    Canadians, ready to make friends.

What do immigrants bring with them to Canada? They bring:

... EDUCATIONAL AND PROFESSIONAL
QUALIFICATIONS.
More than 50 per cent of university graduates, post-graduates and high-school graduates, who came to Canada in the last decade are from South America, Africa, the Middle East, East Asia, and the Far East. One in six visible minority immigrants has a university degree, as compared to one in thirteen other Canadians.

... CAPITAL AND ENTREPRENEURSHIP:
In the period 1983 - 85, immigrant entrepreneurs brought in over $1,500 million dollars to Canada, started businesses, and created over 18,000 jobs–in other words, an average of over three jobs for every immigrant in this class. in the later half of 1980s, immigrants invested over three billion dollars in Canada.

Eighty per cent of immigrants chose to come, of their free choice. Only twenty per cent were compelled to seek sanctuary.

All "law and order" problems in today's society were not brought in with immigrants' luggage. Any expert will tell you that these are the result of unpredictable economic and social changes in our own society, caused by transformations in many countries of the world.

... All that immigrants seek is a fair, level playing-field, in which their skills and expertise get equitable recognition, they have equal opportunities with all other Canadians to compete on their merits and they can find their job, place, and settle down in our society as USEFUL, PROUD, CONTRIBUTING CANADIANS.

" SO WHAT IS THE BEEF ABOUT IMMIGRANTS ? "

Why do so many see this level playing field as velvet-glove mollycoddling of immigrants to the detriment of born Canadians ? Why do some see it with racist-coloured glasses ? Let us sum up both sides of this melee, which has a strong bearing on our vision of FUTURE CANADA.

THE CASE OF THE ANTAGONISTS:

- It attempts to right old wrongs. But people do not buy group guilt.
- Disadvantaged applicants are flooded with jobs.
- A warm glow of condescension is the result.
- Equal rights do not mean identical rights.
- We can become a cacophony of envious, paranoid social and racial minorities.
- It does not address the REAL problems of the POOR.
- It is a politically driven cultural hoax.

THE CASE OF THE PROTAGONISTS:

- Freedom of speech does not mean freedom to offend.
- No individual is entirely defined by a cultural label, any more than he/she is by a radical label.
- Culture is the collective outcome of centuries of human experience. IT IS A COMMON HUMAN HERITAGE.
- No culture, no race, no nation, no gender, no history, no religion is NOBLER THAN ANY OTHER.
- The way to a truly just society lies through EQUAL OPPURTUNITY AND PARTICIPATION BY ALL GROUPS AT ALL LEVELS.
- Let Canadians experience the reality of our society daily, whether looking UP, DOWN, or SIDEWAYS on the self-perceived STATUS TOTEM POLE.

IN THIS SITUATION, CAN WE EVER BUILD A NATIONAL IDENTITY BASED ON UNITY IN DIVERSITY? Is there a professional approach to the POLITICS OF EXCLUSION? What are our supporting features and what should be our line of action? Let us prise the door open for a look at basic definitions, and to develop our perception of FREEDOM WITHIN THE MARGINS.

WHAT IS NATIONALISM AND NATIONAL IDENTITY?

1. In the light of the preceding incontrovertible facts and the REALITY of the increasingly diverse make-up of our society, influenced by large numbers from Third World backgrounds, let us see some recent pronouncements on Nationalism and Canadian identity.

2. Nationalism is an idea that taps into patriotism, loyalty, and attachment to a geographic entity as a nation, rather than merely political nationalism. Relations between and among ethnic groups, and group status should provide the linkage to such a political system.
3. Canadian Nationalism is based on the concept of voluntary Nationalism–The population chooses to be part of a Nation. It has no territorial aspect.
4. CANADIAN NATIONALISM can successfully co-exist in a pluri-ethnic society, if we can meet some of the following basic needs of any civilized society:

   • Relations among components in the society are REASONABLY HARMONIOUS.
   • There are shared interests, collective memories, and promises of a rewarding future, outweighing PARTICULARISTIC bonds.
   • OVERARCHING SYMBOLS exist that appeal to various ethnic and other groups, (e.g., National Flag, National Anthem), which instill NATIONAL PRIDE in all citizens.
   • Institutions flourish that foster SHARED GOALS, INTERESTS, AND LOYALTIES.
   • There is CREDIBLE political leadership.

In order to work on a collective basis, we have to look at certain basic principles for adoption, together with the governing factors that relate to these principles. They are: RESPECT FOR INDIVIDUAL LIBERTY, CIVIC COHESION INTERNAL TO OUR SOCIETY, AND ACADEMIC AND COMMUNITY EDUCATION FOR IMPROVED CROSS-CULTURAL INTERACTION. How do we go about this, without giving the impression of REGULATION OR IMPOSITION ? Whatever we do has to be perceived and accepted by the entire community as a SELF-ELEVATING EXERCISE IN EMPOWERMENT.

The methodology would call for adoption and sincere practice with full conviction and open embracing of principles such as KNOWLEDGE OF THE RULES, UNDERSTANDING OF A COMMON, ACCEPTED NATIONAL WAY OF LIFE, CLARITY OF NATIONAL GROUP, FEASIBILITY OF POLITICAL CHOICES, and FAIRNESS AND PERCEIVED FAIRNESS AMONG GROUPS. THE NEED IS FOR A DYNAMIC CIVIC CULTURE. DIFFERENT GROUPS HAVE DIFFERENT IDEAS ON THE DISTINCTIVE FEATURES OF A "NATION." THE LEADERS,

TOGETHER WITH THE ENTIRE COMMUNITY, HAVE TO
PRACTICE WHAT THEY PREACH AND BE SEEN TO DO SO.

SOME NEEDS THAT GOVERN AN ACTION PLAN

• PLURI-ETHNICITY should empower the INDIVIDUAL to
stand at the crossroads and select from THE FULL RANGE of
roles within a host society. It is then synonymous with
FREEDOM.
• PLURI-ETHNICITY should see beneath differences and
IDENTIFY SIMILARITIES. It will then lead to EQUALITY
OF OPPORTUNITY. Distinctive or exclusive displays of
cultural heritage should be broadened on a cross- cultural base,
for WIDER AUDIENCES OF DIVERSE BACKGROUNDS,
AND SHOULD STRESS SIMILARITIES. They should not
leave the impression that they are used as a bargaining chip in
the power game.
• Such a pattern of society should work in concert with other
strategies to achieve a MEANINGFUL SENSE OF CANADA
AS A NATION, where EVERY CANADIAN can find a place,
FREE of the UBIQUITOUS HYPHEN. It would then be seen
AND ACCEPTED as a FREE CHOICE.
• In evaluating such a choice before deciding on it, we should ask
a number of questions:

  • Does it replace the assimilative "BE US" society of the
  melting pot by the equally divisive "BE YOU" of the
  composite pattern?
  • Is it a half-hearted attempt to deal with very fundamental
  problems and perceptions?
  • If it is tokenism, assumed out of some collective guilt
  complex, can it ever work?
  • Is it designed by political image makers? If so, can it
  outlast changing political perceptions?

THE LIKELY THORNS IN THE BUSH

Before we decide to look ahead and take measures to foster the
growth of such a pattern within our society, we would do well to
perform a SELF-ANALYSIS, to eschew possible negative leads and
focus on positive lines of action. Some examples are:

  • There is a tendency to label anything and everything as
  the outcome of a western, white, racial power syndrome

with colonial overtones, as it relates to Canadians from previously colonized countries. Racism is inherently abhorrent, whatever color or shade it takes. The answer to any racist attitude is not counter-racism. The view that all things Western are inherently corrupt, is as unacceptable and nauseating as RACISM AND SEXISM.

* If advocacy of communication and interaction through portrayal of cultural riches and heritage is perceived to be carrying different features to the point of exclusivity, as a bargaining tool in the political or economic power game, it will continue to be divisive. the risk of such a practice is that it does not contribute to cohesiveness but arouses acute awareness of blocks.

* Can multiculturalism be viewed and understood as trans-culturalism in preference to pluri-ethnicity, so as not to offend the sensibilities of an increasing majority of canadians, say, second and third generations, who do not see themselves as attached to any ethnic affiliation or carry a hyphenated chip on their shoulders?

* Now is not the time for Canadians to ANOINT each other with labels.

* Success will no longer depend on who you know but what you know, what you believe deeply, and what you have the courage to practise and sincerely for all to see and accept on its inherent merits.

THE ENCOURAGING STRAWS IN THE WIND

* Equality and fairness in a democratic society
* Non-manipulated consultation, openness, and dialogue
* Accommodation, appreciation, acceptance
* Inherent merits of diversity, not just a tool for preferential claims or quotas
* Compassion and generosity from the heart and not just from the lips
* Non-violent resolution of conflicts, consistent with a commitment to personal freedom and peaceful social change
* No back-room agendas or veiled self-interests
* Cultural adaptation and trans-acculturization, which demand, on all sides, a lot of HUMAN SPIRIT AND CREATIVITY

WHERE IS THE SUPPORT FOR THIS VENTURE?

- We derive our support from our American-ness: we do things differently. We have roots as deep in our Canada, as the adherents of old home country value systems do there or here.
- None of this is static or etched in stone or engraved in parchment. Value systems have completely changed within one generation, right in the home countries; and yet we seek, pitiably, to cling to them, RIGHT HERE IN TWENTY-FIRST-CENTURY CANADA.

Every attempt to impose the OLD WORLD on us has been a failure.

Quebec nationalism was born out of the painful attempt to escape colonial dependance on France, and have Quebec's distinctiveness protected in the Canadian scenario. Nor could ardent devoteers transplant Old Mother England in the wilderness of North America. Jacksonian democracy fought British constitutional practices.

As a people, we have accepted group/community distinctiveness on a common Canadian identity base.

- We know, deep in our guts, that we respect diversity.
- As Canadians, we do things differently from all other nations.
- Our Federation and Charter of Rights are unique, carefully tailored and re-tailored to MEET OUR OWN NEEDS AND VALUES as these evolve from time to time.
- The provincial and federal divergencies in viewpoints arise out of an acute sense of geography and territorial protectiveness.
- Economic grievances tend to be portrayed as political grievances.
- Regionalism is an expression of more deeply rooted inequalities. The discontent is not with Canada but with the nature of political institutions, and arises out of the immutable features of economy and geography. In this process, regional influences mitigate against a common national identity.

AS WE LOOK AHEAD, WE HAVE SOME EXCELLENT POINTERS

RUBEN NELSON, the eminent Canadian futurologist, recently gave refreshing food for thought to a Calgary audience of professionals. He pointed to the recent upheavals all across the world, earth-shaking changes in social patterns, value systems, and pecking orders. He called on all listeners to ponder deeply on fundamental reorientation of our ideas of society, community, diversity, understanding and acceptance of values, human dignity, individual liberty, accommodation, and mutual respect. THIS IS WHAT WE HAVE TO LOOK AT, FROM A COMMUNITY PERSPECTIVE.

A HARD-HEADED LOOK AT OUR FUTURE NATIONAL ECONOMIC AND POLITICAL PROSPERITY:

A consultant group, on behalf of the Montreal Board of Trade, recently highlighted three concurrent crises in Canada today:

* the recession, which is cyclic;
* constitutional impasse;
* massive de-industrialization of Canada.

Homing in on the last issue which was, of most interest to them and, down the line, to all of us, they stated that Canadian public policies have resulted in considerable economic distortions. The consequence is a large-scale migration of businesses and enterprises out of Canada. In recent times, Canada is losing as many as one thousand jobs a day. They termed this "competitive handicaps induced by policies".

In order to overcome these handicaps, they recommended A team approach, harmonization of public policies, and a pro-active national policy. If team strategy is implemented, the very real advantages of Canada will be fully harnessed to ensure our future prosperity.

These two examples from vastly different angles of vision, a futurologist and a business consultant, point to their similar prognosis—a shared team strategy.

WHERE DO WE BEGIN, WHERE DO WE GO AND HOW SHALL WE ACHIEVE OUR GOAL?

The various facets of the analysis are summarized below:

- We do need "freedom within the margins."
- We need to sit in a circle and look at one another in mutual understanding and respect.
- We need to understand the reality of our built-in diversity. We cannot just wish it away.
- We have to cleanse our minds of all cobwebs and crawl out of our mental cocoons.
- We have to make close friends with our NATIVE BRETHREN and appreciate, in mutual respect, their HERITAGE as part of the CANADIAN PATTERN.
- There is a clear and bright lesson for us in the fast-changing, mind-boggling events all round us in the world of today.
- We have to be humble and grateful for all the rich endowments of our beloved country, the envy of most other countries of the world.
- We have to understand and perform our duties to our country before we claim our rights.
- We have to transform education, and not only in the academic sense, into a learning adventure for our future generations and also for all of us older Canadians.
- We have to develop deep conviction and an abiding faith in our country and learn to demonstrate national pride.
- we shall do so not because we aspire to it, but because we fully deserve it as "one Canadian nation" among nations of the world.

Are we ready for this enterprise ? Let me conclude with short quotes from two luminaries of our generation.

WE SHALL NEVER BUILD A NATION, WHICH OUR
POTENTIAL RESOURCES MAKE POSSIBLE, BY DIVIDING
OURSELVES INTO ANGLOPHONES, FRANCOPHONES,
MULTICULTURALPHONES OR WHATEVER KIND OF
PHONEYS YOU CHOOSE. I SAY–CANADIANS FIRST, LAST
AND ALWAYS.

–JOHN DIEFENBAKER

WHERE THE MIND IS WITHOUT FEAR
AND THE HEAD IS HELD HIGH
WHERE KNOWLEDGE IS FREE
WHERE THE WORLD HAS NOT BEEN BROKEN UP
INTO FRAGMENTS BY NARROW DOMESTIC WALLS
WHERE WORDS COME OUT FROM THE DEPTH OF TRUTH
WHERE TIRELESS STRIVING STRETCHES ITS ARMS

TOWARDS PERFECTION
WHERE THE CLEAR STREAM OF REASON
HAS NOT LOST ITS WAY
IN THE DREARY DESERT SAND OF HABIT
WHERE THE MIND IS LED FORWARD
INTO EVER-WIDENING THOUGHT AND ACTION
INTO THAT HEAVEN OF FREEDOM, LET MY COUNTRY
AWAKE.

–Nobel Laureate poet Rabindranath Tagore

THIS IS NO UTOPIAN DREAM
UNITED WE SHALL SUCCEED
DIVERSE THOUGH OUR ORIGINS ARE
WE ARE CANADIANS FIRST–WE ARE CANADIANS LAST
IN OUR MOSAIC WE BLEND
THE RICH TAPESTRY OF ALL HUMAN CULTURES
AND STAND TOGETHER AS LEADERS
FOR EMULATION BY ALL COUNTRIES
ONE WORLD–ONE CANADA–ONE SOCIETY
PEACE, HARMONY, UNDERSTANDING, RESPECT.

–ANONYMOUS

SO WE BEGIN OUR JOURNEY, NOT SITTING ON THE
FRINGE, LOOKING IN OR OUT WITH SUSPICION, BUT
HOLDING HANDS IN JOYOUS SMILE
RIGHT AT THE CENTRE AND BEAMING OUTWARDS WITH
SOCIAL RICHES AND DIVERSITY.

PART VIII

ARTISTIC TAKES

Sandra Vida
The New Gallery
Calgary

Art and its Gatekeepers

Since space is limited, I will as concisely as possible, define "what is marginal art?" in my own terms and then describe a hypothetical example of decision-making regarding art selection and presentation. And just for good measure, I want to make reference to the title of the conference that gave rise to this volume, "Freedom within the Margins", since I feel a personal affinity for this concept.

I must admit I had serious qualms about appearing on a panel of "Gatekeepers". I had never heard this term before, although I've been involved in visual art in one way or another for about twenty years. The word immediately conjured up a scene from one of my favourite books, Virginia Woolf's *A Room of One's Own*. The scene takes place in the year 1929. Woolf is strolling on the grounds of the mythical University of Oxbridge, doing preliminary thinking for an essay on "women and fiction". She suddenly recalls an excellent essay by Charles Lamb, remembers that the manuscript is located in the library of this very college, and decides to go and take a look at it for inspiration:

> "I was actually at the door which leads into the library itself. I must have opened it, for instantly there issued, like a guardian angel barring the way with a flutter of black gown instead of white wings, a deprecating, silvery, kindly gentleman, who regretted in a low voice as he waved me back that ladies are only admitted to the library if accompanied by a Fellow of the College or furnished with a letter of introduction."(p. 134)

Ancient history, you may say, and rather quaint. But try as I might, this image of the black-cloaked gatekeeper hovered over my deliberations for this essay. I recalled that gatekeepers facilitate access, but they also deny it.

But for the moment, I'll move on to the question "What is marginal art?" (My first thought was "Isn't all art, or all *good* art, marginal" in some way, that is, critical, removed from total immersion in society's value systems? But perhaps that's too easy an answer. Is marginal art what is excluded? If so, I reasoned, perhaps I should start with what is regarded as "official" art. I marched to the shelf in my studio and pulled down H.W. Janson's *History of Art*. This volume, subtitled "A Survey of the Major Visual Arts from the Dawn of History to the Present Day", published nearly thirty years ago, was the one I studied at university, and this is what he has to say about "official art":

> The author of a history of art for the general reader faces one dilemma at the outset: should he proportion his book to give equal weight to every significant area? If not, what should he leave out?...Behind our interest in the past lies the question.."How did we get to where we are now?" For the historian of art, "now" means the living art of our century: this art is the product of Western civilization on both sides of the Atlantic. We have, accordingly, discussed in this book only those elements outside Europe and America that have contributed to the growth of the Western artistic tradition: prehistoric and primitive art, as well as the art of Egypt, the ancient Near East, and Islam. Three major areas have been omitted--Indian Asia, China and Japan, and pre-Columbian America-- because their indigenous artistic traditions are no longer alive today, and because these styles did not, generally speaking, have a significant influence on the West. (p.ix)

How safe, comfortable, and even smug he sounds to us now, undisturbed in his monocultural dream of excellence and knowledge. Aside from the exclusion of certain cultural groups, there is another rather glaring omission in my version of Janson. Apparently, from the "Dawn of History to the Present Day", not one work of any significance was produced by a person of my gender. Naturally, this information tended to, in Virginia Woolf's words, "lower my vitality" in regard to the art profession.

To be fair, I made a trip to the library to see how the newer versions of Janson had changed. The second edition, published in 1977, is much like the first. By 1986, H.W. had died and passed his black cloak and keys over to his son. This version opened the gate to include the work of thirteen women artists (from all eras), although the language to describe these artists is distressing: "wife of", daughter of', "was inspired by', "continued the work of', "was indebted to", and so on. This version acknowledges, for the first time, "black artists" in a quarter page outline, although only one name is mentioned. There is also the addition of two pages on "Indian art."

In the latest edition, 1991, which is still the standard reference at most art colleges, the same number of women appear; two black artists now appear, called "African American;, and in the "Indian section" the word "primitive" no longer appears. As well, some of the language to describe the women artists is less blatantly patronizing.

Obviously something had changed, some adjustments had been made, however minor and seemingly tokenistic. I can't help thinking that what had occurred was not the result of a miraculous change in the Janson family, but a response to concerted pressure on the art world by excluded voices that could no longer be ignored in the name of "historic continuity." Let me move on quickly to my "hypothetical story" about art and decision-making.

Once upon a time there was an artist. As a child, she was constantly making things. And she was always writing little plays and songs and forcing her family and friends to watch her perform them. When she went to school, she was told that art was a bad career choice, and unsuitable especially for a woman, except as a hobby. She was encouraged to study literature, and psychology, which she did. But she continued to make things. At University, she was told that no one but white male Europeans created art works of any significance from the "Dawn of History to the Present Day." She thought she was an artist, however, and when she graduated, she began to approach galleries with her art work. They told her her work was too weird, too new, too risky. They told her the schedule was full, and it always seemed to be full of mostly male artists.

"To hell with this!" she thought, "I'll start my own gallery." She found a lot of other young artists who felt the same way. (Some of her women friends felt so strongly about gender imbalance that they created galleries to promote only women artists.) All of them, however, were determined to come up with an "alternative" or maybe even a better model. They were going to throw out concepts like bureaucracy, hierarchy, and traditional definitions of "quality", and replace them with group decision-making. They were going to keep the overhead low and the artist fees high. They were going to value process over product. They were going to create a "parallel" system where others who felt excluded could participate.

262 / Sandra Vida

It all sounds hopelessly idealistic. Surprisingly enough, these "artist-run centres" are still around, about eighty of them in Canada. In some people's eyes, they've been around so long, in fact, that they have become institutions themselves, where other artists may feel excluded. They are now supported by government grants and large memberships. And they often work in collaboration with the more traditional galleries. But their emergence, and their continued presence, has affected and altered the whole aspect of art practice and presentation.

So to get back to my story, there are two possible endings:

Choice 1: And so, the artist found herself part of the mainstream after all, and lived happily ever after.

Choice 2: And so, the artist had to keep moving and changing in order to keep her "oppositional" status, and began to define it as a conscious and positive position.

My point in recounting this story, which strangely enough is very similar to my own personal history, is to recognize several important things.

One is that the definitions of what is "marginal" and what is "official" are constantly shifting. What seems natural and proper in one generation appears smug and authoritative and exclusionary to another generation, or another cultural group. Likewise, what seems idealistic and foolish to one segment of the population seems an absolute necessity to another. The power shifts and the personnel changes. But structures of domination and subordination still operate, even if they become invisible, or become internalized.

I thought again about the idea of "gatekeepers." One Aboriginal artist uses words like "finders" and "keepers." These rather loose titles appeal to me somewhat, signifying on the one hand a proactive searching, and on the other a kind of "reverent caring for." I would align myself more with the "finders" but I still feel that even these notions resonate with an uncomfortable power differential. Some art is good, some art is bad, and *someone* (perhaps in a black cloak, with a set of keys) *knows the difference.* Who? Someone like H.W. Janson?

True, at The New Gallery in Calgary, decisions *are* made as to which projects are supported. *Who decides* is a changing group of artists from the community. We are more comfortable with a sort of communal, flexible, and community-based definition of art. The system has its own flaws, but it acknowledges that definitions change.   In artist-run centres, we have deliberately tried to eliminate words like "curator,' "critic," and "director" (and "gatekeeper," now that we know about it), and to replace them with words like "facilitator" and "coordinator," more slippery roles which can be filled by fellow artists as well as by "art professionals."

And we continue to place a kind of holy faith in the consensual decision-making process, in round-table discussion, and in peer assessment, trying to keep in mind that access to the system is still unequal. We realize that new systems may be emerging that need support and space to develop, support and space which *we* may have to give up or at least *share*.

The last point I want to make is, again, about the difference between "marginality" that is imposed (a forced exclusion that privileges one gender, class, ethnicity, region, age group, or medium over another) and "marginality" that is chosen as an oppositional stance. On a personal level, as a woman artist I still feel overlooked and excluded in some arenas by the dominant culture. In another way, I feel that I have chosen marginality: in working in the "alternative" artist-run system, in working with under-represented media like video, performance, and installation, and in calling myself a feminist. I'd like to close with the words of someone who has clearly articulated and defined the marginal voice, bell hooks:

"I am speaking from a place where I am different, where I see things differently. I am talking about what I see. ...To speak about that location from which work emerges, I choose familiar politicized language, words like "struggle, marginality, resistance", I choose these words knowing that they are no longer popular or "cool"--hold onto them and the political legacies they evoke and affirm, even as I work to change what they say, to give them renewed and different meaning..   I am located in the margin. I make a definite distinction between that marginality which is imposed by oppressive structures and that marginality one chooses as a site of resistance--as location of radical openness and possibility. ...We are transformed, individually, collectively, as we make radical creative space which affirms and sustains our subjectivity, which gives us a new location from which to articulate our sense of the world."

Gatekeeper's Forum

I have undertaken to explore gatekeeping from the administrative point of view. I am an administrator in a large institution. As an assistant director, I share in the overall management of a large multidimensional facility with an operating budget of approximately eight million dollars and a staff of 130. As director of programs, I am responsible for the public face of this institution–exhibitions, educational programs, public events, and extension services. It sounds awesome. But right off the bat, I want to make it clear that I am proud of the Glenbow. Most days I wake up before the alarm clock goes off. I am challenged by what we do and what we're striving to achieve. I like the people I work with. I love what I do.

I am not a curator, although was one in a not-so-distant past life. The decisions I participate in making are most often negotiated in the boardroom, not the artist's studio. However, these decisions are instrumental in shaping the institution and the choices we make.

What I'd like to do is to explore those decisions on two levels: first, as they represent the institutional infrastructure, and second, in how they are manifested (what results they produce).

The institutional infrastructure is navigated via its mandate. That mandate is that we are a public institution–we serve the public. Not only are we non-profit, but we spend your money on you. The money you pay at the door, spend in the shop, give back to the government in the form of taxes, goes into a pot that is managed and allocated to give you something back–to provide public service.

Before I get into "what you get," though, I want to stick with this institutional infrastructure a bit more to acknowledge the tools that are used to manage this responsibility, and to get down to the "art specifics." Your money is used to support collections, collection management, exhibitions, and programs in cultural history, ethnology, military history, mineralogy, the library and archives as well as art at the Glenbow Museum.

But in this essay we are concerned with art. How is your money managed to collect art and to exhibit art at the Glenbow? What tools are used to manage your money in providing art to the community? How do we manage the choices we make on your behalf?

There are policies.

COLLECTING POLICY

The collecting policy is a policy that Glenbow will collect historical art to the present day taking into account, as collecting criteria, aesthetic merit, documentary importance, required storage, condition of the work, historic value, or potential. There are procedures to carry forward this collecting policy:

(a) Funds for collecting are raised by a non-profit, arms-length, volunteer society called the Glenbow Museum Acquisitions Society (via lottery, dinners, seeking private donations). They raise approximately one hundred dollars per year (not bad in this economic climate).

(b) Curators select, using the collecting criteria and responding to what is available, what is affordable, what fills a gap in the collection, and what represents current artistic endeavours and critical thinking.

(c) The curator presents this selection, with rationale, to a collections management committee made up of volunteer representatives of the community.

EXHIBITION POLICY

The exhibition policy is that Glenbow will offer exhibitions and programs that address those issues that are of interest and concern to the general public and that are meaningful, relevant, and entertaining.

PROCEDURES

Curators field requests from outside the institution (about ten per month), as well as seek exhibitions (through their collegial contacts), as well as propose their own exhibitions. These recommendations for hosted shows and proposals for in-house shows go to an exhibition committee made up of two curators; a director, an assistant director, programs; and assistant director, finance and community relations; an assistant director, technical services; a chief curator; a head of public relations and marketing; and a head of education.

The selection criteria includes achieving a balance among the local, regional, national, and international; historical, modern, and contemporary; media–painting, sculpture, photography, prints, new media, performance, film, video, craft and architecture; the potential for new knowledge; the audience; the potential for public knowledge; and funding.

These recommendations then go to a program committee of the board of governors–who are also representatives of the community. In my six-year tenure with the Glenbow Museum, this committee has never vetoed a staff recommendation. Although approval and rejection are within their mandate this committee encourages discussion and debate and provides advice and assistance.

These two policies and their respective procedures may sound like a bureaucratic fortress. But remember the public mandate, the responsibility of spending your dollars, and the scope of the institution. These checks and balances are necessary. Accountability is required.

What results are achieved through this process of decision-making? What do you get out of all this structure–policy–procedures? What does an artist get?

If an artist collected or exhibited at a large institution, he or she gets a catalogue, community exposure, potential sales, career advancement, credibility, achievement, and authorization.

If an artist is not collected or shown at the Glenbow he or she can get access to collections and exhibitions; facilities for research; and the opportunity for growth.

The public gets exposure to what is going on; access to a collection; opportunities for critical thinking; educational programs; facilities for research; opportunities for growth, contemplation and provocation; and enjoyment.

Just as the institutional infrastructure is navigated by our public mandate and so we require all those tools of accountability–the work we do, how we interact internally, and the results we provide are navigated by a vision statement. It is because of this vision statement that I love what I do and am proud of the Glenbow. That statement is the recognition, acknowledgement, exploration, and celebration of diversity.

Institutional authority is constantly being questioned. In the olden days, authority centred on the collection–one that reflects Western thinking, values, and conventions. Nowadays the authority is shifting outward. We talk about the public much more, and we talk to the public a lot more–certainly for survival purposes as we require public support for our continued existence–but, also because we yearn to be responsive, reflective, relevant, meaningful.

In the process of carrying out our policies and procedures, we are constantly challenging our own voice and seeking other voices.

We're out in the communities more. Our communication strategies now require more listening than talking. Our exhibitions are striving to explore diversity rather than instruct in a monolithic truth. We're using personal voices rather than institutional language. We're asking questions more than giving answers.

This value shift, as exciting as it is, is not without struggle. It takes time. We can't throw out the collection and start all over again. But through the process of change, what the public is getting is not a temple of truth with one authoritarian voice, but rather a place where many voices can be heard.

Choices still have to be made, and in that regard I suppose the institution still has gatekeepers. But these choices are now inclusive rather than exclusive.

Thomas Heyd
Department of Philosophy
University of Victoria
Victoria, B.C., Canada

Resistances: A Review of "Crowns, Thorns and Pillows"

> Thera ... was the center of an ancient cult in which lyric
> dances of a solemn and austere rhythm, called
> *gymnopaidia*, were performed (Seferis 1977, 61).

Replete with clues, the piece *Crown, Thorns and Pillows* performed
May 1992 in Calgary (capital of the yearly *High Performance
Rodeo*) as part of the conference "Freedom within the Margins: The
Politics of Exclusion," effectively manages to transcend those
clues. The small stage presents us with six crowns on bedpillows on
the right. On the left there are a narrow, wooden ramp and a pile of
time-and glacier-worn rocks. An athletic-seeming man is fully
wrapped in, and tied into, a body-length pillowcase by an older,
greying one. Then the older-seeming man carefully lifts and
carries some more rocks from the audience area onto the stage; after
that he plays Erik Satie's *Gymnopédies* on the piano.

Nothing happens onstage while *Gymnopédies* is played.
Slowly, the piano player goes over to where the wrapped one lies
prostrate; with the help of very long, sharp scissors, he gravely frees
from his cloth-casket the pillow-encased man, who emerges as in
birth.

The birthed man strips down to his underwear; slowly, and
then vigorously, he performs his dance. A country-western song by
Waylon Jennings is played on a cassette player. The birthed one
puts on one of the six crowns. This is a poorly fitting headpiece,
obliging him to carefully balance himself. Precariously he makes
his way up the ramp, only to face the surly, old-looking piano-
player, who climbs up the rock pile and, after a loud verbal
interchange, takes the crown and deposits it on the glacial rocks.

This peregrination is repeated four times; each time the birthed man travels up the ramp in a more prostrate manner. On the second trip he wears a very large, oversize crown slipped right over his head so that it rests on his shoulders; on the third voyage he advances on his knees wearing a thorn crown; finally he crawls up, propelling himself with his bare torso and elbows, while wearing a very heavy, king's crown. Between each Sysiphean journey up the ramp, the surly, old character plays Satie's *Gymnopédies*.

The clues to the piece's interpretation appear to offer themselves fairly clearly. The crowns, signs of authority, are handed over by the birthed man to the father figure; the verbal exchanges terminate each time when the father figure speaks the loudest, final word; the ascents up the ramp by the birthed man, from a free walk to a crawl on his knees to a crawl on his belly, increasingly take on signs of submission. The soft pillows (signs of the comfort of childhood's naivety) on which the crowns rest, as well as the two crowns that look like antlers and horns (signs of the natural and free?), remain behind. At the end of the road/ramp there is the chasm, the unwieldy rock-pile, and the father. Everything speaks for a relatively straightforward interpretation of the piece: from the day of birth on, the man discovers that he is in a perilous place fraught with burdensome conventions, punctuated by oppressive, hierarchical power relations.

Counter to this reading, largely based on the conventional meanings of the gestures exhibited, there militates an unrelenting physicality. The rocks are genuine rocks gathered from an Alberta field, their solidity evident when knocked against by the crowns. The crowns, crafted out of steel, bulkily weigh on the birthed man's head while he balances up the narrow incline. Floor and body surfaces resist the birthed man's intentions to traverse space as their contact increases through his kneeling and prostrate positions. The moment of submission, represented by the handing over of the crowns, is increasingly resisted by *embodiment*.

Embodiment permeates the design of the piece. Contrasting with much performance art that relies on its affinities with conceptual art, this piece betrays a strong commitment to corporeality in its attention to the forms presented: the motions are precise dance movements, the crowns are meditated sculptures. The *Gymnopédies*, played in the manner of a refrain, elicits the context for an alternative interpretation.

Despite the explosive, volcanic fate of the rocks of the Greek island Thera (also called Santorini), the one-time embodiment of the lyric dances, *gymnopaidia*, is indelible. The piece discussed here similarly shows that, even in the representation of oppressive conventions and strangulating, established power structures, physicality offers its resistance. There is a margin, body, that ultimately remains unassailable.

> Let your hands go if you can, to travel; separate yourself
> from disloyal time and sink,
> he who lifts the great stones sinks (Seferis 1977, 65).

AUTHOR INDEX

SUBJECT INDEX

Employment Equity Act 165
equitable participation 171
ethnic identity 78, 203, 207, 209
ethnic origin 205
ethnic literature 46-49, 61,62
ethnic studies association viii
exclusivism 4

F
female ethnicity 63
female centred 63
feminism 63
feminist spirituality 32
folkloristic scholarship 79
    functionalist approach 77-78
    Flemish Canadian Family
    78-84
French-Canadian minority
164,165
Franco Albertans 164

G
German Canadians 208
    cultural rights 213
    ethnicity 206
    first generation German-
    Canadians 209-210
    origin 205
    preferred immigrants 207
    second generation German-
    Canadians 215
Glenbow Museum 265-267
    collecting policy 266
    exhibition policy 266
    procedures 266-268

H
health behaviours 129-133
    exercising 134-137
    effects of social roles 130-133
health issues
    immigrants and refugees 120
    global vision 124-126
    public policy 125
    local action 124-126
health promotion program 119,
121
hermeneutics 8
hermeneutics of suspicion 8
human rights 163

I
immigrant women 87, 91
immigrants in the workplace 150-
151
inclusivisim 4
ideology 11

J
Jewish literature 43

L
liberal humanist tradition 62

M
magical realism 54-59
marginal art 260-262
Mennonites 219
multicultural communication 11
multicultural issues in the
workplace 145, 152
multiculturalism vii, x-xi, 3, 5 ,7, 8-
10, 13, 62, 144, 156, 163, 164, 233-
235
    canadian model 243-245
    gender issues 238-239
    multicultural rhetoric 237
    state imposed 233-235
    racist bias 235-236
    systemic racism 238-239
    visible minority 238-240
    world view 234-235
multicultural women's group 88

N
narrative self 6,7
nationalism 248-249
Native women 111
    Bill C-31 111, 113, 115
    Indian Act 111-114
    Tabique Indian Women's
    Group 113, 114
neo-pagans 19-20, 28
nordic myth 72

O
occupational health and safety
143, 144, 156-157
    biopsychosocial paradigm
    145